'2017

At Home
with the
Armadillo

GARY P. NUNN

GREENLEAF
BOOK GROUP PRESS

This book is a work of creative nonfiction. The events portrayed
are from the author's memory and personal experiences.

Published by Greenleaf Book Group Press
Austin, Texas
www.gbgpress.com

Distributed by Greenleaf Book Group

For ordering information or special discounts for bulk purchases,
please contact Greenleaf Book Group at PO Box 91869, Austin, TX 78709,
512.891.6100.

Design and composition by Greenleaf Book Group
Cover design by Greenleaf Book Group
Cover photograph by Valerie Fremin Photography
Back cover photograph by Scott Newton
Flag image © Bruce Stanfield; armadillo image © Juli Gin.
Used under license from Shutterstock.com

Cataloging-in-Publication data is available.

Print ISBN: 978-1-62634-487-7

eBook ISBN: 978-1-62634-488-4

Part of the Tree Neutral® program, which offsets the number of trees
consumed in the production and printing of this book by taking proactive
steps, such as planting trees in direct proportion to the number of trees
used: www.treeneutral.com

Printed in the United States of America on acid-free paper

17 18 19 20 21 22   10 9 8 7 6 5 4 3 2 1

First Edition

*This book is dedicated to the memory of my parents,
William and Flossie Nunn, whose discipline, guidance, and
direction have kept me "between the ditches" when I swerve
and have allowed me to survive this incredible journey.*

Contents

Foreword

WHERE DO WE TURN to learn about the bright and energetic artists who carved out the progressive country music scene in Austin, Texas, that came to be known as "Redneck Rock"?

Look no further! Here is a spotlight on one fine fellow, standing tall in the midst of some of the most daring singers and players of then and now. He broke the mold and dashed into prominence with a sound all his own—some country, some blues, some rock, and a lot of enthusiasm.

We're speaking of Gary P. Nunn.

A heaping helping of Texas and a bit of Oklahoma brought forth not only an interesting and unique sound, but also one stalwart individual who blossomed into a great writer, songsmith, and Texas music icon.

Yes . . . early on, Mr. Gary P. Nunn deftly twisted his own form of entertaining storytelling into a strong sonic statement that lives on today. Who can ever forget the unbridled blasphemy of Gary's wondrous composition, "London Homesick Blues" from 1973?

Since then, he's been charging down a curvy, cool path and delivering a splendid string of songs to sing along with.

With Gary P. Nunn continuing to invite us into his ever-emerging brand of blues, country, and rock 'n' roll, we can indulge ourselves in a most rewarding form of entertainment that only GPN can deliver.

Sing it!

Billy F Gibbons
August 22, 2017

Chapter 1

Sonny Boy

THE DAY HAS ARRIVED for my procrastination to end and for me to begin the project I have been contemplating for years. It's hard to know where to start, so I'll just start at the beginning. I intend to just write off the top of my head, see what comes out, and let an editor do his or her job.

I was born on December 4, 1945, in Okmulgee, Oklahoma. The story is that my father, William Ulysses Nunn, drove my mother, Flossie Loraine Crocker Nunn, to the hospital in the school bus, as their '43 model Kaiser was broken down. They forded the iced-over creeks that crossed the county's dirt roads from their home in the small, rural community of Eram, where they were employed in the public school system.[1]

My father was the superintendent. He taught math and science, coached girls' basketball and softball, and my mother taught second grade when she didn't have babies to care for. They lived in an apartment inside the schoolhouse, as that was the housing provided

---

1 Eram was also the hometown (really just a rural community, not really a town) of Anita Hill, who gained national recognition as the lawyer who accused Supreme Court nominee Clarence Thomas of sexual harassment during his confirmation hearings in 1991. Hill's introductory statement mentioned she was from Eram even though she was technically born in Lone Tree. (It's not where you come from; it's where you go.)

for them. I had two older siblings, the oldest being brother Max, who was five years older than me, and sister Judy, who was three years older. Our lives naturally revolved around the school.

My first memories are of my mother in a small room in the schoolhouse. I recall the sunlight shining through an elevated window illuminating the dust and lint suspended in the air. I was sitting on her lap. She was reading a letter aloud to me from my Uncle Robert and Aunt Mary Lou, my dad's brother and sister-in-law, announcing the birth of their first child, Tollie—a family name borne by my fraternal grandfather who had come down the family line through a connection with a family by the name of Tallifero.

My memories of the five years we spent in Eram are dominated by scenes of basketball games; of school Christmas assemblies where my dad played Santa and every kid got a brown bag of hard candies and Brazil nuts; of me trying unsuccessfully to get a bottle of Grapette or Nehi Red or RC Cola out of the coin-operated pop machine (without inserting any coins!); of boys on their knees in the dirt shooting marbles ("shootin' 'doo-gees'" it was called); of girls playing Jacks and London Bridge Is Falling Down; and of the school playground where students played a game called "Work-Up," a baseball-type game played with a softball and few gloves, if any. Breaks from class for recess, lunch, and "School's out" were announced with a handheld bell. Almost before the bell quit ringing, boys and girls from first grade through high school would race out to the ball field.

The game of Work-Up started with three batters: In a race to decide who would be first, the first kid to touch home base was the first batter, the second kid was second batter, and the third kid to arrive was the third. The next in line to touch home base was the catcher, then the pitcher, then first base, second base, and so on. Slow pitch softball was the format, so all could play—boys and girls, large and small. When a batter struck out or when an out was made, that person had to go to right field, and everyone would move up a position—the catcher would become the batter and so on. If you caught a fly ball, the batter would exchange positions with you. If you didn't make an out, you got to continue batting. The games would start early, before school, and go till the first bell. First graders and seniors together—all the kids played happily for twenty-five minutes or so till the hated bell rang. Play would often last till dark for the kids who lived close by and didn't have to ride the school bus.

Of course, I was too young to play with the big kids at Eram because I hadn't started school yet, but that's all I could think about, and I lived for the day when I would be old enough to play. This is where my love of baseball and sports in general began.

IN 1950, WE MOVED to another small country school in a community called Olney, which was near Coalgate. Ada was the nearest town of any size, about forty miles away, and that's where my brother Steve was born. At Olney, we lived in a teacherage that was provided for the superintendent's family on the school grounds, which occupied ten acres or so. The teacherage was an old converted Army barracks that became available in the years just following World War II. There were no toilet facilities, and we shared the privy outhouse that was provided for the school. Our living quarters were in the front half of the building, which was divided into three rooms. The front room served as the living room and my parents' bedroom. When we had company, my folks would surrender their bed to them and sleep on a quilt pallet on the floor—a common practice in our family when there was a shortage of beds. Baby brother Steve slept in the room with Mom and Dad. The middle room held the kitchen, dining room, and a back portion, which served as a bedroom for me and my brother and sister. I slept in a metal child's bed. A door at the back of our bedroom led directly into the school cafeteria, where two or three school cooks wearing starched white uniforms and hairnets cooked nutritious home-style meals.

My dad fenced off a wooded area adjacent to the school property and built a barn to store hay and feed. We always kept a milk cow and a couple of hogs (that we fed with the slop from the cafeteria). It was my brother Max's chore to slop the hogs every day after school and milk the cow every morning. It was my chore to get up at 5:00 a.m. and accompany him—rain or shine, sleet or snow. Max was only eleven years old at the time, and I was only six, but this was an every-morning occurrence for the five years we lived in Olney—except during our holiday trips, which were always to my grandparents' farm near Hanna, Oklahoma. I'll write more about those days later.

I remember some trying times for my brother Max on bitterly cold mornings when the cow would frequently either kick over the bucket or step in it, despite the metal hobbles he put on her back legs to prevent her from doing it. This always resulted in a lot of hollering (a typical Nunn family trait inherited from Grandpa Tollie) at the cow, and I believe this is when my brother started cussing.

Olney was only a slightly bigger school than Eram, having around one hundred students in all twelve grades. Like Eram, elementary school had first and second grade in one classroom, third and fourth grade in another, fifth and sixth in another, and seventh and eighth together, with one teacher teaching both grades. It was a good system, and all the kids learned reading, writing, and arithmetic. The high school, which was constructed of stones found locally, was at the other end of the schoolhouse. This was the early '50s and a boy's typical attire was Levi's blue jeans, which, when new, were rolled up several inches to allow for shrinkage and potential growth yet unrealized. A typical summer shirt was a white T-shirt or a short-sleeve, cotton plaid button-up shirt. It was fashionable in those days to roll up your sleeves. Some of the older, more rebellious boys would push their Levi's down on their hips and stow a pack of Lucky Strikes in the roll of their T-shirt sleeve. I suppose by this time, they had been exposed to Marlon Brando in the movie *The Wild One* and used him as their role model.

My dad didn't approve of this style at all, and it was usually those boys who made the most trips to his office. Everyone knew about the possibility of a session with my father's wooden paddle wrapped with athletic tape at the business end! Girls wore shirt-waist cotton dresses, or skirts and sweaters, and bobby socks with black-and-white saddle oxfords. None of the kids ever got too out of line because anyone who crossed my dad's discipline line got the dreaded wooden paddle across his or her backside. There were very few disciplinary problems at school or at home because the same rules applied in both places in those days.

My first- and second-grade teacher was a very special lady who had a great influence on me. Her name was Lola Gatlin. By the time I was five, my mother had a hard time keeping me in the house, and I would sneak out and climb through an open window of Mrs. Gatlin's first- and second-grade classroom. There was no such thing as air-conditioning back then, so the windows were always open during the warm weather seasons. Mrs. Gatlin didn't mind me sneaking in and let me stay. Eventually, my dad would find out and come and make me leave and go back to the house. However, I paid attention while I was there and learned a lot of what was being taught to the real first graders. I turned six in December 1951, but my dad held me back and didn't let me start school till the next year. I was thrilled at last when time came for me to enter first grade.

Since I was familiar with first grade schooling already, first grade was a snap—straight As all the way. Second grade was easy too, since I had been exposed to what the second graders were learning too. It was much the same when I went to the next teacher for third grade. Life was school and playing ball with the big kids. Summertime was short pants, bare feet, catching buzzing cicadas and fireflies, homemade ice cream, an occasional watermelon, *The Lone*

Ranger on the radio, and staying out playing till after dark. When we came in, Mom was there with a wash pan full of warm water, and she would give us a washcloth scrubbing from head to toe to remove our covering of sweat and dirt.

SINCE MY DAD WAS the school administrator, his duties required him to make a trip on Saturdays to nearby Coalgate, the county seat of Coal County, to do whatever business he had in the courthouse there. He would take me with him and drop me off at the movie theater. He always gave me a quarter, which was good for the price of admission, a pop, a box of popcorn, and an all-day sucker. On Saturday mornings, they showed ongoing serials of Westerns featuring Roy Rogers, Gene Autry, Lash LaRue, and Hopalong Cassidy, but my very favorites were Red Ryder and Little Beaver; Little Beaver, played by Robert Blake, was an American Indian boy and the sidekick of Red Ryder, and he rode the prettiest paint pony bareback. *That's what I wanted to do!* Oh, how I pined to have a pony to ride. I had the greatest time in my dreams, when I'd even dream that I had one. But when I woke up, I'd run outside, only to be disappointed with the reality that there was no pony.

But one day, my dream did come true! With no advance notice or fanfare, my dad came home with a full-sized paint horse! I was in heaven! Her name was Nellie Belle, and she was a good mare, very gentle and easy to handle. I would get a couple of washcloths from the house and tuck them in my short pants for a breechclout, raid my mother's lipstick to use for war paint, and stick a hawk's feather in one of my dad's neckties tied around my brow like Willie's bandana. I was the next best thing to Little Beaver that a tow-headed, sunburned kid could be. I rode her bareback all over the dirt roads of the countryside. The only bad part was that I had no one to share my fun with because none of the other kids around had horses.

Then one day my dad up and sold Nellie Belle. She was no trouble that I could see, but I guess we couldn't afford the extra expense, and my parents were planning to locate to another school.

OUR LIVES REVOLVED AROUND school, of course—and church. My mother came from a family of Baptists, and she made sure that we got raised in a Christian manner. My love of music began at Olney, where there literally were no churches as it was so sparsely populated. So the folks in the community organized a Sunday school there in the combination gym/auditorium at the school. We had our classes in the same rooms where we went to school. Mrs. Gatlin was my Sunday school teacher as well as my classroom teacher: I think I might have been what you call the teacher's pet! The congregation met on Sunday mornings, and hymns were sung, prayers were prayed, and news announcements of the area were read.

The school gym was also made available for funerals and what were called "singing conventions," where folks would gather occasionally on Sunday afternoons; they would bring food, socialize, visit, gossip, talk politics, and sing hymns all afternoon. It was a diversion from the normal routine at least. Entertainment in Olney was limited to an occasional "donkey basketball" game, a pie supper, a cakewalk[2], or a rare family trip to Wapanucka or Coalgate for a movie, which my mother characterized as "bang-bang-shoot-'em-ups."

---

2 The pie suppers and cakewalks were ways to raise money and bring boys and girls together. In the pie supper, the girls baked the pies, and the boys would demonstrate their preference for a particular girl by bidding on her pie. The winner won the opportunity to sit with and share the pie with the girl. It was a chance to do a little courting and sparking in public. In the cakewalk, the boys marched on a circular path made of numbered squares drawn in chalk on the gym floor as music played. The numbers corresponded to a number assigned to each cake. When the music stopped, a number was pulled out of a hat. The boy standing on that number got to eat the cake with the girl who had baked it.

Donkey basketball was a great and humorous form of entertainment where a basketball game was played by two teams mounted on donkeys that were provided by traveling showmen who visited country schools with a school bus loaded with a dozen or so donkeys.

We didn't have a minister, so there was no preaching and no sermons. Mr. Riley, the local mailman, was the head of the loosely knit, nondenominational congregation. (I was always trying to get close to him, as he owned a Shetland pony farm, but I was too shy to ask him if I could come to his place to play with them.) I first sang in front of an audience at these Sunday morning services. My friend Alan Morrison and I sang together—no doubt a children's Christian song, the name of which I don't recall. From that point on, if there was any sort of music going on, I found a way to be right in the middle of it.

From time to time, fundamentalist Christian groups would hold revivals in the gym for a few nights running, and that's where I saw people actually talking in tongues! It was a wild scene for a little kid to see the worshippers become possessed with the spirit of the Lord. As they were overcome, they began raising and waving their arms toward the heavens, uttering undecipherable sounds, and they would sometimes roll around on the floor as if overtaken by some sort of epilepsy! This must be where the term holy rollers originated. *Sun-ditty-ah, sun-ditty-ah* was the sound they uttered repeatedly during these sessions of apparent religious ecstasy.

My dad hired his brother Robert to teach and coach at the school. He and his wife, Mary Lou—who was beautiful, part-Cherokee, and whom I always adored—moved to Olney and lived on a one-hundred-acre farm they had bought in partnership with my folks a couple of miles down the country road. My people had all come from the land, and the path to upward mobility required the ownership of a piece of ground. They bought some registered Hereford cows; a brand-new little Farmall Super C tractor with a plow, a disc, and a harrow; and tried to farm a little. But as is so often the case, small operations cost more than they bring in, so they eventually sold the land when it came time to move to the next school.

MY DAD AND UNCLE Robert taught me how to swim in the Clear Boggy River near Olney, and swimming became another of my passions. It was always so hot in the summertime, and swimming was so cool and refreshing. It didn't matter to me if it was in a river, a creek, or a stock pond. I just loved the water. At least once a summer, we would pack up for a picnic day trip and go to a place called Ballard Park, somewhere down around Tishomingo. There was a dammed-up creek with clear, green water that passed through a swimming pool and a gristmill that was not in operation except for show. The moving water turned its big waterwheel, and my first near-drowning experience was there. When we arrived, I already had my swimsuit on. I jumped out of the car, ran to the pool, jumped in at the deep end, and sank straight to the bottom. My dad had to fish me out.

In those days, there were few dams to control flooding, and when we would have a big rain, the creeks and rivers would get up and out of their banks and spread out over the countryside. I can recall times when we drove to Coalgate after some of those rains, and as we approached the Clear Boggy River, we would see it completely out of its banks and covering everything as far as you could see. My dad, with maybe the whole family in our '50 model Chevrolet, would just drive off into the water as if he was unconcerned about any danger that might be involved. Nothing ever happened, and we always made it through with no problems, but thinking about it today, it's not something I would ever consider doing. Seems like there was a lot more chance-taking back then. Perhaps it could better be described as doing whatever needed to be done to solve the problem at hand.

On other occasions, we would go to Sulphur, Oklahoma, which was aptly named, as the air and water were saturated with H_2S, hydrogen sulfide—commonly known as "rotten-egg" gas. Sulphur had the first real swimming pool that I ever swam in, and the odor that permeated the area was quickly forgotten by the thrill of being able to swim in a real swimming pool. I nearly drowned there also! Once again, my dad was there to save me. I had a fair complexion, and I would always get sunburned. We were totally unaware of the dangers of sun exposure back then, and we didn't even use suntan lotion. Sunscreen was unheard of, but sunburned or not, those were the happiest of days for me!

I wanted to play baseball by then, even though Olney had no baseball program for kids my age—just a high school baseball team for boys and softball for girls. We had a couple of baseball gloves around the house, but I had no kids to play with. My dad did play catch with me and always coached me at the same time. He would hit me ground balls, and I got pretty good at scooping them up. I would also pester my older brother Max, who would rather have been reading than playing ball, till he would come out and play with me. Even being five years older and not particularly athletic, he did have incredible upper body strength, and he could throw really hard. He would pitch, and I would catch. I was only about eight, and he would try his best to "burn me out" throwing as hard as he could, but I learned to catch anything he threw. Sometimes I would exaggerate his burning me out, by taking my glove off and moaning and groaning about how he was hurting my hand. He seemed to derive a great deal of pleasure from that, and when I yowled about how much his pitches were hurting me, he would throw his head back and howl with laughter. His pitching did hurt, but it was worth it just to have someone to play pitch and catch with, and I suppose this is where I gained a lot of skills that served me well as I grew up and later had the opportunity to play team baseball.

I loved playing the game and fantasized about playing for the St. Louis Cardinals, whose games we could pick up on KMOX, the powerful 50,000-watt radio station out of St. Louis. Though I was a small kid, I was always pretty good at whatever sports I tried, and most sports came natural to me. I was a good climber too. Climbing trees to their highest limbs was my thing—or I'd climb to the top of the schoolhouse. My dad promoted my climbing abilities, and he'd brag to visitors that I could climb to the top of the fifty-foot flagpole by the schoolhouse. They would offer me a nickel to do it, and I always did.

It was about this time that my folks decided we kids should all take piano lessons. Mrs. Stalder, an elderly German woman, taught piano in Coalgate, so my Saturday trips to town switched from being for cowboy movies to piano lessons. I took to it pretty well. Mrs. Stalder entered her students in a contest at Southeastern State College in Durant, and I received top honors for my level. I can recall it to this day, and I still can play the song I performed. It was called "The Dirigibles." I remember the age spots on the backs of Mrs. Stalder's hands, her diamond ring set, the clicking of her painted fingernails on the piano keys, and the stars she would stick on the music to signify that you had performed her assignments satisfactorily. I only took lessons for about a year, but I learned to read music, and those lessons gave me a firm foundation and familiarity with music that has served me well.

Everyone around Olney lived on small farms. They survived on the vegetables they grew and canned from their gardens. Those same vegetables (ground corn mixed with water) fed a hog or two that people would butcher and hang in the smokehouses that everyone had back then. People milked a cow for milk and butter and had as many beef cows as their pastures would support. Other than farming, there were few jobs in those days. You were a schoolteacher, a postman, a county employee who kept the county roads graded, or an administrator or law enforcement official of the county government or the military.

There was not much money circulating, and most people had very little. People who talk about poverty today would be shocked at the desperate situation of the poor families around Olney back then. The only cash crop grown in the countryside was cotton, which was ready for harvest in late October. Since there was no source of additional labor available when all the cotton was ready for harvest, school was dismissed for a few weeks, and many of the schoolkids worked picking cotton for the local farmers. They moved from field to field as each was completed. They picked the cotton bolls by hand and stuffed them in sacks with straps that were looped over their shoulders. The pickers dragged the heavy cotton duck sacks that were anywhere from six to twelve feet long depending on the strength and capacity of the picker. My sister Judy was a really good cotton picker. She pulled a nine-foot sack and could pick two hundred pounds a day—she was only eleven or twelve years old. One time during cotton-picking season, my father pulled Max out of the bathtub and gave him a few straps across his naked backside with a belt because my sister had picked more cotton that day than he had.

Of course, the cotton patch was where all the kids were, so that's where I wanted to be. I begged my mother to let me go pick cotton too. She relented and made me my own cotton sack out of a one-hundred-pound flour sack. She sewed the shoulder strap on it, and I joined the other kids in the fields. Cotton picking is backbreaking work: You either have to bend over or you have to go down the rows on your knees to avoid bending over to pull the bolls, which have hard hulls with very sharp points. Either way it's hard work, but with all the camaraderie, joking, teasing, and such that goes on, it was enjoyable too. When your sack was full, you took it to the loading wagon and weighed in. That's where the expression "sack and all" comes from . . . "It weighed in at sixty pounds, 'sack and all.'" I think I spent a couple of weeks picking cotton with the kids. We got paid three cents a pound.

My pay ended up being $1, but it was the first money I had ever made working—besides what I got climbing flagpoles—and I was so proud. I searched through the Sears, Roebuck and the Ward's catalogues (where my mother did all her shopping) for something I could order for $1. During my search was the first time I saw guitars offered for sale.

And I had my first taste of tobacco in the cotton patch. Some of the older guys kept pestering me to chew some Days Work chewing tobacco . . . "Come on, you little sissy. You want to be a man, you have to chew tobacco." I resisted because I knew my parents would be very upset, but the boys continued to pester and pressure me until I finally gave in and put a "chew" in my mouth. It wasn't long before I became deathly ill. I spent the rest of that day throwing up and turning green in the shade under the cotton trailer. I never put chewing tobacco in my mouth ever again. Lesson learned.

THE SUMMER OF 1955 rolled around, and my dad had accepted another school superintendent's job in a small town further west called Bradley. He had bought a new '55 Chevy—a 6-cylinder, four-door sedan with "three on the tree." Seems we got a new car every five years. As was his nature, he would spend months dickering over the price. When he pulled into a service station for gas, he would tell the attendant, "Fill it up with schoolteacher's gas." We were always poor, but never destitute, and we managed to have the basic necessities of life—but certainly no frills. Right before we moved, Dad had bought a raffle ticket and ended up winning a brand new '55 Ford with a big V-8 engine—so we had two brand new cars when we moved to Bradley. We sold the Ford sedan for $1,700, which was probably the biggest windfall my folks ever had. Uncle Robert, who always helped us move, brought his Ag teacher's pickup with sideboards, and we hauled all our belongings in the back of that little truck to Bradley.

Bradley wasn't just a school out in the country but was actually a little town with a population of a few hundred souls, several churches, a little store with a gas station, and a few paved streets. The school sat at the bottom of a long hill below the level of the town, and a creek bottom ran along the south side of the school. It drained into the Washita River that ran just east about a mile or so. A levy protected the school ground, which made the whole area a great outdoor playground. When it rained, my friends and I would go down to the river and play in the rising water that was red from the clay in the soil. Most summers, groups of gypsies in horse-drawn caravans could be seen camping along the Washita near the bridge that crossed it a mile or so east of the school. I repeatedly asked my mother if I could go down and visit with them. "No. No. No. Don't you ever go anywhere near those gypsies!" I didn't, although I was mighty curious about those exotic people who lived in horse-drawn caravans.

Broomcorn and alfalfa were the cash crops in the Washita River Valley, and there were broomcorn fields just north and across the road, and all down in the river valley. The laborers who harvested it were called "Broomcorn Johnnys." They cut each head of broom straw with a short, snub-nosed knife.

Bradley was quite a step up from Olney, and I was excited to be entering the fourth grade in a new place. Once again, we moved into the front portion of a US Army barracks building that sat perpendicular and just a few steps from the high school end. The school cafeteria was in the middle, and the other end of the barracks building was occupied by Vera Mae Eubanks, a widow-woman schoolteacher and her two sons: Dean, who was my brother Max's age (fifteen), and Dale, who was a couple of years older than me. Max bonded with Dean, who was already smoking Lucky Strikes and was a bit of a wise guy—though very likable. Dale let me tag around with him.

I was really fascinated by pigeons, and Dale got me into keeping them. He would go out to barns on nearby farms at night and catch wild pigeons by shining a flashlight in their eyes. After catching the birds, we cut their flight feathers and put them in a coop. The gentling process took place while the flight feather regrew: We would go out and catch them and then handle and pet them so that they became tame and familiar with us rather quickly. Like any animal, they quickly learned where the dinner table was and who was doing the cooking. During this flightless period, we prepared for when their flight feathers grew back by training them to go through a one-way door in the coop from the outside much like a dog uses a doggie door.

We constructed a landing platform on the outside, and we taught them to enter the coop by pushing them through the gate made of movable sticks hanging down from inside. The birds could easily see and be pushed through it to reenter the coop. It didn't take them long to catch on, and they were always anxious to return to what had become their new home. Of course, they would eventually pair up and mate, build nests and lay eggs, and make the coop their nesting area as well. So, by the time they had regained their ability to fly, they had nested and were familiar with how to return to and enter the coop. It was exciting when the day came to release them to the outside world to see whether they would come back. They always did. We would take a few birds some distance away and release them, and invariably, they would beat us home. From that point on, we let them fly freely. It was so fascinating to observe their behavior that I spent many a Saturday afternoon in the coop, oblivious to anything in the world but those birds.

MY DAD ORGANIZED A 4-H Club in Bradley, so I joined and raised a Duroc barrow (a neutered male pig, for those unfamiliar with barnyard terminology), and my sister fed out a Hereford steer. We took our animals to show at the Oklahoma State Fair in Oklahoma City, the first city of any size I had ever been to. We stayed in the Black Hotel in downtown OKC. That hotel was a first for me, with its uniformed porters, marble floors, and porcelain bathroom fixtures. My pet hog was overweight, and he got culled in the first round and went straight to market. I think he brought about $30. But I was sad because I had become quite attached to that big fat red hog. From then on, I always silently referred to an oversized boy with dark red hair as "Duroc."

Bradley had an outstanding high school basketball team coached by a man named Lee Freeze. Man, those kids could play! That was when I really got into basketball. In those small schools, they would start you in basketball in elementary school, and I had started back in Olney in the first grade. Since my dad was the superintendent and had the keys to the gym, I had the opportunity to play there year-round. I was a pretty athletic kid and learned quickly how to dribble, shoot, and drive for a layup. We would suit up and play a quarter or so before the older kids' ball game. Coach Freeze seemed to take an interest in me and let me shoot on the court during high school practice. As long as I didn't get in the way, I could hang. Seems I always liked to be around kids older and bigger than me because they were doing the things I wanted to do. In sports, it was always a challenge to be able to play with the big boys.

Come summer after my first year at Bradley, I was ten years old and had finished the fourth grade. My dad decided that we kids should have something constructive to do, so he arranged for Max and me to go stay with and work for his brothers, Joe and Samuel. They lived in and around Hanna, where my grandparents from both sides of the family lived. Hanna was the center of our family life and where we always went for holidays and trips to visit the kinfolks. Uncle Samuel lived just down the road from Grandma and Grandpa Nunn. Joe was newly married and had just returned to the States from a tour in the Army in post-war Okinawa. My maternal grandmother, Grandma Crocker, lived in a big two-story house in town with my mother's sister, Verna Green, and her husband, Ira Earnest ("Fat") Green. It was an unlikely match between my rather spinster-like "schoolmarm" Aunt Verna and "Fat" Green, a harmless and likeable nonpracticing Jewish fellow who had a taste for whisky. I learned he was Jewish years later when he confided that fact to me as we drove around the countryside trading pulls off a pint of whisky. He told me how he was related to the Jewish community in nearby Henryetta, and how Jewish people stuck together and helped each other, and how he could lay his hands on money if it were necessary. Until that point, I had never encountered any Jewish people. I think Aunt Verna more or less insisted he at least pretend to have converted to the Christian faith, as the Crockers were strict Baptists all the way.

Living in the area as well was my Aunt Billie, my dad's sister, who was married to Logan Mouser, a local boy who farmed and worked for the county road gang keeping the dirt roads graded and in passable condition. Uncle Joe and Uncle Samuel were partnered in the commercial hay-baling business. They baled hay for people who had hayfields but no farming equipment, as well as for American Indian families who owned lots of property they didn't develop or farm. They baled everyone's hay "on the halves," which meant they took half of the hay in pay for the baling. They either sold it or used it to supplement their own hay crop for feeding their cattle through the winter. As soon as school was out, Max and I were shipped off to Hanna into the care of Joe, Samuel, and their wives, where we worked the hayfields for the rest of the summer. Sometimes I stayed with Samuel and his wife, Velma, who had two daughters, and sometimes I would stay with Uncle Joe and his new wife, Della. All my aunts—Della, Velma, and Billie—were pregnant that summer.

Since Max was older, he was assigned the job of mowing the hay, as that required more care and attention, and I was given the simpler job of raking the new-cut hay into windrows after the hay had had a chance to shed the dampness of the overnight dews. I was put on an old Avery tractor that had one wheel up front. Uncle Joe gave me a short lesson in operating the tractor and side-delivery raking apparatus and told me to "get going." I quickly learned how to operate the outfit and would stay on the tractor until I was told I could quit. Most days, we would get to the fields around 8:00 a.m. and work till noon when the aunts would bring us a home-cooked meal or a bologna sandwich; there was iced tea or Kool-Aid—always heavily sugared. That experience inspired me to write a blues-type song I called "Come and Get It While It's Hot," which I recorded live on an *Austin City Limits* performance in 1983. With only a short rest, we were back on the tractors and wouldn't quit till sundown or we had finished mowing and raking the field.

Uncle Samuel, an Army veteran of WW II, was not the early riser that Joe was. He would sleep in a bit and have the same breakfast of eggs, sausage, toast, and a couple of cups of coffee every day. Velma doted on him and waited on him hand and foot. Samuel and Velma both smoked cigarettes, much to the disapproval of my father, who was a teetotaller in every respect. But they would enjoy a leisurely smoke, and then Samuel would take his time shaving at a wash basin on the enclosed back porch, lacing up his combat boots from the Army, and donning his long-sleeved cotton Army shirt. Maybe you've heard the expression "shade-tree mechanic"? Well, Samuel would putter around under the shade tree, where he worked on tractors and equipment and sharpened mower blades. Then he'd fill up a couple of five-gallon gas cans, a five-gallon can of water, and get in his old pickup and head out to join us in the hayfield—usually later in the day after the hay was mown and raked and had plenty of time to dry.

He operated the baling machine that picked up the raked rows of hay, pushed them through the compressing and wire-tying mechanisms, and finally deposited the eighty- to ninety-pound square bales on the ground behind it. After Uncle Samuel came the hay truck onto which the bales were lifted by hand to a stacker on the truck. Max and Uncle Brother, another of my dad's brothers who lived at home with my grandparents, would "buck" the heavy bales and put them on the truck bed, with the aid of a "hay hook" used to lift, handle, and stack the bales. Uncle Brother was a "little different," but he was capable of incredibly hard work. When the truck was loaded to the max, and the hay tied down with lariat ropes, it would be driven to a barn and unloaded—again lifted even higher off the truck and into the hayloft of the barns where it was stored out of the rain. It's hard to imagine the incredibly hard labor this work required in the hot summer heat. Imagine lifting those bales up over your head with leaves and dust raining down in your face. I escaped that backbreaking work since I wasn't big enough to buck bales. I drove the truck or pickup while the hay was being loaded: That's where I learned to drive. I wasn't big enough to see over the steering wheel, and my legs were barely long enough to push and release the clutch pedal, but I would ease the truck along, stopping after short intervals as the hay was loaded. Sometimes Joe would send me to Dustin, several miles away on the main highway, to get the mower sickle blades sharpened. Crazy! I was ten years old and couldn't see over the steering wheel, but I did it, and it made me proud to think I could do a man's job. This is how the summer passed, with only a few breaks, from Memorial Day till Labor Day.

We did get some breaks. When we had finished one field and were waiting for another to be ready, we got to take a bath in a galvanized tub or in the stock tank. Or we got to go "uptown," such as it was, to one block of the few surviving buildings that remained standing in what had been a bustling little community with three cotton gins, a bank, drugstore, a couple of grocery stores, a two-story mercantile clothing store, and a "picture show." It was common to see American Indian families in wagons pulled by horses or mules uptown on weekends and holidays. Lots of folks would come to town. They'd park their cars and pickups in the middle of the wide street and stand around and visit and catch up on the local gossip.

Uncle Joe would always take me with him pretty much everywhere he went when I wasn't riding the tractor. He was fun to hang with and was always teaching and coaching me about farm work, or Nunn history and philosophy, or telling me stories about living in Okinawa and the Geisha-girl housekeeper he had there, or just "pulling my leg," which he seemed to take great delight in. He always carried the .45 caliber automatic that was his sidearm as a lieutenant in the Army. A couple of times he would say, "Look under the car seat and see if you can find a little brown paper bag." I would find a pint of whisky, and he would uncork it and take a swig. He had a taste for the brown water and that is where I got my first taste of whisky. I didn't like it then, and I never developed a taste for it. Another lesson learned.

I liked hanging with Joe more than Samuel, since he was more fun. He was the youngest of my dad's six brothers, with thirteen years separating them. He was playful and humorous and was always going places and doing things away from the farms. He had been to college at Oklahoma A&M; then, he'd been to Korea and, of course, Okinawa.

SOMETIMES I WOULD STAY with Grandma and Grandpa Nunn and Uncle Brother. Brother was not mentally retarded, but he had some characteristics about him that prevented him from leaving home and living a normal life. He was socially awkward and had the habit of blurting out in public what was considered best left unsaid. But he was tolerated and accepted as a member of the community. He was well known for his loud outbursts at local Hanna High School basketball games as his booming baritone voice excoriated the referees in no uncertain terms for all to hear. It was a source of good-natured humor for most, and no doubt a source of embarrassment to his family. He knew all the verses to every song in the hymnal! I think he could be characterized as an idiot savant. He loved to play dominos and was always going on about "Cactus Clay" (Cassius Clay, who took the name of Muhammad Ali).

Brother Nunn, besides being an invaluable source of labor during hay season, was charged with doing all the chores around my grandparents' farm: feeding hay to the cows in the wintertime and feeding corncobs to his team of mules, Old Sam and Old Surry. Oh, he would cuss those mules! You could hear him all the way from the barn to the house, cussing a blue streak. Cussing was forbidden in the house, but he took full liberty to express himself while out of doors. Uncle Samuel planted a corn crop every year that was gathered by hand, tossed into a team-drawn wagon, and stored in the corncrib. Mules and horses love hard corn on the cob and can strip a cob clean with their teeth. The leftover cobs were a source of ammunition for corncob fights between the older cousin kids and the younger ones during family gatherings.

On warm summer evenings while I was staying at the grandparents' house, Brother and I would occasionally walk the two or
so miles to Hanna to the picture show. This was about the funkiest
movie theater you could imagine. Of course, there was the little concession area up front with a popcorn machine; pop was iced down
in a round washtub; and there were boxes of Baby Ruths, Butterfin-
gers, Peanut Rounders, and Paydays. The theater had rough wood
flooring with an aisle down the middle of the forward-slanting
floor, with about ten handmade slat benches on either side. The
projector was in the back of the theater, and there were occasional
interruptions for the changing of film by the concession keepers.
Forty people would have been a "full house," but it was never full.
The "bang-bang-shoot-'em-ups" were a welcome source of entertainment and relief from the normal routine of baling hay. After the
show, Brother and I would walk the two miles back to the house in
total darkness. If we happened to be walking home under a bright,
moonlit sky, we would cast moon shadows on the dusty road, and
Brother would relay his fantasies of what he would do with this or
that woman if he ever got the chance. That old movie house building stood empty for many years after it was closed. You could look
inside and still see the old projector, rusting in the dusty gloom of
the true last picture show.

One of the highlights of the summer was the annual Fourth of
July picnic in the nearby town of Vernon. Vernon exists (as it did
then) from the remnants of an all-black community that was established in 1911. Cattle, horses, and mules roamed freely in Vernon—
fences were nonexistent except for a few pens around town to hold
hogs or milk cows. Every once in a while, you would see one of the
Indians sleeping off a bender, sharing a shade tree with cows taking
their midday lay-down.

Cooder Fields, the principal owner of most of these stray cows,
horses, and mules, was the de facto leader of the black community,

and he owned a piece of property that contained several vacant lots full of weeds. In the middle of the property was a small open-air wooden dance floor of sorts and a jukebox snuggled inside a small doghouse for cover. On the Fourth of July, Mr. Fields would string up a few lights and throw a barbeque. Uncle Joe took me with him. Most of the whites, except for the hard-core Baptists and followers of the Church of Christ (who knew there was probably some whisky-drinking going on in the shadows), would come for the rare chance to eat barbeque and cold watermelon, drink iced-down pop, listen to the jukebox, and watch intrepid teenagers do the Bop on the mini dance floor. I remember Max, who had let his hair grow in the fashion of James Dean that summer, doing the dance with Susan Hopkins, who still lives in Hanna. I also remember eating Cooder Fields's barbeque, and my mouth burning like he had put lighter fluid in the barbeque sauce. Because of that experience, I was reluctant for many years to eat barbeque. Some memories you just can't forget!

I might take this opportunity to comment on the state of race relations during those days. I would say simply that it was very bad for the blacks. They were segregated into their communities, their schools, in public restrooms, in restaurants, and so on. Most whites referred to them with the N-word. But my family always used the term *negro,* which was polite. The only work available to blacks was primarily limited to hoeing cotton in the summertime and picking cotton in the fall alongside farmers' kids and white adults—everyone was just looking to get a little cash in their pockets, as there was very little cash money moving around. The young blacks had to leave home if they wanted to have any chance at all of escaping abject poverty their whole lives. Many did escape by joining the military. Some managed to go to college despite the many barriers. Some became teachers and came back and taught in the old school building that stands in neglect today. My people appeared comfortable around blacks, and it was common to stop in the little store there and buy a pop and stand around and visit a bit. The whites, the blacks in Vernon, and the Indian kids all grew up around each other and knew each other despite the segregation. But there was very little interaction among us. Cooder Fields always had a good horse with him, either up in the back of his beat-up pickup with no sideboards or in a funky stock trailer that couldn't really restrain any animal that wanted to escape. He was an excellent horseman and cowman, and he got around a lot. He interacted with my uncles and other locals, but that was pretty much the extent of it. The races lived separated.

There was a story around the countryside that illustrates my family's relationship and attitude toward the black members of the community. It went something like this . . .

> There was a handsome young man, whose name was Sonny Boy, who lived in the country and was blessed with the gift of gab and a pleasant, outgoing nature. He had traveled around a bit, did his time in the Army, worked on a pipeline in the Dakotas, and in general had seen some of the world outside of McIntosh County. He considered himself somewhat of a dandy when he came back home.
>
> He reached a marriageable age and set about to find himself a suitable wife. There were several eligible young ladies about, and he courted them all, but there was one in particular who was universally viewed as the most beautiful. She had several suitors seeking her hand. Sonny Boy pressed his suit, outmaneuvered his rivals, and won the prize he sought.
>
> They were married and settled in and began their life together. All went well for a while, but soon it became apparent that perhaps they weren't so well suited for a

life of marital bliss. They found themselves disagreeing on most issues that confronted them—even those of the most trivial nature. Arguments between them were a daily occurrence, but divorce was a religious and social taboo, so they continued to live together in a Mexican standoff and at perpetual loggerheads with each other.

Now Sonny Boy was smart and quite ambitious, a deal maker who pursued every opportunity to accumulate land and materials that would one day be useful in fulfilling his dream of building a showplace cattle ranch that would be the envy of all in the countryside. Consequently, as the years went by, he had accumulated a lot of building materials and would store them on his place until he could get around to completing whatever project he had in mind.

There were black people who lived around Sonny Boy, and there was one in particular whose name was Slim. Now Slim was a man of full-blood African descent with skin as black as night. He had a great sense of humor and a pleasant, friendly air about him.

His perpetual smile displayed his pearly white teeth that gleamed in stark contrast to his black skin. Slim had gone out into the world and done well for himself, putting in his years working at a government job. He had saved his money and had a good retirement income. He returned to the area to retire, bought a piece of land, put a nice mobile home on it, and proceeded to clean it up, building fences, and sheds and chicken coops, and he made it a real nice place.

As he and Sonny Boy were neighbors, they became friends and would help each other out working cattle, fixing tractors, building fences, lending each other equipment, and the like. One day Slim was hanging around at Sonny Boy's place, and he happened to notice several thirty-foot creosote telephone poles that Sonny Boy had salvaged lying on the ground. They were just waiting in the weeds for Sonny Boy to get around to the project he had envisioned for them.

Slim says to Sonny Boy, "Sonny Boy, why don't you give me those telephone poles laying out there in the weeds? I could use those for corner posts in the new fence I'm building!"

Sonny Boy says to Slim, "Why, hell no, Slim—I'm not giving you my telephone poles!"

Slim says to Sonny Boy, "Well why not? You're not using them!"

Sonny Boy says to Slim, "Well Slim, I've got a wife I'm not using too . . . but that doesn't mean I want *you* to have her!"

HANNA IS IN THE area originally granted by the federal government to the Muscogee-Creek Indian tribes, who had been removed to Oklahoma (designated Indian Territory) back in the 1800s during Andrew Jackson's presidency. The land was granted, "in common," to the tribe as a whole. In 1887, Congress passed the Dawes Act. It provided for the surveying of the "reservation," its division into 160-acre parcels, and legally deeding it to the head of each Indian family. This had the effect of transferring the ownership of the lands from the tribe "as a whole" to individuals who were free to develop the land as they saw fit—as personal property owners for their own private benefit. In Indian tradition, history, and culture, the idea of one man owning one piece of property was ludicrous. Man does not own Mother Earth. Mother Earth is for all creatures to share. Spiritually, they were likely not equipped to embrace a concept that was taboo, and the plowing up of the land would certainly "make the spirits angry."

Consequently, many of the Indian people, having no apparent alternative, fell into decline, living in houses built for them by the government and collecting checks for support; they did not pursue the idea of developing their property for their own support and benefit. The overall effect of the law was that many were forced to sell their properties for failure to pay taxes, mismanagement, or due to alcohol problems and other reasons. Therefore, white farmers and ranchers inevitably ended up owning a lot of the property. Most of them were not much better off than the Indians, but they had a different idea about profiting from ownership of the land, and they were willing to work from daylight till dark. I come from those kinds of people.

My great-grandparents settled in Indian Territory in the late 1800s, probably around the time the Dawes Act was passed. Beyond the effect it had on the Indians, another result of the act was that it encouraged whites to move into Oklahoma. When you are people who have nothing, never had anything but hand-to-mouth poverty, certainly don't own any property in a land where the rulers hold all the property and make all the rules, the lure of owning your own land was irresistible. Rarely, if ever, in the history of mankind has there been a situation where there was so much unused land that the ruling class could benefit from by making it accessible to people without property. Whites poured into the open lands that had been freed up for settlement by the acts and policies of the federal government. Soil conservation and crop rotation were unheard of, and stories are told of how old-time farmers would brag about the number of farms that they had "worn out." This practice eventually led to conditions that caused the great Dust Bowl of the 1930s.

THE NUNN FAMILY TREE can be traced back to Revolutionary War times and to the well-known historical figure Francis Marion, the celebrated "Swamp Fox," who was the tormentor of British forces during the war for independence. I have the idea that my people on the Nunn side were probably immigrants to America by way of James Oglethorpe's Georgia penal colony, which was a way for people in England who were primarily in trouble for indebtedness to be pardoned and deported to America. I'll have to consult with my cousin Sherrie Nunn Flud, who is the genealogist in the family, but I think they came by way of Arkansas most recently and before that, by way of Georgia. From Georgia, and as a part of the massive wave of western migration, the Nunns made their way to Oklahoma and settled among the Muscogee–Creek Indians along the Canadian Rivers in east central Oklahoma. Life was total self-sufficiency. You grew a garden, fattened hogs, milked cows, cut wood for cooking and heating, dug wells and drew water, and burned coal-oil lanterns for light. You would clear some land and grow a cornfield to feed your mules and horses and have some pastures for making hay to get a few cows through the winter. Your only source of income for the most part was to grow a cotton or onion crop and get a little cash to buy the kids a pair of shoes and a winter coat maybe. Even up to the time when my parents were growing up, that's the way their family survived. I don't think the Depression years changed their lives very much, as things had always been that way. Depression—what Depression?

The older brothers started coming of age along with World War II. Five of the Nunn brothers served—the only exceptions being Brother and my dad. He told me he went to enlist on several occasions but was always turned down. He was, by this time, a college graduate, married with two kids, and a school administrator and teacher. He said he asked the draft board why he was denied acceptance, and they told him, "Your mother already has five sons in the war, and that is enough for one family." In my grandmother's house, there was always a little wooden plaque hanging on the wall with five stars in a circle that was given to her by the government: All of her boys returned safely from the war. Walter, the oldest, was career Army. He was a combat instructor for British troops in England and served in military intelligence there. He was in England on D-Day but was not deployed in the invasion. Samuel was a good large-equipment operator, so he was employed building roads and airfields and such. He served in Egypt: There's a family photo of him standing in front of the Pyramids. John was an Army combat captain and was with the American infantry forces that swept through France and Germany to Berlin. He married a young German woman he met during the occupation and brought her back: I have five German-speaking cousins. Robert joined the Navy, and he served at naval air stations in Fort Worth and San Marcos, Texas. Joe, the youngest, was in the Army National Guard and, as I've mentioned, later served in Korea and Japan.

After the war, Walter came back to Lawton, Oklahoma, and continued to work for the Army at Fort Sill as a meteorologist. He married Lena Holmes from Hanna, and they had two sons, Brian, who was Max's age, and Milton, who was a couple of years younger than me and the boy cousin closest to my age. They spent about four years living in Germany and returned to Lawton around 1956. After he retired from the Army, Walter went to college, got a degree, and taught school long enough to have a teacher's retirement as well as a military retirement.

Samuel returned to Hanna, married Lena Holmes's sister, Velma, and settled into farming and ranching and driving a road grader for the county. They had three daughters: Patricia, one year exactly younger than me, Sherrie, and Sheila, the youngest.

John brought home his new German bride and settled in Columbia, South Carolina, near Fort Jackson, and served until he retired from the Army with the rank of major. He died of a heart attack in his early fifties.

Robert pursued his education and followed in the footsteps of my dad. He became an Ag teacher and a coach. He married the beautiful part-Cherokee maiden Mary Lou Helms, who was a teacher as well. They had three children: Tollie Boy, Karen, and Tanya.

Joe married Della Patrick from nearby Dustin, and they had one daughter, Joann.

Billie, the youngest and only daughter, married local boy Logan Mouser, and they had four children: Bonita, George, Joyce, and Billy Jack. I am mentioning my aunts, uncles, and cousins here, as they will likely be appearing from time to time in this telling of this story. This is it for the Nunn side of the family.

My mother's side—the Crockers—was similar in a lot of ways, yet very different. I know very little about the Crocker side beyond my mother's father, Robert Crocker. He died of tuberculosis at a relatively young age in a sanatorium in Texas. My grandmother, Lottie Patton, was half-German on the maternal side of her family. Their family name was Stumbaum. They were very strict Baptists, whereas my father's side was Church of Christ; we were raised Baptist. The old saying goes that when a couple gets married, the husband takes the wife's religion, and the wife takes the husband's politics, and this will make for a happy marriage. The Crockers retained the German quality of frugalness and a strict adherence to Christian doctrine. It was "waste not, want not" in that house.

There were rarely any leftovers at their kitchen table when the meal was over, though as a family, they seemed to be much better off than the Nunns—and slimmer. They all had regular-paying teaching jobs, and my mother's older brother, Earnest Crocker, became a wealthy man. There was no smoking or drinking allowed in their house, and the utterance of profanity and vulgarity was strictly *verboten*. This was unlike the Nunns—who generally were not smokers or drinkers except for Grandpa Tollie and some of the boys who had been in the Army—who would have an occasional drink on holidays . . . *mostly*. They never poured cocktails, but some of the boys managed to have a "pint to sneak a pull on," on special occasions.

The Crockers and their wives and husbands were all schoolteachers, and all were strict Baptists. Grandma Crocker, whose single sinful vice was "dipping" Garrett Bros. snuff, lived to her nineties, and she dipped till the day she died. She lived in a big two-story house that she shared with my mother's sister, Verna, and the aforementioned Fat Green. Family gatherings there were rather somber affairs around the dinner table with discussions about the weather, church, school, and other family talk. After dinner (dinner was the noonday meal; supper was the evening meal), they would retire to the living room parlor or to the front porch swing for more of the same. Of course, there was no TV, and certainly no thoughts of how to keep energetic kids entertained. We had to sit quietly and listen, or be constantly admonished with "Hush, now" or "Don't do this, don't do that," or go outside. Voices were never raised in animation of any sort, except to scold children. Along before dark, the visitors would say, "Well, I guess it's about time for us to go home," and they were gone. (I might mention a Crocker of note: The son of my cousin Margaret, Bill Self, is the head coach of the Kansas Jayhawks basketball team.)

When we stayed there overnight, we kids would sleep in the small, unheated, and unair-conditioned upstairs—under a pile of handmade quilts in the winter and sweating in the unventilated bedrooms in the summer. The adults rarely ever went upstairs, and it was not really fixed up at all except with beds for company. I liked it up there, though I wasn't allowed to be there except to sleep. It was cozy and mysterious. I could dream about baseball, swimming in a real swimming pool, riding horses, chasing outlaws, singing a song, and getting the girl.

The Nunns, on the other hand, were not nearly so strict, and there was much more fun to be had in staying at Grandma Nunn's house out in the country where the chatter around the table was filled with life and laughter and lively conversation and debate. The house itself was, I must say, a very poor house by comparison with Grandma Crocker's house "uptown." It was made out of nothing more than barn wood. It had a sheet-iron roof and was set on stacks of large sandstone rocks as a foundation. I'm surprised it never blew away as it didn't appear to be attached to the rocks in any way. I would characterize it as a tar-paper shack, but there was no tar paper; no insulation whatsoever, and the few cracks in the walls were covered over with newspaper. The floors were only partially covered with worn-out linoleum. There was a front porch, then two separate rooms across the front, both of which had screen door entrances from the porch. The room on the right held an iron double bed frame with a featherbed where Grandma slept, and a frayed-around-the-edges couch, and that's about all the space there was in that room. There was a mirrored dresser with drawers that was covered with porcelain figurines or other modest mementos of their lives. There were no closets in the house, so Grandma's dresses were just hung up on a rack in the corner, with the few private things she owned stuffed in a small chest of drawers. Despite its small size, I witnessed many a family discussion and a few family rows in that room filled with uncles and aunts—with Grandma standing or sitting on the couch or the bed.

On the left side at the front of the house was another room of equal size. There was another double bed covered with a home-made quilt in the back corner, a small table with chairs suitable for a game of dominos or dinner for kids, and a good-sized pot-bellied coal-burning stove. Someone delivered a supply of coal on a regular basis. The left front room was, I guess, the family room because that's where the fire was. Domino games were pretty much going on all the time as Tollie and Brother both liked dominos and didn't get much chance to play unless there was company around. We kids were new meat and they would play with us . . . deaf Grandpa and crazy Uncle Brother! It was a learning experience, and I learned how to play dominos pretty well. I don't ever remember being cold in that house though winters could be brutal.

Grandpa's room was an add-on off the back of the house and was barely large enough for his bed; any extra space was taken up by the accumulation of a lifetime of newspapers, magazines, clothes stuffed in corners, and stacks of papers he had written. Sadly, they were thrown out when he died. When Cousin Milton and I would go in his room to greet him, he'd be lying back there in his deaf solitude. We'd yell to him, "Hello, Grandpa!" and he would say, "Is you Walter's or William's boys?" We *were* Walter's and William's boys.

Connecting the front part of the house to the back was a middle room, once again with a double bed, and that's where Brother slept. When I stayed there, I would sleep with Brother. There was a screen door leading to another porch on the right side of the house that had its own door to the kitchen. The kitchen was on the back of the house. A lot of gatherings concentrated in the kitchen around a circular table. Grandma Nunn cooked sausage or bacon with eggs and toast every morning of the world. Grandpa Tollie would shuffle in, take his seat, and proceed to drink his coffee by shaking his shaky hand and spilling the coffee into the saucer. Then he'd loudly slurp the coffee out of the saucer. Grandpa was totally deaf and blissfully unaware of the disapproval about his horrible table manners expressed by Grandma and the omnipresent aunts in the kitchen with her. He was removed from participating in conversation due to his deafness, but every now and then he would burst forth with some story about something that happened way back when. No one would listen or quit talking, so his story would go on unnoticed.

He was the classic cantankerous old man who came from a time long past and was generally an embarrassment to everyone in the family—especially my dad and Uncle Robert, who were the two most straightlaced of the family. He would curse when he was angry and stomp through the house raising holy hell! He smoked a pipe with Prince Albert tobacco that eventually led to mouth cancer. He had had surgery, and he bore a scar across his sunken left cheek that proceeded through his upper lip. That's where I got my first taste of smoking tobacco. It tasted awful and the pipe burned my mouth. I never could develop a taste for smoking a pipe.

From the stories I heard, the young Tollie Nunn was some kind of character in his day. Apparently, he had a rather "artistic nature"— which was his way of justifying his avoidance of hard work after his boys got big enough to cut firewood, feed the stock, and hoe cotton. He was known to hang out for extended periods with the Indians, write poetry, make pottery, go on long horseback trips to San Antonio, and catch the train to El Paso. He wore a gun on his hip, and there's a story that he killed a man in El Paso over a card game. He was quite a "rounder–sounder" and spent a lot of time away. Grandma said, "He would come home just long enough to get me pregnant again."

He was very hard on his boys and a rather tyrannical father, never hesitating to whip them with the nearest willow switch or trace line from the mule harness at the slightest provocation. He always kept a pint of Old Charter Whiskey under his mattress, and that was the inspiration for the song I wrote called "Well of the Blues" that Jerry Jeff Walker recorded on the *Walker's Collectibles* LP. All I could gather about his politics is from a story about the time a Ku Klux Klan member came by his house in his Klan robe and hood, threatening him regarding the way he should vote in the next election.

He reportedly replied to the fellow, "I know who you are, and if you come around here threatening me again, I'm gonna shoot you dead!"

Grandpa always had a pistol under his mattress. One time, all of us cousin kids were there, and he summoned us all out to the front porch. He had his pistol in his hand. He told us to look to the high bank across the dirt road that passed in front of the house. There was a red pocket-sized Prince Albert can over there. He said, "Now you kids watch this," and he fired off three shots at the can. He sent us racing across the road to retrieve it. Sure enough, it had three bullet holes in it. Something tells me he was playing a trick on us, but we never knew for sure. He was known to be a good shot, and everyone in the countryside knew he would not hesitate to pull a gun if threatened, so nobody ever messed with him. He had a short fuse and a terrible temper that tended toward loud and violent outbursts, a characteristic inherited by several of his kids and grandkids. My uncles would be playing "Moon" at the kitchen table after supper at Grandma's house, and disagreements would fester into loud arguments. A couple of times they nearly came to blows. It was classic blustering but does go to illustrate the nature of the genes they inherited from Tollie. Fortunately, in that regard, I think I took after my mother's side of the family.

My Grandma Nunn supplied the calming influence, and I never once saw her lose her steadiness. Her story is interesting. Her father, Charles Ferguson, was a coal miner in Bristol, Tennessee, so she, like Loretta Lynn, was a coal miner's daughter. He brought his family to Oklahoma in the late 1800s. His story is that he was born a Floyd, but raised in a family of Fergusons, and he took the name. Supposedly, a branch of that Floyd family eventually bore the fruit that was known as "Pretty Boy" Floyd. My dad made the trip to Sallisaw in northeastern Oklahoma to attend his funeral when he was eventually run to ground.

There were eight children in the family: Ethyl, Bethyl, Berthyl,

Bessie, Woodson, Mammie, Claude, and Maud. She told me that most of the folks in Bristol, Tennessee, were English and spoke with a distinct English accent that she could imitate quite well despite the seventy years since she had heard it. Ethyl Nunn accepted her lot with no complaints and went about her duties making the best of what she had. She was married to Tollie Nunn, for whom she had to care and from whom she got very little help. He was a handful just to live with and kept her barefoot and pregnant her whole young life.

She had fifteen or twenty grandkids, any of whom might be in and out of her house at any time. On holiday gatherings—which was every holiday—she would have them all coming in and out all day long, with the accompanying slamming of the screen doors. They all had to be fed and provided with a bed. Since Uncle Samuel and Velma lived about a mile west down the road, and they had a good-sized house, and my Aunt Billie and her husband Logan lived east of Hanna, there always seemed to be beds for everyone somewhere. Of course, us kids had to double up. Thinking about it, it's hard to imagine how they did manage to accommodate all of us when we were all there at once. Once I asked her if she had any regrets. She rolled her eyes back in her head as if to find the answer up there and said, "Yes. I do . . . I think if I had it to do all over again, I wouldn't have had so many children."

Another of her quotations that has always stuck with me came forth one day when I was grown and visiting with her. She was commenting about bull riders, as the subject had come up in conversation, and she said, "Bull riders, musicians, and politicians are all 'counted sorry.'" Counted sorry was a common expression that connoted good for nothing! I always kept her words in mind and have tried to make sure that I never fell into the "counted sorry" category.

Chapter 2

Home with the Armadillo

AT THE END OF the summer of 1956, I was relieved to be able to return home to Bradley and reunite with my family. School was back in session, I had kids my age to play with, and the normal routine returned. I felt a sense of pride that I had done a lot of man's work that summer—I had learned how to drive a truck, operate a tractor, and lots about tools and the servicing and maintaining of equipment—even though I received no praise, thanks, or money for all the work I had done.

The praising of kids for a job well done was not part of my family's makeup. They didn't dote, pet, or worry about things like their kid's self-esteem. Self-esteem, for them, came from discipline, accomplishments, honesty, integrity, and the living of a clean, Christian life. Birthdays were seldom taken note of and certainly there were no birthday parties or gifts. But as a kid, I guess you don't miss what you are unaware of. Though I never doubted my parents loved me, the outward display of affection was rare.

Nevertheless, once I returned home and school got going, I was a happy camper. I got back into school and playing ball and tending my pigeons. One of the kids in town had a Cushman 3-horsepower motor scooter that I coveted. Elvis Presley was creating a stir with the song "Hound Dog," and songs like "Party Doll" by Buddy Knox and "Great Balls of Fire" by Jerry Lee Lewis that my folks regarded as vulgar were playing on the radio and on jukeboxes in the cafes in Chickasha.

In the fall of 1956, a presidential campaign was in progress. Dwight Eisenhower, the Republican candidate, was running for a second term against Adlai Stevenson. My dad wore an I LIKE IKE button, and there was a lot of discussion and debate going on. People would say, "Are you for him or are you 'agint' him?" referring to Eisenhower. Seems my dad was the only one around who supported Ike. Mrs. Rayburn, my fifth-grade teacher, was an outspoken Democrat and had no reservations about engaging her boss in lively debate.

I often wondered why my dad was Republican, as he had lived through the Depression and the Roosevelt years and had served in the Civilian Conservation Corps (CCC), a "make-work" program created by the Roosevelt administration for unemployed young men not in the military. In the late 1930s, he joined in the CCC building roads and bridges in national parks in the mountains of Colorado and in Lufkin, Texas. He also built jetties along the Texas coast around Rockport and Port Aransas. Palo Duro Canyon Park is a good example of projects built by the CCC. The men slept in tents and lived quasi-military style. My dad sent all the money he earned to his mother and dad for their support.

Considering the hard times and the absence of work in the country, one would think that he would have thought that the make-work programs of the New Deal were worthwhile, and he would have given credit to Roosevelt, but that was not the case. He would often complain bitterly about Roosevelt, though I can't recall any specifics of the complaints. This was my first awareness of anything political. My dad's not being a Democrat later had significant negative effects on his career in the school business.

EISENHOWER GOT ELECTED, BASKETBALL season arrived, and attention focused on the Bradley Dragons team. Local fans would pack the gym for home games and follow the team to the area schools. I spent all my Saturdays and Sundays bundled up in warm clothes in my pigeon coop or in the gym with my brother Max. I was suiting up with the fifth-grade team, which was coached by Lee Freeze, the high school coach. While I would practice dribbling, shooting, and driving for layups, my brother would stand at midcourt and hurl the ball toward the basket. He became quite proficient at making goals from half-court.

At Christmas, we were back to Hanna. Christmas trees back then were not the beautiful spruce trees grown for that purpose today, but rather, scraggly cedars that Brother had cut and dragged in from the woods. They were strung with a few lights and ornaments, as well as a string of red berries that lent themselves quite well to Christmas tree decoration. Tollie would get up and dress around six every Christmas morning, probably have a nip off the pint of Old Charter from under his mattress, and stomp through the house banging his walking cane on the floor and yelling, "Christmas gifts. Christmas gifts!" There would be a pair of socks from Grandma and a cap pistol with plenty of ammunition (rolls of paper caps that popped when you pulled the trigger) under the tree for me. I was happy with it, and I spent the holidays outdoors playing cowboys or soldiers—me and Cousin Milton at war with Max and Milton's older brother Brian. Corncobs from the barnyard supplied more ammunition: hand grenades thrown from the hayloft at the enemy below.

Uncle Walter was an avid hunter, and I loved to accompany him on hunting trips through the woods. I thought I was a big boy, as I got to carry a little double-barrel .22/9 mm gun that Uncle John had brought home from the war and given to Grandpa Tollie.

The 9 mm shot a little buckshot shell a bit smaller than a .410. There were lots of bobwhite quail, cottontail rabbits, and squirrels in the trees. Occasionally we would "tree" a possum. We'd take the game back to the house to skin and clean it. Grandma cooked whatever it was and served it for the next meal. Possum stew is not half bad, though a bit greasy. It was, no doubt, a welcome source of protein during the hard Depression years when there was little else to eat.

After Christmas, it was back to Bradley, basketball, and school. Someone had taken note of my keeping pigeons and gave me several pairs of White Kings, Fantails, and Racing Homers that upgraded my pigeon flock with exotics in addition to the common barn variety I was keeping.

Dale Eubanks was the younger of Vera Mae Eubanks' sons. They lived on the other side of the barracks building from us. Dale had a job breaking Shetland ponies for a prominent local alfalfa farmer and rancher named Adam Brown. He raised four or five Shetland colts every year, and Dale had full control of the ones that were coming two years old in the spring. It was Dale's job to break them to ride and to gentle them and make them suitable for sale. He asked me if I would like to help him. A chance to ride ponies! My dream came true! I was in heaven! Every afternoon after school, we went up to Adam Brown's place up the hill on the edge of town. Dale would take the oldest and largest and start riding him: Old Buck was the name of the first pony. When Dale got him going to a certain point, he would turn him over to me, and he would start the next one. Tony was next. I would ride Buck, and he would ride Tony. When he finished with Tony, he would turn him over to me, and he would start the next, a little dapple palomino named Star with a white mane and tail. We'd ride till dark and walk back down the hill, usually late for supper.

We enlisted our next best friend to join our mini-equestrian band of cowboy-horsemen. By the time spring came, we had five ponies totally broken to ride and gentle as big dogs. We'd spend all weekend on extended daylong rides all over the whole countryside. We'd strap on our holsters with cap pistols and have good guy–bad guy chases at full gallop with cap pistols blazing. We'd go skinny-dipping in Adam's Hole and just turn the ponies loose—they were trained to come back to the whistle. We even had a hideout; some sort of underground cellar-type thing that we had discovered in our explorations. It was in a field of weeds and just up the hill from the schoolhouse. We'd "borrow" costume jewelry from our mothers' and sisters' jewelry boxes and put it in a fruitcake tin—that was our "treasure," which we kept "stashed" in our hideout. I got in trouble over that for sure. It was a total fairy tale come true for a kid like me, and those were the happiest days of my life!

Once again, school was out for the summer, and a couple of days later Max and I were delivered back to Hanna. The happy days of riding horses and playing cowboy were gone, and it was back to real work. Max and I knew the routine and hit the ground running. Again, we were shuffled around and were staying with Joe and Della some, or with Samuel and Velma, at Grandma Nunn's, or at Billie and Logan's. All the aunts had new babies (Aunt Velma had Sheila, Della had Joann, and Billie had Billy Jack), so sometimes, on off days, I was assigned to them to help look after their kids while they did garden work or gathered wild berries or "sandhill" plums for the making of jams and jellies. That summer I spent more time at Billie and Logan's. I carried Billie's two-year-old Joyce around on my hip quite a bit, and Uncle Logan had me trapping gophers in his peanut patch. With a shovel, I would dig a shovel's length and expose the gopher tunnel six or eight inches underground.

The gopher trap was a wooden cube about three inches wide and five inches long and open on the bottom and back. A trap mechanism sat inside. A hole to allow light in was drilled on the front side exposed to the outside. The trap would be set in the gopher tunnel and covered with dirt except for the side with the hole. When the gopher would see the light, he would move toward the light to cover it and be caught in the trap before he reached the source of the breach in his tunnel. Of course, there were so many it was impossible to rid a field completely. Gophers could do a lot of damage to the peanuts developing underground.

As Max and I were a year older by this time, and experienced hands, Joe would put us in the fields early in the morning, leave a five-gallon water can, and he'd go off looking after other business; sometimes he wouldn't come back till dusky dark. Those were long, hard days, and I would get so sunburned that my lips were blistered and swollen. Since I was getting no praise, or pats on the back, or signs of appreciation, I began to lose my enthusiasm for driving a tractor around all day in a hot, dusty field. Keep in mind that I was eleven years old and had absolutely no contact with any kids near my age. I had taken a baseball and a glove with me that summer, but the only thing I could do was to throw a ball up in the air and catch it myself . . . pretty boring play. I swiped one of Velma's menthol cigarettes and smoked it out behind Samuel's barn. It made me sick, and I felt guilty. To prevent being caught, I washed my own mouth out with soap, as it would surely be reported to my dad if I got caught, and that was a prospect I did not want to chance. I was not a happy kid.

By this time, Grandma Crocker and Aunt Verna had a new television, and their first air-conditioner window unit was installed in the living room/parlor in their house uptown. I started taking every opportunity to stay at their house and sit in an air-conditioned room watching television—especially *The Mickey Mouse Club* that featured the kids' cowboy series "Spin and Marty." It beat the heck out of trapping gophers or riding a tractor all day in the burning heat. Before long, Uncle Joe would be knocking on the door, and we were back in the hayfield.

Right as school let out for that summer, Lee Freeze, the basketball coach, had gotten wind of some school-teaching jobs in Brownfield, Texas. He traveled out there and accepted a junior high counselor's job for himself, an elementary teaching position for his wife, Rulene, and one for Verna Mae Eubanks, who was Rulene's sister. Before we left to go to Hanna, they had come driving up in front of our Army-barracks house, and we went out to greet them. They informed my dad that there were additional teaching jobs available out in Brownfield and encouraged him to check them out. Little did I know that after Max and I had been delivered to Hanna, my folks had driven out to Brownfield, interviewed, and decided to apply for jobs there.

The thought of moving to Texas sparked great excitement for me. I had no idea what Texas was like, but to me, it was where all the cowboys were, and everyone lived on big ranches and rode horses and worked huge herds of cattle—and that was perfect in my mind. But I didn't have the time to dwell on it that summer.

It was pretty much drudgery in the hayfields, as I had been assigned another duty to add to the raking of the hay. The old baler had developed a problem. The mechanism that cut and tied the baling wire around the square bales was malfunctioning, and it would not return completely to its start position for the next bale. It required a large rattail wrench to be inserted into position, and the tying mechanism had to be moved into place or it would fail to tie the next bale. It fell on me to sit on the rectangular tube behind where the finished bales passed, and insert the point end of the rattail wrench to nudge the tying mechanism back to its proper position. Otherwise, untied blocks of hay would be delivered out the backside. A plunger pushed the hay being gathered on the front side, and every time it made a plunge, it would scatter dust from the hay into the air and into my face. The baler would bounce around due to the uneven ground, and I was being tossed and bucked around back there with dust spewing in my face. We baled hundreds of bales that way in the heat of the afternoons.

By the end of the day, I would be covered in dust and sweat and completely exhausted. My bottom was raw from sitting on the U-shaped steel tray that ran the length of the bale chute. Of course, the hay had to be picked up, so I would drive the truck while Brother, Max, Joe, and Samuel "bucked" and stacked the hay on the truck. Then it was on to the barn. We would get back to the house, and Brother and I would go for a bath in the stock tank. It was damned hard work! With no TV or AC, after supper we went straight to bed with the windows open and praying for a little breeze to blow through. It was so hot I would sleep in my jockey briefs with no cover.

I had mixed feelings about the situation. I felt a sense of pride that I was just a little kid who could do a man's work without complaint, and that I could help my uncles do work that had to be done. Farming life in general appealed to me as it seemed to be a lifestyle one could derive a great deal of satisfaction from, what with the husbandry of land and animals, and the planting and watching crops grow to produce food. I continued to learn a lot about the use of tools and the maintenance of farm machinery and the care involved in raising cattle. On the other hand, I was homesick and lonesome for companionship with kids my own age. I needed some praise from the big boys for the work I did, and I needed a sense of belonging to the team.

I stayed mostly at Samuel and Velma's house when we were working the hayfields. Samuel had bought a brand new International Harvester tractor that was parked out behind their house. It was a huge step up in quality and was bigger and more powerful than what they'd had before. It even had an enclosed cab on the top with an air conditioner. One morning, no one was home except for Aunt Velma, and I went out and climbed up. I wanted to check out the new tractor. The gear shifter had some symbols on the dash that

I assumed were put there for the benefit of non-English-speaking operators—of which there were none in Oklahoma. There was a symbol for a rabbit and one for a turtle. I quickly deduced that the rabbit was for fast and the turtle for slow. Upon seeing this, I ran into the house and told Aunt Velma, "It's really neat how they put the symbols of a rabbit and a turtle in Samuel's new tractor!"

Well, Velma was incredulous. She said, "That's not true, you're telling me a story." The word "story" was a word commonly used to avoid saying, "You're telling a lie."

"No, I swear, the new tractor has a rabbit and a turtle on the dash."

Determined to catch me in a fib, the little woman went out and climbed up into the tractor cab to see for herself. Sure enough. She came back in a bit of a huff. The small humor I enjoyed in that moment was about all the humor I had that summer, and I still break into laughter thinking about it.

Time dragged by and it was getting toward the end of July. One morning, I was out at Samuel's outdoor "shade-tree workshop" filling up five-gallon gas cans. Velma came out the back door and hollered to me, "Your mother just called, and y'all are moving to Texas!"

A wave of complete happiness and joy washed over me, and I was overcome by a feeling of ecstasy that had to come close to what the fundamentalist Christians experienced when they were speaking in tongues and rolling on the church house floor. I bolted up, knocked over a partially filled gas can, and pogo-jumped around, clapping my hands. I sang out over and over as loud as I could,

> "Oh, how I'd love to live in the Lone Star State
> I'm gonna be happy, it's gonna be great
> It won't be long, and I can't wait
> Oh, how I'm gonna love the Lone Star State."

No sunburned, towheaded, wannabe ballplayer/cowboy could have ever been happier than I was at that moment.

Chapter 3

Moving to Texas

IT WAS THE BEGINNING of August in 1957. We had worked hard in the hayfields those last days, and I was still going to be raking hay and riding the back of the dusty, bucking hay baler for another week or so, but I didn't mind. We were moving to Texas! When my dad came to pick up Max and me, I recall him talking to Uncle Joe as we packed for the trip back to Bradley. Joe was so involved in conversation with my dad that he didn't once recognize Max or me for the work we had done; nor did he thank us or offer us even a five-dollar bill to acknowledge it. I was hurt, as I had tried so hard to please Joe and make myself a "hand" to him, proving I could do what I was told to do. Without saying goodbye to anyone else in the family, we loaded into our '55 Chevy and drove back to Bradley. I was relieved and excited about the future.

In my absence, my pigeon coop had been invaded by rats and most of the birds had been killed, except for the White Kings and a few others. I opened the coop and set them all free. They were still hanging around the day we packed our furniture in Uncle Samuel's borrowed flatbed hay truck and headed for Texas. Mom and Dad and little brother Steve rode in the truck, and Max drove the car with sister Judy and me aboard. We got a late start and had to drive all night, arriving in Brownfield close to sunup. We had left Oklahoma behind.

The Freezes and the Eubanks had moved at the beginning of that summer and were well established in their homes when we arrived. Max and I were deposited at the Eubanks' little stucco house, which was a common building style on the older homes there. We bunked in with Dean and Dale Eubanks. Mom and Dad unloaded and stored all our furniture in the Freezes' garage and stayed with them across town, with Steve and Judy sleeping on pallets on their floor. My parents placed a mattress on top of the furniture stored in the garage and made their bed there. We relied on the generosity of our Oklahoma friends for a couple of weeks while my folks finalized the purchase of the first house we had ever owned at 1304 E. Broadway, just on the edge of the nicer part of town and a few blocks from the high school.

We finally got moved into our new home and began our new life in a three-bedroom brick house. It would be considered small by today's standards, but compared to the Army barracks buildings we had lived in, it was a castle! Sister Judy was a teenager, and she could finally have her own room. Baby brother Steve was just coming six, and he still slept with her in her room. Judy didn't mind, as this represented no change: She had always shared a bed and nurtured and cared for baby brother Steve. She was just happy that she finally had her own room and a new bedroom suite. Max and I had our own room, and we shared a bed as we always had.

It may sound primitive and as if we were impoverished Okie hillbillies, but everything is relative to what you're used to. This was a giant step up for us in terms of our lifestyle, even though there still was not much money left at the end of the month from my folks' meager salaries teaching school. They taught school for over thirty years and never made more than $30,000 a year combined salary. At Brownfield, Mom got a position teaching second grade, which she preferred, but Dad did not get a principal's job. The superintendent told him if he would teach math, he would be in line for the next principal's position that became vacant.

Max and I stayed with the Eubanks, and Dean took Max under his wing and showed him around, as they were both seniors in high school. Dale was closer to my age, and I bonded with him. He had a new pony to ride—a Cushman 3-horse motor scooter—and a paper route, so we were mobile. He familiarized me with the lay of the town and introduced me to Johnny Knox, who lived up the street and had a scooter too. We rode around double on his motor scooter. He took me to the beautiful city-operated swimming pool, the Little League ballpark, the high school, the junior high, and the city's several elementary schools. He showed me around the downtown, which had three movie theaters with air-conditioning and soft velvet seats. One was a Spanish-language theater that served the significant population of temporary Mexican workers, called braceros, who were brought into Texas to work in the cotton fields. A thriving business district was centered around the Terry County Courthouse square and a Piggly Wiggly grocery store. To my kid's eyes, walking into that Piggly Wiggly was like walking into an HEB Superstore today. We could shop without driving thirty miles! Brownfield was just a wind-blown West Texas town in the middle of a giant cotton field, but it was a real town and a far cry from the hayfields-and-dirt-road-backstreets and last-picture-show existence from which I had just escaped. I thought I had died and gone to heaven. Not only did they have paved streets to ride a bicycle on, a beautiful swimming pool with diving boards, Little League baseball, but also band, and something with which I was totally unfamiliar—football! There were no horses to ride, but there was so much more that I didn't care.

I ENTERED JUNIOR HIGH in the sixth grade. Dad taught seventh-grade math. No more two grades in one room with the teacher teaching all the subjects. In Brownfield, we had a different teacher and a different room for every subject. We had our own lockers, and we mixed with kids in the seventh and eighth grades between classes. I'm sure this all sounds like no big deal to the reader today, but to me, back then, it was an exciting new world, and I was looking forward to living in it.

Brownfield offered junior high band in the sixth grade. I had always gravitated to music and wanted very much to take band. I wanted to play the trumpet, because at that time Big Bands had been the dominant musical style, and the trumpet players were always the featured musicians. In other words, they were the stars of the band. Dad informed me that he didn't have the money to buy a horn, but I persevered, enrolled in band, and was supplied a used horn from the school stock.

I started band in the sixth grade and played the trumpet, but my band director, Mac Jones, wanted me to give it up and convert to a baritone horn. The baritone horn is a valve instrument that looks like a miniature tuba. It's voiced in the same range and has a tone similar to a trombone, but not as brassy. I think this was because there were already five or so trumpet players in the band and no baritone horns. I was disappointed, as my goal was to be the first-chair trumpet player and the star of the band, and the baritone horn was definitely not going to make anyone a star. My dad was in on the plan too, and they informed me about it one day after school. I asked them why. "Well, Mr. Jones says your lips are too big to play the trumpet," my dad told me. You see, my lips are rather large, and the mouthpiece for the trumpet is very small. The mouthpiece for the baritone is larger, similar to the trombone. I was rather dubious about the reason they gave, and I said to them with some emotion, "That can't be right—Louis Armstrong's lips are four times bigger than mine!" Nevertheless, I was converted and moved to the baritone section next to seventh-grader Bill McGowan.

Being flexible and versatile would be a reoccurring theme in my life. It seems I was always the utility man, assigned to filling the slots that were necessary, but not glamorous; doing the things that nobody else wanted to do, like playing secondary or supportive roles. I justified and accepted it by assuming an attitude that championed the importance of being Number Two. Actually, in the long run, it served me well and laid a solid foundation for my career.

Mac Jones was fresh out of college. This was his first job, so we were all beginners. I loved sitting in the trumpet section, because it was somehow the "cool" section other than the ultra-cool drum section, where the drummers were always goofing off. A lot of the kids I had classes with were in the band too—mostly girls, who played clarinets and flutes. It was fun, and I enjoyed band and loved Mr. Jones, who would play a large and influential part in my life as time went by.

My dad bought me a used bicycle and had it cleaned up with new handgrips with plastic tassels hanging from them. I immediately got a paper route job. I threw about thirty afternoon papers a day for the *Odessa American*. My route included the whole town! Most people read the *Lubbock Avalanche-Journal*, but they didn't need any carriers and the *Odessa American* did. Their subscribers were people who worked in the oil fields out west of Brownfield, and the *Odessa American* kept up with the West Texas oil business news. After school, I would come home and roll my papers, hang the paper bag across my handle bars, and ride my bicycle from one end of town to the other—north, south, east, and west. Man, I was one tired puppy when I got home from throwing those few papers.

I think I made seven or eight dollars a month for my efforts. Plus, I had to collect once a month from the few scattered customers. Up to that point in life, I was not having any luck making money for all the work I did. Then I started thinking, *How I can do less work and make more money?*

I WAS DYING TO have a motor scooter. In Texas, you could ride a scooter with no more than 3 horsepower at the age of twelve. Cushman and Allstate (Sears) made a little red scooter powered by a 3-horsepower Briggs & Stratton engine, and Cushman made the Cushman Eagle, which had an 8-horse motor. It was bigger and faster and was designed more like a motorcycle. That is what the big boys rode. Vespa had a scooter that wasn't much different from the ones available today, but there was only one in town. They were regarded as sissy scooters even though they were fun to ride. There was a little "scooter gang" in town who called themselves the Eagles. They wore leather motorcycle jackets, slicked back and oiled their hair, and swaggered about pretending they were Hell's Angels. People called them "thugs," but they never seemed to get in any trouble. They would take the guts out of the exhaust pipes, and those Cushman Eagles would roar like Harley hogs. They'd come thundering to school every day and cut a few donuts on the school yard grass and then "rack off" the engines a few times before shuttin 'em down.

My dad always talked about what he would do if his ship ever came in, and one of the things he wanted was a Harley-Davidson Super Glide, the top of the Harley line. So when I turned twelve, he told me he would get me a scooter if I got a paper route that would pay for it. He told Max the same thing. I suppose he thought he could live vicariously through us and would enjoy seeing his boys riding in the wind, as he probably would never be able to do. Dale

Eubanks put in a word for us with the local distributors of the *Avalanche-Journal*, and we both got offers to take over routes that were being vacated.

As soon as we secured the jobs, Dad went to Lubbock and bought two used scooters—a 3-horse Allstate for me and a Cushman Eagle for Max! The deal was that we had to pay him back from the money we earned throwing papers, and we could never take the guts out of the exhaust pipes. Hey, that worked for me.

The Lubbock paper was a daily—morning and afternoon publication. If you bought a $1.50/month daily subscription, you got a paper every morning, including the Sunday morning—a big, thick paper with all the additions and inserts by commercial retailers. Or, you could take the afternoon paper, which got you the evening edition and the Sunday morning paper. Or, you could take just the Saturday morning paper. All subscribers got a Sunday edition, so my Sunday route totaled about 350 papers. The papers were delivered to our front porch every morning at four o'clock, in bound stacks. Max and I would get up at 5:00 and roll the papers, put them in cotton-paper bags, throw them across our scooters, and go throw our routes. His was on the north side of the Tahoka Highway, and mine was in the nice neighborhoods a few blocks south of where we lived.

Most mornings we were back to the house by 6:30, and we could sleep another hour before school. During the week, we could get all our papers in one bag for our morning routes, so we just had to make one trip. On Sundays, because we had another hundred or so extra Sunday papers, and they were so big and heavy, we'd have to return to the house a couple of times to reload the bags and then complete the route. We'd have a full bag across our lap, another on the buddy seat, and the space across our laps was stacked with as many as we could handle. Mom and Dad would often get up with us and help roll the papers. On snow days, Dad would take me in his car. I did this every day from the sixth grade all the way through high school, and I got pretty good at throwing papers. You had to compensate for your speed and throw the papers well in advance of your scooter, but I could hit the front door of the houses at thirty miles per hour cruising down the early morning streets in the dark with no hands on the handlebars. In the wintertime, we attached windshields and put on Naugahyde windbreakers. When I was westbound on mornings when the wind was blowing thirty miles per hour out of the west, that little 3-horse scooter could barely buck the wind. But when you got turned around and going with the wind, you could sail down the streets dodging the tumbleweeds that shared the road and the wind with you. It got mighty cold out there some mornings with the wind and rain and sleet blowing in your face. Combine that with the dust blowing off the newly plowed cotton fields in the early spring, and I'd get home covered in ice mud! Once again, on top of all this, I had to collect from each of my 350 customers once a month and report to my distributors. I never made more than thirty dollars a month—a dollar per day—but I didn't mind. I had wheels, I had mobility, and I had freedom, as long as I did what I was supposed to. This was better than having a horse! The scooter and the paper route became a daily part of my new life in Texas.

BUT I DIDN'T ALWAYS do what I was supposed to. We lived about five blocks from the high school, and Max would leave his Eagle parked in the garage and walk to school. Dad had given him strict instructions to always take the key out of the scooter. As I went out one morning, I noticed the key was in the Eagle. I thought I would be smart, and I decided to ride the big Eagle to school. Then, as now, and always in my life when I did something wrong, it wasn't long before I regretted it. I got to school early and took

Nancy Noel, my classmate and the first girl I ever kissed, for a spin. It was unfamiliar and exciting to have a pretty girl so close with her arms wrapped around me. I was taking full advantage of the opportunity to show off. I dropped her off and decided I would ride over to Dale Eubanks' house and ride with him back to school. On the way, I was crossing an intersection when I noticed Coach Niles and Coach Jones, the junior high sports coaches, waiting at a stop sign on my left. I waved at them, and that's the last thing I remember. An elderly gentleman didn't see me as he was making a left turn in front of me. I crashed head-on into his car, was thrown forward, and my head hit his windshield! I was unconscious in the hospital until late that afternoon with a concussion, but I had escaped any serious permanent injuries. A scar under my right eyebrow is the only remnant of what could easily have been the end of me!

When I awoke, my mom and dad were there, along with several kids from school who had come to see about me. My dad was not pleased that I had taken my brother's scooter without permission, and under normal circumstances, I would have gone a few rounds with him with one of his hands around my wrist and the other holding a belt. But since I was in the hospital with a concussion, I escaped facing the consequences. He was, no doubt, relieved that I wasn't dead. Later that evening, I was alone in the hospital when the elderly gentleman came by to see how I was and to express his concern for me and regrets for his part in it all. That was the only time I ever saw or knew anything about that man, but I always appreciated that he came by to check on me.

Since I was a new kid in school, naturally no one knew me, and I didn't know anybody. But after that mishap, everyone in school knew who I was—so there was a positive that came out of it. After a few days, I was back in school, and everyone greeted me and asked how I was. From that point on, I was no longer an unknown outsider, and that accident helped me as the new kid in town become known and accepted. My brother was not too happy with me, but the Eagle was not severely damaged. It was repaired without too much expense, and soon we were back in business. A life lesson was learned.

THE FALL OF '57 had surrendered to colder weather on the Great South Plains. The cotton harvest was coming in, and the local farmers and merchants were experiencing a boom in business. There were lots of Mexican braceros with their shiny combed-back hair, khaki pants, and long, pointed shoes downtown on the weekends. The new model cars were out, and we began to see a lot of '58 Chevys and Pontiacs and Fords around town. Most of them were two-door hardtops, manual, 4-speed transmissions, with the largest V-8 engines available. Gasoline was about nineteen cents a gallon. The Brownfield Cubs played their last football game (in the old stadium) without advancing to the playoffs, and basketball season arrived.

In Brownfield, like in all Texas towns, football is king. Kids in Brownfield were not even introduced to basketball until the seventh grade. I was in the sixth grade, but I already had five years of basketball experience when I got to Brownfield. I have the feeling that my former coach from Oklahoma, Lee Freeze, who was junior high counselor, and my dad, who taught seventh-grade math, were visiting with Coach Niles and Coach Jones in the teacher's lounge one day when they happened to mention to the coaches that little Gary Nunn might have the ability and experience to play on the seventh-grade basketball team. They had my schedule changed, and I was assigned to the seventh-grade basketball team instead of sixth-grade PE. The guys who went out for basketball had just finished their first football season and were the best athletes in the seventh grade. As it happens in school society, this made them the most popular kids and members of the in-crowd. Here I was, a barely-twelve-year-old sixth-grader and a starter on the seventh-grade team! This also made me a part of the in-crowd and, again, had the effect of raising my profile at a new school, even though I had only been in town about four months. Things were going good, and I began to lose the feeling of being an outsider.

I made it through basketball season with flying colors. It was amazing how quickly the inexperienced seventh graders developed and became good basketball players. I bonded with those fellows even more than I did with my own classmates.

They started preparing us for seventh-grade football in the spring of sixth grade. I went out for my first taste of football with my own classmates. We were all anxious to begin our football careers and be like the high school players, vying for the coveted spots of quarterback, tailback, and fullback. The positions they placed us in were, for the most part, the positions we played all the way through high school. Coach Clifford Niles was head coach, and Coach Coy Jones, a Brownfield native who rode a Cushman Eagle to school every day, was his assistant and the line and defensive coach. They were great guys, as were all the coaches I played under during my school years at Brownfield. So were all my teachers, and all of them had a very positive influence on my young life.

Since I was a schoolteacher's kid, I was expected to perform and behave in such a way that reflected well on my parents and their reputations, and I did the best I could to please them. That seems to be a reoccurring theme in my life, as my primary motivation has always been to not disappoint anyone who had expectations of me. I was expected to make not just good grades, but straight As—which I did all the way through high school. It helped that my mother, every evening after dinner, would say, "Get your homework done." She would help me if I needed it, as would Dad. Before every exam, she would review all the material with me, so I was totally prepared and I aced all the tests. I never took a final exam in my twelve years of school, as you were exempt from finals if you had straight As. My curfew was ten every school night until I graduated from high school. After all, I had to get up at five to throw my paper route.

Finally school was out, and growing grass and pleasant weather meant it was baseball season. For the first time in my life, I had the opportunity to play real baseball, organized Little League baseball! Real teams with matching uniforms and names like the Yankees, the Braves, and the Cardinals. I was twelve, and that was the oldest you could be for Little League. I tried out and was assigned to the Yankees. The big-league Yankees were my favorite team, with Mickey Mantle and Yogi Berra—my heroes! We'd play late afternoon and twilight games in the Little League ballpark. I was a scrappy little second baseman and could get on base by hook or by crook. I would steal about every base. My years of playing Work-Up with the big kids back in Oklahoma paid off, and I made the All-Star team.

Dad had summers off, but he didn't like to sit around and do nothing, so he would look for a summer job to keep himself occupied. Our neighbors, the Shirleys, who lived across the alley directly behind us, were wealthy and were members of the country club. Jane Shirley was the granddaughter of M.V. Brownfield, after whom the town was named. She came over and asked my dad if he would be interested in keeping the country club swimming pool, teaching swimming lessons, and lifeguarding for the country club kids for the summer. He agreed. Granted, it wasn't much of a job for a grown man, and it paid very little, but he accepted the offer, and I was the beneficiary.

Dad's job at the country club pool gave me access to the pool too. You've heard the old saying, "Possession is nine-tenths of the law." My motto has always been, "Access is nine-tenths of possession." I had total access to the country club swimming pool seven days a week! I took full advantage. I'd get my ball-playing buddy,

Conrad (Connie) Vernon, and we'd jump on my scooter and ride
the five miles or so east on the Tahoka Highway to the country club,
where we'd spend all day playing "dibble-dabble" with the country
club kids in the pool. We would get offers to caddy for golfers, and
we could pick up a few bucks if we chose to. That was back before
golf carts. We also had access to the golf course, and we could play
for free if we wanted to and we did. This was my introduction to
golf. Unfortunately, I never took a lesson until much later in life, so
I couldn't hit the ball well at all . . . and still can't hit it that well. It
was a cool summer—spending all day every day in the country club
pool, playing golf, or attending Little League baseball practice and
games—with total mobility on the scooter.

I was always looking for a chance to make an extra dollar. Occasionally, one of the older boys from a farming family would pay
Johnny Knox and me three dollars apiece to ride our scooters out to
a cotton field to move a quarter mile of irrigation pipe. We'd shut
down the big irrigation motors and disconnect the pipe. Cold, clear
water drained out from the pipe. It's hard to imagine the amount
of water that was pumped from the Ogallala Aquifer considering
most of the cotton fields on the south plains were irrigated. Without irrigation, dryland farms produced only a fraction of the cotton
of those that were irrigated.

Sunday mornings after the paper route and a couple more hours
of sleep, my mother would get us all up and dressed, and we'd attend
Sunday school and church services. Sunday dinners were always a
special treat, with roast beef or fried chicken, mashed potatoes and
gravy, green beans, corn on the cob, fresh-baked rolls, and a pie
or strawberry shortcake for desert. Sunday afternoons lots of kids
would go to the matinees at the Regal Theater on the courthouse
square downtown or gather on the expansive lawns of the Goodpasture house across the street from the high school for games of
flag football or flying model airplanes. Grady Goodpasture was the

acknowledged richest man in town. He owned the grain elevator, the town's largest structure on the west side. Mr. Goodpasture was apparently a very reclusive man, because I don't recall anyone ever saying they saw the man. In any case, we played touch on his huge green lawn anytime we wanted, and no one ever came out of the house to run us off, so I suppose he provided it for our benefit. Sunday evenings, we were back at the First Baptist Church for services.

IN THE FALL OF 1958 when school started, I discovered I could no longer read the writing on the blackboard. I was sent to the optometrist, where I was fitted for glasses, and my lifelong status as "four eyes" began! I hated wearing glasses, but the improvement in my vision was so dramatic that it was obvious I seriously needed them. Football season began, and we picked up the training started the previous spring. We suited up in the "red and white" and played games every Thursday, but I had to wear ugly "athletic" glasses that smashed your face when you took a hit.

The seventh- and eighth-grade teams played in the brand-new Cub Stadium or traveled to play the teams in our district. We'd load in what we called the "Yellowhound" and head off to one of our district rivals in Levelland, Lamesa, Seminole, Andrews, Monahans, Pecos, Fort Stockton, or Odessa Ector where we played two games. It's a long way from Brownfield to some of these towns. After the games, we'd go to a local restaurant, and they would feed us a chicken-fried steak if we won—a hamburger if we lost. We'd play Hearts with the coaches, and that made the trips go a lot faster. Sometimes it was long after midnight before we got home, but I loved every minute of it.

In the seventh grade, home football games presented an interesting situation. I was on the football team and in the junior high marching band, which marched at home games. I was expected to play *and* march, so during halftime, I changed into my band uniform and went to march with the band. I had persuaded Mr. Jones to let me play a valve trombone when we marched. For all practical purposes, it was identical to the baritone, but it just wasn't as cool as a trombone. After the halftime band performance, I would rush back to the locker room, put my pads back on, and head out with the team for the second half of football. In the eighth grade, I was allowed to play the bass drum.

When basketball season rolled around, they put me back to play with my classmates. They were good athletes and progressed rapidly, and it wasn't long before we were all playing at the same level. But for some reason, I didn't bond with them the way I had with the older guys the year before. We got along fine, but we didn't pal around and never developed really close, long-lasting relationships.

SEVENTH GRADE ENDED AND summer and baseball were again in the air. My brother had graduated from high school and gone off to college, and I graduated and inherited his Cushman Eagle. No longer was I stuck with the dinky 3-horse Allstate: I had a mount equal to the big boys'. I was thirteen and advanced to Babe Ruth League baseball, which included thirteen-, fourteen-, and fifteen-year-olds. Once again, I was "drafted" by the Yankees and played second base.

Still always looking for a way to put a little money in my pocket, I got a job at the local A & W Root Beer Drive-In "jerking" sodas, peeling potatoes, and washing dishes. I could have free hamburgers and drink all the root beer floats I wanted. I worked there most of the summer doing six-hour shifts for fifty cents an hour, less taxes. At one point midsummer, I discovered my boss was shorting me on my wages, and I confronted him about it. He huffed and puffed, obviously annoyed that he had been caught red-handed shortchanging a kid, but he paid me what he owed me and fired me on the spot! I didn't mind too much, as the job had prevented me from going to the city pool until late in the afternoon, when most of the kids had already gone home. I used the extra time running and getting in shape for the upcoming football season.

When eighth grade came around, we were big-time upper-classmen in the junior high school. I was the starting wingback in our wing-T offense because I didn't have the size or speed for one of the prized backfield slots. Most of the starters on offense were also starters on defense. I was small, but I wasn't afraid to hit, and I played corner back on defense. I was the punter, and on the kickoff and punt return teams, so, like most of my teammates, I was on the field on almost every play.

One day after football practice, we had showered and dressed and headed en masse from the field house, when I heard someone comment, "Did you hear? Alton Nicholson's dad bought him a guitar."

Chapter 4

Enter Guitars

I HAD NEVER HEARD of Alton Nicholson, as he didn't play sports and wasn't part of the "jock" crowd. My interest was piqued, however, at the mention of one of my classmates having a guitar. Rock-and-roll music had been around a few years with Elvis, and once, my brother and Dean Eubanks sneaked out of the house on a school night and went to Lubbock to see Jerry Lee Lewis at the Cotton Club. But I was pretty much oblivious to it. I was taking band, and Big Band music was more my thing; I was too busy to have any extra time to pay much attention to rock and roll, but the thought that a kid in town had a guitar was absolutely intriguing, and I couldn't resist the temptation to explore the situation. I soon found out where he lived, and after football practice I rode my Eagle to his house and knocked on his door.

Alton's mom, Imogene, answered the door. "Is Alton here?" She escorted me back to his bedroom. He was sitting on the edge of his bed with a brand-new Fender Duo-Sonic guitar! Wow, it was beautiful, so slick and shiny, a light-buff color with a white pick guard. He had a 45 rpm record player going and was listening to a single of "Sleep Walk" by Santo & Johnny, a tune that's still a classic today among guitar and steel enthusiasts. He was taken aback a bit to have a stranger walk into his room but warmed up to my presence when he realized how taken I was with his guitar. This was the beginning of a relationship that would last until our senior year in high school. From that point on, I spent every minute I could spare at his house. I loved that guitar, and I wanted so badly to have one of my own.

Christmas came around and two other classmates, Gary Carr and Mickey Beck, got guitars and funky little amps for Christmas. They started hanging out at Alton's house, trying to learn to play a popular 45 single, "Honky Tonk," a guitar/saxophone instrumental tune by Bill Doggett. It was the first song you learned on the guitar, as it was basic and simple enough for a beginner to pick up on. I didn't have an instrument, so I would sit and play drums with my hands on my thighs, wishing I had a guitar to play with them.

Every year along about February the local Lion's Club sponsored a talent show at the high school auditorium. There was a junior high and a high school division, and we thought about entering the junior high competition.

A couple of bands in high school had instruments and played dances around town. The Tremelos were led by the Rayburn twins, Donnie and Ronnie. One of them played a beautiful red Gibson ES-335, and the other played drums. The Rayburns were identical twins, so I couldn't say which one played what. Another band was the Emeralds: They were seniors and had two Fender Stratocasters—top-of-the-line Fender guitars. They also had drums and bass. Doug Coppock played lead, Jimmy Green played rhythm guitar, Don "Skeebo" Skiles played drums, and Morris (Moss) Tyler played a Fender Precision Bass. We were particularly impressed by the Fender bass that Morris played. It was so much larger than a regular-size guitar, with its big strings, *l-o-o-n-g* neck, and *h-u-u-g-e* tuning keys—very impressive to kids in the eighth grade!

They had quite a repertoire of guitar instrumentals, a few vocals, and they played occasional dances for the high school kids. In the early '60s, they went to California and cut an instrumental single on Indigo Records called "Dreams and Wishes." Don Skiles lived a block or so from Alton's house on Reppto Street, and we would go over there and listen to them practice. They had Fender amps with reverb, which really enhanced the sound of the guitars, and we would watch and listen in awe as they practiced. They took an interest in us and would take the time to show us a few things.

We told them we wanted to enter the talent show and implored them to help us. They made up a guitar instrumental they called "Rebel" and taught it to Alton, who was quite adept at picking out guitar licks. Gary Carr and Mickey Beck would just play basic rhythm. I was to be the drummer, even though I had no drums.

I asked Fred Smith, the high school band director, if I could borrow some things from the band hall. I guess he trusted me as we lived practically next door. He told me to go in the band hall and get what I needed. So on the afternoon of the evening we were scheduled to perform for the talent show, I went into the band hall unsupervised and got a snare drum and stand, a marching snare and stand for a tom-tom, a marching bass drum, and a cymbal—from which I removed the hand holder. Then I borrowed a bass drum pedal, a drum stool, a cymbal stand, and a pair of drumsticks from one of the Rayburn twins. This completed my makeshift drum kit. I moved the instruments to the auditorium stage, adjacent to the band hall, and proceeded to assemble my kit. I attached the bass drum foot pedal to the marching bass drum, which had no stoppers to prevent the bass drum from sliding, mounted the two drums on their stands and the cymbal on the cymbal stand, and placed the stool in position. I had never sat on a drum kit or ever practiced with a kit with the band, but I was full of confidence that I could pull it off. I rushed the short distance home, cleaned up, put some Butch Wax on my flattop haircut, donned a white sport coat and black snap-on bow tie that was our uniform for the show, and rode my scooter back to the high school. Backstage, I clutched the borrowed pair of drumsticks to my chest and tried to calm my nerves.

When it came our time to play, we plugged in the three little amps, and I reassembled my drum set behind the red curtain. The curtain rose, and there we were, staring at a packed auditorium! The whole junior high school was there to cheer us on. We began the song, and I started banging away on the drums. I was doing okay, but it didn't take long for my complete lack of experience to catch up with me. The stage was polished hardwood, and since the bass drum was not set on a rug and had no stoppers, it started sliding forward on the slick stage floor with every hit of the foot pedal! How was I to know? At one point, I had to quit playing and reach forward to pull the bass drum back into position, but it didn't seem to matter, and we made it through the song. The audience, led by our classmates—especially the girls—went crazy! After all the contestants, including the high school division, had performed, the winners were selected by an audience applause meter. When the emcee said, "And now, let's hear it for The Rebels!" the applause meter must have pegged out! The Beatles couldn't have gotten a bigger response. After the show, all the girls, in their mutton (pronounced *moo-tahn*) fur coats and cancan petticoats, rushed backstage all excited and full of praise, hugs, and kisses! Well, from that point on, I was hooked. I envisioned every show would be like that!

Now I'll relate what was one of the most embarrassing moments of my career. I had been elected the president of the junior high student council for my eighth-grade year. Part of the responsibility of that honor was to emcee school assemblies and lead the student body in the Pledge of Allegiance. Immediately following our triumphant win at the talent show and having our pictures on the front page of the *Brownfield News*, the junior high principal invited us to perform for an all-school assembly. I walked out on the stage in front of the whole school and said, "Let's all stand for the Pledge of Allegiance." I put my hand over my heart, leaned into the microphone, and began, "Our Father, who art in heaven, hallowed be thy name." The whole school burst into uproarious laughter! I was mortified. I'm sure my face got red as a beet, but I collected myself and proceeded to lead the pledge. The laughter continued for the longest time!

From that point, the Rebels started to get better organized. Gary Carr dropped out. Maybe he felt that playing in a band wasn't his cup of tea, or perhaps his parents decided that they would nip this rock-and-roll thing in the bud before it got out of hand. Alton decided that we needed a bass player, and that was to be me. Mr. Nicholson went to Harrod Music Company on Avenue Q in Lubbock and bought a brand-new, 1960 model Fender Precision Bass. Alton said, "You're the bass player from now on," and that was the beginning of my bass-playing career that lasted till 1979. I took to the bass naturally, but I wasn't getting any closer to my dream of playing guitar. Once again, I was maneuvered into playing a secondary, supporting role.

Alton had decided and arranged for Jerry Don Purtell to be the new drummer in the band. Jerry Don was in high school, had his own kit, and was an experienced player, but he only played with us till the end of that school year. We got our buddy Johnny Knox, who had played drums in the junior high marching band, to join. His parents bought him a brand-new set of Premier drums. We changed our name, and Alton, Mickey Beck, Johnny Knox, and I, from that point on, became "The Premiers." For once, we had a complete band, with a full complement of instruments. I bought a blonde Fender piggyback Bassman amp that I played for years. We started adding more instrumentals to our set list—several Ventures tunes like "Walk Don't Run" and "Perfidia" and Freddie King's classic "Hide Away." We bought a little Bogen PA that consisted of two twelve-inch speakers with the backs open. You could put the amplifier inside the two speakers, snap the cabinets together, and walk out the door with the whole PA system in one hand. I started singing a few vocals like "Johnny B. Goode" and "Bony Moronie."

I was the lead and only singer and booked all the shows, but Alton ran the band with a firm hand. He had a way of intimidating me, and I kowtowed to him. It was the only way we could get along, as he was going to run any band he was in. I went along to get along. There was no alternative except to quit the band, and I wasn't prepared to do that so I endured it. I looked for ways to get things done that didn't require direct confrontation with Alton.

My eighth-grade year came to an end, and I applied for a job working for the Brownfield school system. Because of my grades, I had been exempt from taking final exams, and the school system assigned me to the groundskeeping crew. I say crew . . . there was just this one man who was my supervisor plus me. I was put to work immediately, and guess where? Right there at the junior high school. All the other kids were there taking finals, and I was out on the school lawn (which also served as a football practice field) moving irrigation pipe and pushing a lawn mower right in front of my classmates. It was more than a bit inglorious in my mind, and not a fitting finale to a school year where I had been a straight-A, honor-roll student, a first-team football and basketball player, president of the student council and honor society, and a player in a rock-and-roll band. I admit I was a bit ashamed and embarrassed to be out there working in plain view of all my classmates. I went home after work that day and expressed the feelings I was suffering to my mother.

She sat me down and said, "Work is honorable. You never need be ashamed to do any kind of honest labor." She had a way of conveying moral lessons in the plainest of terms. I always kept this in mind when I found myself having to do menial work. Another important lesson was learned. Mom was a simple, humble woman, but she possessed a clear moral and ethical compass that has kept me (pretty much) on the straight and narrow.

While reading a biography of John Adams by David McCullough, I ran across an account that John Quincy Adams wrote about his mother, Abigail Adams, who was equal to John Adams in every way. As it reminds me so much of my own mother, I thought I might include it here:

> My mother . . . was a minister of blessings to all human beings within her sphere of action . . . She had no feelings but of kindness and beneficence. Yet her mind was as firm as her temper was mild and gentle. She . . . has been to me more than a mother. She has been a spirit from above watching over me for good, and contributing by my mere consciousness of her existence, to the comfort of my life.
>
> Never have I known another human being, the perpetual object of whose life, was so unremittingly to do good.[1]

WE GRADUATED FROM JUNIOR high in the spring of 1960. In Texas, you could get a car driver's license at the age of fourteen providing you had taken a driver's education course. Consequently, many of the kids graduating from the eighth grade enrolled in a summer school driver's education class. In a couple of weeks, we had completed the course, taken our driver's license test, and received our driver's licenses—fresh out of junior high. Immediately, many of the kids' parents bought them used cars, and some of the kids from wealthier families got brand-new, top-of-the-line models.

---

1   David McCullough, *John Adams* (New York: Simon & Schuster, 2001), 623.

Johnny Knox, our drummer, got a fully loaded '57 Pontiac Bonneville two-door hardtop. My dad arranged for me to get a new
Cushman Eagle, as I still had my paper route. He took a summer job with the USDA transporting braceros from El Paso to
Brownfield in a school bus. He seemed to be happy to get out of
the house and see some country. He always spoke of the Mexican
laborers in sympathetic terms. I suppose with his background, he
could relate to their situation.

I worked all summer, mowing the weeds around the schoolhouses and moving irrigation pipe on the football field. Toward
the end of summer, I was invited by my friend Buzz Steele from
the class ahead of me (who I had played basketball with as a sixth
grader) to spend a week at Lake J. B. Thomas near Big Spring. He
also invited Tommy Harris and another classmate who is a devout
Christian and holds a prominent position and may not appreciate
my mentioning his name.

In those days, the closest liquor store was in Slaton, about forty
miles from Brownfield, and as soon as everyone got their driver's
license, kids started driving to Slaton to buy beer. It was unbelievable, but if you had a fake ID and were big enough to see over the
counter, they would sell beer to kids! For our trip to the lake, someone had gone to Slaton and bought four cases of Coors, one case
for each of us.

We pulled Buzz's family boat down to the lake and spent a week
painting the lake house, drinking beer, water-skiing, and, in general,
having a teenage ball away from our parents' supervision. When the
week was done, we packed up and headed back home. All the beer
had been consumed except for a six-pack that I had left from my case.
Everyone in the car was putting pressure on me to share the remaining six-pack, but I adamantly refused, much to the annoyance of my
buddies. When I got home, I hid the six-pack in some shrubbery out
in the yard. Well, anytime I ever did anything shady, instant karma

intervened. It was no time before my dad came in the house with the six-pack in hand. *Uh, oh!* Busted! I expected the worst. *I'm gonna die!*

He gave the beer to Mom, and she immediately went to the kitchen and poured it down the drain. He told me to follow him back to his bedroom. I just *knew* he was going to tear my ass up! I remember noticing a Sonny Liston boxing match on TV, and the thought occurred to me that he might punch me out. He sat down on the bed and said very calmly to me, "Son, did you know that one out of four people who ever take a drink become alcoholics? I want you to always remember that." He dismissed me and went back to watching the fight. That's all he ever said to me about drinking, and I confess that every time I ever popped a top on a beer, his words were there ringing in my ears. Several years later, I wrote a song inspired by that event called "The Well of the Blues" that Jerry Jeff Walker recorded on his 1974 MCA record *Walker's Collectibles*. The lyrics go like this:

> Well, the preacher man bad-mouths the bottle
> Momma pours it down the drain
> Old grandpa keeps it within reach
> To ease his favorite pain
> And all year long, teetotaller songs
> Echo grandpa's fall
> But on the holidays, everything's okay
> Even the judges forget the law
> *Chorus*
> The well of the blues never runs dry
> It never gets full enough of whisky and rye
> The well of the blues.

We entered high school as lowly freshmen, endured some soft-core hazing from the upperclassmen, but we were full of anticipation and the excitement of being in high school. Football season began, couples started pairing off, going steady, and dating. I tried to go with some girls that I liked, but nothing ever clicked, so I focused on schoolwork, working up new songs at Alton's house, and playing dances with the band. We charged a one-dollar cover and usually made fifteen or twenty dollars apiece. I never got an allowance, but I always had a little money in my pocket.

My dad had bought me a Remington automatic 20-gauge shotgun the previous Christmas. After football practice, I would go dove hunting with Coach Niles and Coach Jones in the grain sorghum fields just outside of town. This was my first taste of real shooting, and it was cool to go out in the fields with the coaches. On more than one occasion, my classmate Biff Davis and I would ride our Eagles east to Post, Texas, where Biff's grandfather owned a big ranch teeming with birds. We would make the fifty-mile trip on a major highway with our shotguns across our laps! One can only speculate what would happen today to two fourteen-year-olds who got caught openly carrying shotguns on scooters on a public highway!

The Premiers started playing at the "Teen Canteen" at the Presbyterian Church after football games and at dances in nearby towns like Seminole or Levelland on Saturday nights. Occasionally, I would rent the National Guard Armory to promote a dance there. Once I even booked us a gig at a teen club in Ruidoso, New Mexico, a mountain resort town about two hundred miles west of Brownfield. I have no idea how I ever pulled that off.

The summer after my freshman year, Connie Vernon and I got jobs lifeguarding at the city pool for a dollar an hour: It was my dream job. The city pool was the center of social activity and the place to be in the summertime. We had to take a lifesaving course to qualify. We would show up at the pool at 9:00 a.m., police up the pool area, and clean the dressing rooms. At ten, the kids taking swimming lessons would show up, and we taught the lessons.

I didn't know a thing about teaching swimming except what I had picked up from my dad, who had given lessons at the country club. I started the lessons with the dead man's float. I had the kids push off the side, in the shallow end, in a prone position with their arms outstretched and their faces down in the water, and kick their feet for as long as they could hold their breaths.

I discovered that the key to teaching kids to swim was to have them become comfortable with swimming underwater. Once they became aware of their natural buoyancy, they wouldn't panic and fight to stay above the water. Soon, I would take them to deeper water at the ladder and have them swim along next to the poolside underwater, come up for breaths as needed, and then go back under and continue until they reached the next ladder about fifteen feet away. If they gave out or started to panic, they could reach up and grab the drain that ran along the pool's side just above the water line. When they could all get from one ladder to the next without grabbing the drain, I would take them to the low diving board. I'd have them jump off the board toward the nearest ladder in the corner of the pool. I would instruct them that when they emerged from the jump, to take a breath, go back under, and swim toward the ladder. When they needed a breath, they would surface, grab a breath, and go back under and swim till they reached the ladder. By the end of the two-week term, I would have most of them jumping off the high board. I taught scores of kids how to swim and got a great deal of satisfaction from seeing them learn and become comfortable in the water. I've often thought learning to swim underwater is a metaphor for survival in the real world as well.

I worked at the pool that summer and the next. The high school football coaches—Coach Doug Cox, the head coach, and his line coach, Coach Charlie Keese—were the managers of the pool and our bosses. Early in the summer after my sophomore year, the coaches went away for a couple of weeks to coach training. They put Connie and me in charge of everything besides running the cash register, which was handled by Coach Cox's daughter, Gina, with her little sister, Lela Ann, minding the concession stand. Our duties included the cleanup, swimming lessons, opening and clos- ing, lifeguarding, vacuuming the pool, and cleaning and changing the water filters.

The water filtering and chlorination system also had to be attended to, and that duty fell to me. The chlorine gas was encased in large iron cylinders that had to be adjusted properly to release the chlorine gas into the pool water as it circulated through the filtering system. One morning I was opening the gas valve with a wrench when a blast of chlorine gas was released directly into my face! I quickly shut off the valve and, choking and coughing, exited the building that housed the filtering system. I'm lucky that I wasn't exposed to more chlorine gas since it's very poisonous and can cause lung damage and even death. That was the second time (not including the near–drownings) in my young life that I had narrowly escaped serious injury or death. I always wondered when the third strike would come my way, so I took note to do my best to avoid it.

Later that summer, Connie's family invited me to join them on a vacation to Mexico. Connie's grandparents came along too, and Con- nie and I drove them. His parents and his two younger sisters drove in a second, identical, new Oldsmobile. We entered Mexico at the border near Roma, Texas, where we stopped to buy Sanborn's Mexi- can insurance, and reached Monterrey the first night. We checked into a hotel, and to our surprise, Connie's dad told us we could go out on the town for a while if we wanted to. We caught a cab that took us to a bar and had a beer—apparently there was no age limit in Mexico. Some girls propositioned us, but we declined, being the fifteen-year-old virgins that we were. We spent the next night in San Luis Potosí, and by the third night we reached Mexico City.

First thing that morning we got up, had breakfast, and headed out on the street sightseeing. We toured a small Catholic church, the first I had ever set foot in. There was gold all over that church—the first gold I had ever seen. As we all exited the church, we were approached by a man who offered to be our guide and show us the sights. Connie's dad declined, and we proceeded to walk down the street. We hadn't walked a couple of blocks when Connie's dad turned around and said to us, "Well, Goddammit, if you boys don't want to hang around with us, y'all can just get out of here and do whatever the hell you want to do!" We were dumbfounded. *Hell, we're a couple of dumbass kids, and he's going to turn us loose in a foreign country?* I think it was just his way of justifying giving us the freedom to explore on our own without being tied to Mom and Pop, Grandma and Grandpa, and a couple of preteen sisters. They walked down the street and left us standing there. We looked at each other, shrugged our shoulders, and wondered what we were going to do then. All we knew about Mexico City was the name of the hotel.

We turned around and started walking back toward the church, when we encountered the same guy who had offered to be our tour guide. He had witnessed the scene and seemed to sense our dilemma. He said, "I can show you guys around. What would you like to do?"

We asked him, "Well, what's the deal?"

He said he would take us where we wanted to go if we would pick up the cab fares and pay him a certain amount for his time. The only thing we knew about Mexico City was that we had heard about the "Thieves Market." We had both planned to buy a Mexican guitar while we were in Mexico, so we asked him to take us there. Jesus, how naive were we? Two teenagers without a clue headed off to the Thieves Market with a stranger, and nobody on the planet knew where we were or where we were going! Those were different times for sure. Nonetheless, he took us to the Thieves Market, and we found a guitar shop where we bought two inexpensive classical guitars. We visited a few other shops and looked around. I got the idea that I wanted to buy a pair of pants, as I had noticed men in a fashionable style of pants with slim legs and a nice flair at the bottom—really cool and different from the blousy-legged dress pants that were the style at home. We looked around a bit, and I found just what I was looking for. I bought them, and when I got back home, I wore those pants every time I played in the band.

We got back to the hotel, *no problema*, and made an appointment to meet our guide the next day. I had the phone number of a girl who lived in Mexico City, who had gone to a ritzy girls' school in Gulfport, Mississippi, with Jane Hackney, a classmate of mine from Brownfield. I called her up, and she invited us to a party that night at the Chapultepec Club de Golf. Our tour guide picked us up in a cab, and we spent the whole evening looking without success for that club.

The next day, we hooked back up with the family to visit the main tourist attractions, like the Metropolitan Cathedral, the Floating Gardens of Xochimilco, and the National Museum that houses the famous artwork of Diego Rivera. We climbed to the top of the Teotihuacán Pyramids and saw the house where Leon Trotsky was murdered. We drove around the National Palace and Chapultepec Park, the very site where the Texas Rangers and the US Army overwhelmed the defenders in the battle that ended the Mexican-American War in 1847.

We then made the drive south to Acapulco and checked in at the Las Brisas Hotel, the location for the Elvis Presley movie *Fun in Acapulco*. We had our guitars and were able to attract a few local beauties by singing Everly Brothers songs around the pool—which was built so the ocean water filled it. We had dinner at the famous restaurant in the El Mirador, where you could watch the cliff divers. One evening Connie and I hailed a cab and told the cabby to take us to a nice place, which he did. It was very nice, one of "those" bars that featured white tablecloths and a higher class of "sporting" ladies. Or course, they approached and propositioned us. Connie accepted the initial invitation and disappeared. It wasn't long before he came roaring back into the bar area, belting out, "Goddamn, Nunn, are they trying to screw you too? Let's get the hell out of here!" Apparently all the user fees had become too much to bear. So we split with our virginities still intact.

When it was time to make the trip home, we stopped in Taxco, the famous gold and silver mining town, and Connie's folks did a bit of shopping and bought a few silver pieces. The next stop on the leg home was the city of Guadalajara. Connie and I went out to a famous restaurant called Bajo el Cielo de Jalisco, where we saw the most fabulous fifteen-piece mariachi band—another first for me. I loved the trumpets and the violins and the passion they sang their songs with. The hotel where we stayed had a ten-meter diving tower, and we were the only ones in the pool. Since I fancied myself to be somewhat of a diver, I just had to dive off that tower. That evening, I came down with "Montezuma's Revenge." The next day, we headed for home, with me suffering from the worst case of amoebic dysentery. It was the most miserable trip, and by the time we got home, I was down to 130 pounds.

When Connie and I dropped by the swimming pool, my coaches looked at me and said, "What in the world happened to you?" The loss of weight was serious, as we were to start football practice soon thereafter. I did suffer greatly through those first two-a-day practices in the 100-degree Texas sun, but we had a kick-ass team our sophomore junior varsity year, and we went undefeated. Connie was our quarterback. We both made the varsity basketball team as starting guards, and we were both good baseball players and played on the high school team. We cruised through the tenth grade!

THE SUMMER AFTER TENTH grade, my dad started back with his getting-out-of-the-house job of shuttling the braceros from El Paso to Brownfield and back. He was in and out all summer, but Mom was home, and she always had a nice lunch of vegetables fresh from the garden waiting when we came in from our summer jobs.

She always excused herself at 12:30 to watch her favorite soap opera, *As the World Turns*. It was the one and only indulgence she reserved for herself, as she could only watch it in the summertime. We would jokingly remark to her as she left the table, "There she goes. She's gonna watch *As the Dinner Burns*." It was some rare, good-natured family humor that we enjoyed at her expense, but she took it in stride and would dismiss us with a *Pshaw!* and a wave of her hand as she retreated to the living room.

Football season was approaching once again, and I started training by running the mile or so to the swimming pool, back home for lunch, back to the pool for an afternoon of lifeguarding, then back home at six when the pool closed. But none of it did anything to help me in those grueling two-a-day practices that began a couple of weeks before school started.

Despite my small size, I graduated from the wingback spot, which was basically a blocking position that didn't see any ball-carrying action, to the fullback slot that was very much a part of the offense. I never learned to be an evasive runner, but I loved to hit and I didn't mind taking a hit—coaches love that. Never once did one of them take me aside and say, "You should try harder to avoid contact, rather than seek it out, and you'll be a more productive ball carrier."

I've often thought that if I had been a coach, I would have focused on teaching the kids not only the "what to do," but I would have also taken the time to explain the "why you do it" too. You don't score many touchdowns engaging your would-be tackler in contact, but I did manage to score a few.

I decided that I wanted to take choir for an elective my junior year. A. V. Wall, the choir director, was a very gifted and talented man. He was young and handsome and had the most beautiful tenor voice. I had seen him perform with the Lubbock Symphony Orchestra back in junior high when Mac Jones sometimes took me with him to those concerts. I recall his breathtaking performances of show tunes like "The Sound of Music," "Singing in the Rain," and "On the Street Where You Live" accompanied by a full orchestra. It was awesome!

He had the kind of talent and good looks that could have made him a star on Broadway or in Hollywood, but his passion was teaching and exposing high school kids to vocal music.

I was a three-sport-a-year "jock," and choir was considered "sissy" in general, but I convinced a few of my teammates to take choir, and we ended the stigma. I placed myself in the baritone section, but it wasn't long before Mr. Wall moved me to the tenor section, and I became the first tenor, which meant I got to sing the lead tenor parts. Over the next two years, Mr. Wall would have a tremendous influence on the path my life would take.

After the midterms and Christmas of my junior year, Mr. Wall put us to work on the stage production of the hit Broadway show *Oklahoma*. We were all excited about it as it meant we would have our first chance at acting as well as singing. I auditioned for the leading male part of Curly and for the part of Will, the second leading part. I thought I had a good chance of getting the lead role since I was the first tenor. I could nail the opening song, "Oh, What a Beautiful Morning." However, it was not to be, and I was cast in the tertiary role of Ali Hakim, the Persian peddler. It was the most difficult role to play and consequently the most difficult to cast. It required me to learn to speak with a Middle Eastern accent, and there were no featured songs for that part. Again, my versatility and adaptability placed me in a necessary but difficult supporting role.

Danny Thurman was cast in the lead part of Curly. Jane Weiss was the obvious choice to play the lead female role of Laurey: She was beautiful, had a good voice, and was about two inches taller than me. Danny was taller than Jane, and I suppose it was determined that visually he paired better with her.

In any case, I accepted the role, and we dove into rehearsals during our choir period and two or three evenings a week too. But I got in trouble with my basketball coach, Elroy Payne, as he discovered that our performance of *Oklahoma* fell on a date when we had a scheduled district basketball game. When he found out I was going to miss a game, he benched me until we had finished the show. That was the first and only time I had ever been benched, and it was excruciating to be forced to sit on the bench for those games. It felt like punishment for overachievement, and that didn't seem fair at all. Soon after that, I tried out and was selected for the all-state choir, but I was forced to turn down the opportunity because of basketball.

But during those evening rehearsals, Mr. Wall did something for me that changed my life.

I had always lacked self-confidence even though I excelled to some degree in most everything I attempted. If I brought home a report card with one A- during one semester, my dad would say, "What's your problem? You need to bear down and straighten yourself out." If I got three hits, stole six bases, and scored three runs in a baseball game, he would say, "You could have done better." It sometimes seemed to me that the guys I wanted to be friends with rarely reciprocated, and the girls I liked never responded.

However, after those evening rehearsals for *Oklahoma*, several of us would sing songs from the show on our own. I would play the piano by ear, the cast would gather around, and we would sing songs like "Out of My Dreams." One evening during one of these sessions, Mr. Wall came by, put his hand on my shoulder, and said, "I think it's great you're playing the piano by ear. You seem to have a special talent, and I hope you will keep it up."

It was the first time in my life that anyone had ever given me any real praise and encouragement. At that moment, I got the idea that what I was doing was okay. It only took one person that I respected, giving me those few words of praise, to set me on the course my life was to take.

My brother Max was in college at North Texas State, which was and still is noted for its music school. Many of the greatest jazz musicians who played for the Big Band orchestras of the day were North Texas grads. Max majored in music even though he hadn't had a lot of music experience or training, except for the piano lessons we took from Mrs. Stalder back in Coalgate. This was during the time that Dave Brubeck came out with his classic *Time Out* LP, which included the timeless jazz classic "Take Five." Max would bring home other albums by the Stan Kenton Orchestra, Duke Ellington, Dizzy Gillespie, Thelonious Monk, Miles Davis, Charlie Parker, and the Bill Evans Trio. That was a pretty heavy dose for a kid out in West Texas. "Listen to this," he'd say. "This is gonna blow your young mind," and it did. I bought a little Zenith stereo record player and had gotten hold of a blue stage light that I kept in my room. I would turn on the blue light and listen to those great jazz albums until the wee hours. The blue light and the jazz music seemed to match my perpetual bluesy mood.

I collected a few albums that I also listened to a lot—but with the lights on. The Everly Brothers were one of my favorite groups, and I loved their songs and their perfect two-part harmony. Connie and I could do a pretty good job together on their tunes. I learned a few too, with one of my favorites being "Love Hurts."

Another of my favorite groups back then was Peter, Paul and Mary, who were part of the coming era of the folk-singing Hootenanny scene. Acoustic folk groups like Peter, Paul and Mary, with their songs "500 Miles," "This Train," and "If I Had a Hammer;" the Kingston Trio, with their huge hit, "Tom Dooley;" and the Serendipity Singers were huge stars. I started playing along and learning these tunes on the Mexican guitar, and Connie and I and some other kids from choir started getting together at school on lunch breaks and at house parties to sing some of them. It was refreshing to play and sing acoustically without the *bang-boom* of electrified playing, which to me always seemed too loud. My hearing today is a testament to that.

Max started bringing home Bob Dylan and Ravi Shankar. This is when things started to change culturally, as Bob Dylan, having taken up where Woody Guthrie had left off, released social consciousness into the atmosphere. Many of his songs dealt with issues unheard of in pop music, such as war, the Holocaust, the bomb, racial issues, and justice and injustice. Oh, the times, they were a-changin'.

WE FINISHED OUT JUNIOR year in 1963, and I started to work measuring cotton for the Agricultural Stabilization and Conservation Service (ASCS). I had gotten my first car that spring—a 1957 Chevrolet four-door Bel Air sedan, cream over bronze. It had been a doctor's car and was in excellent condition. I paid $700 for it that I had saved since I started my paper route in the sixth grade. The measuring of cotton is a solo job with lots of responsibility, as we were doing official work for the US Department of Agriculture. If you made a mistake or reported something erroneously, you would be summarily dismissed. But it was the best-paying job a kid in Brownfield could get.

My heart wasn't in it. I did the work satisfactorily, but I had no enthusiasm for it at all. It turned out that all the older employees were football coaches from neighboring towns who had done the job for years. They would pull all the lucrative contracts that were a snap to do and paid the most, leaving the difficult ones that required lots of work and time for the uninitiated "grunts" like me. So, once again, I was spending long days out and not making much money.

Chapter 5

Enter the Sparkles

BY THE TIME WE were juniors, I started hearing about a band called the Sparkles. I hadn't heard them play, but some of my classmates had, and the girls were especially excited about them. When it came junior prom time, I had hopes that perhaps our band, which was pretty well established by then, would be selected to play. But Patsy McKinney and her group of friends demanded that we have the Sparkles. Well, the Sparkles played, and oh my God, they were fantastic—a four-piece band with two guitars, bass, and drums. All the members sang, and they wore cool matching suits, did dance steps, and for the finale, they threw their guitars up behind their heads and rocked out while simultaneously doing coordinated dance steps! I think that was where Jimmie Vaughan learned about playing behind his head. Stan Smith, the lead guitar player, was a Chuck Berry master. He knew every CB lick perfectly and sang a half dozen of Berry's most popular songs like "Johnny B. Goode," "Nadine," "Memphis, Tennessee," "Brown Eyed Handsome Man," and "Little Queenie."

Donnie Roberts was a tall, handsome football coach from Levelland who played rhythm guitar and sang harmonies. Bobby Smith played bass and sang all the R&B stuff. They were all good, but the star of the show was Lucky Floyd! Lucky was an incredible drum-mer. He'd been a first-chair, all-state snare drummer from Seagraves High School and the first-chair drummer in the concert band at West Texas State in Canyon, Texas. He was a sticking genius who had natural ability, not only as a drummer but also as a singer, and he could imitate Elvis, Buddy Holly, James Brown, and especially Roy Orbison; plus, he was very funny and a great showman able to bring down the house with a drum solo! The girls swarmed the stage around him and chanted, "Go, Lucky, go!" I was smitten!

After that, I took every opportunity to see them play. If we didn't have a gig, Johnny Knox, our drummer in the Premiers, and I would jump in his '57 Bonneville and drive anywhere they were playing. I started getting acquainted with them, and sometimes Lucky and Bobby would spend the night at my house. I started adding songs that they did to the Premiers' repertoire.

My senior year finally rolled around. By now, I had worked my way up the ranks from wingback to fullback, and finally to starting tailback—the prize running back position on the Cubs football team. I got to wear the coveted Number 30, the number that was worn by all my illustrious predecessors. David Auberg was a bigger, faster, and better running back than I was, but the coaches deemed his skills could be put to better use at the fullback position. Still, I had risen to the top, and I guess I was pretty much a big man on campus—all five feet eight and 140 pounds of me. Yet, somehow, I didn't feel like a big man on campus. That "outsider" thing lingered. I still had trouble making close friends, and I felt alone among my classmates.

All through school, I had briefly dated a few girls, but nothing halfway serious ever developed from it—just prom dates and such. I was always playing at the parties we had, so I wasn't out there on the dance floor mixing it up with the ladies. There was a girl: Pamela Jane Shirley. She was two years younger, so I had never paid much attention to her. Her family was well-to-do and in the upper echelon of Brownfield society. We grew up just across the alley from each other, but there were light-years between her life and mine. I knew her little sisters, Liza Jane and Shirley Jane, and I think I may have taught swimming lessons to her little brother, John Brownfield Shirley. We were all kids in the same neighborhood, and the Shirleys were never anything but polite and friendly to us. At some point, as Pam was getting up around fifteen, she asked me if I'd like to come over to her house and listen to records. Her room had been converted from a two-car garage, and it was situated on the other side of the house from where her family spent their time. So we had complete privacy in her room, and her mother looked in on us only occasionally. I would take the guitar I had bought in Mexico and got her started playing a little. She had a record by the Four Freshmen titled *Love Lost*, a record of romantic ballads sung in four-part harmony. It was moody and bluesy and beautiful, and I could relate to the lonely and love-lost feeling. Apparently, she could as well, as that's the only record she ever played besides one by Johnny Mathis. We would listen to that record over and over and talk for hours. It was the first time in my life that I had ever spent any real time with a girl. She was a bit shy but very perceptive and intelligent for her age, and we would discuss the music and topics of the day. We developed what I would call a real and meaningful friendship. I liked her, I enjoyed her company, and we got along splendidly. She was tall, two or three inches taller than me, very attractive, and I enjoyed spending time with her more than anyone else I knew. This was all new territory for me, as I had never had this kind of friendship with anyone, boy or girl. As time went by, I really started to fall for her. She became my best friend—the only real best friend I had ever had.

Pam was a sophomore and old enough for her parents to let her date. I got up the nerve to ask her out, and I eventually took the plunge and asked her to go steady. This meant that she wore my football jacket, and I would send her white mum corsages with a red Number

30 for her to wear at home football games. We went on dates, "made the drag" from one end of the Lubbock highway to Boston's Super Dog on the other, and then made the obligatory drive to the outside of town to park and neck in the turnrows of the cotton fields.

One Saturday morning after a Friday night football game, everything came to a screeching halt. I should have known something was up because she hadn't worn the mum corsage the night before. She had her mother wear it instead. There was a knock on the door, and when I opened it, Pam was standing there with my letter jacket in her hand. Without saying a word, she reached out and handed it to me. I knew immediately what it meant. We stood there in awkward silence. She offered no explanation, and I was so thunderstruck I was rendered speechless. Then she turned and walked away. My first real crush was crushed before it had a chance to bloom. Not only had I lost my girlfriend, but I had also lost my best friend! Love lost became all too real to me then. I was devastated.

To make things worse, Connie Vernon, the closest thing I had to a pal, immediately started dating her. He would take her out on weeknights, drop her off across the alley, come to my house, and give me the blow-by-blows of their necking episodes—apparently totally oblivious to the pain he was inflicting on me. My loner feelings returned, and I retreated into myself and my jazz and my blue light. There was no going back to a friendship relationship with Pam Shirley, and we rarely had any occasion to speak to each other afterward. Thinking back, maybe there had been no chance for us to have a long-term relationship, but still I missed her and pined for her for a long time.

I DISCOVERED RAY CHARLES about that time. He was the perfect blend of Big Band and the blues, and I became a lifelong fan. I started buying his albums and picking out songs by ear like "What'd

I Say," "I've Got a Woman," and "Born to Lose" on my sister's piano. We added them to the Premiers' repertoire. I kept myself occupied with basketball and was selected all-district. I started wearing coats and ties to school on Fridays when we traveled out of town for ball games. Without me promoting it, all the guys on the teams followed my lead and started wearing ties as well. We began rehearsing for another musical stage production called *High Button Shoes*, but it was not the memorable show that *Oklahoma* was.

We had a good team when baseball season rolled around. We were the same guys who had started out together in Little League, played on different teams together through Babe Ruth League summer ball, and spent the three previous years on the varsity team. I worked my way through the infield from second base to third base, and finally, to shortstop by my senior year. I had never been a power hitter; I just didn't have the natural upper-body strength. Oh, I could get a line drive over second base or to right field and get on base . . . but something happened to change all that. The previous year during spring football training (which consisted mostly of conditioning and running plays in shorts and T-shirts), our coaches introduced a new training technique that proved to be extremely beneficial to me. It was called "isometric contraction." The concept involved pushing on steel bars for a period of seven seconds; then relaxing and repeating. Rope climbing was included as a part of the program to increase upper-body strength. We had to climb a twenty-five-foot oversized rope using only our hands and arms.

I received a 110-pound set of barbells for Christmas, and at first, I could only press the whole 110 pounds once. Not impressive, I realize. But by the end of that isometric contraction and rope-climbing training period, I could press the 110 pounds ten times—a tenfold increase! Consequently, I found myself hitting much better. I was pulling the ball to left field and hitting home runs. Our whole team benefited from that training, and we won our district, even though we had only one dominant pitcher, Amalio Garcia, and a sophomore, Craig Collier, who was pretty good, and who won the games we needed him to win against our less formidable opponents. Our coaches did a great job of utilizing only two pitchers to our best advantage, and we ended up winning our way to the state final playoffs in Austin. It was the first time the Brownfield Cubs had reached the state finals. I had the highest batting average at the state tournament—a whopping .526—which I attributed to the isometric and rope-climbing training.

We used Amalio Garcia for the semifinals game. We won and advanced to the finals, where we were matched with South San Antonio for the final game. They had a team of little Mexican guys who were great ballplayers, and they could really hit. We used our only remaining pitcher, Craig Collier, but sadly, he was no match for their lineup of powerful hitters. They hit doubles, triples, and home runs with regularity and beat us something like 16–2. It was a tough loss for us, but we were proud of being able to scratch and scrape to get as far as we did.

I later learned that the coach of that team was none other than Augie Garrido, a famous baseball coach for the Texas Longhorns who won five national championships for the University of Texas.

We were sacking up our bats when Harold Blackburn, who was really a great coach and an easygoing guy, came over. As we were walking alone together from the field, he said to me, "Well, that's the way it goes . . . moving west!" His comment gave a lighthearted sense of finality to my baseball career and high school years.

BY THIS TIME, THE Premiers had disbanded. We had been together since eighth grade, and Alton's insistence on having his way all the time had begun to wear on me. Besides, by this time, all I could think about was the Sparkles!

I had become pretty close with Lucky and Bobby and would travel anywhere to see them play. They always drew big crowds of kids. One day, I got the big idea to promote a show with them at the Brownfield National Guard Armory. I neglected my cotton measuring work and spent my time driving around to all the neighboring towns like Lamesa, Seagraves, Seminole, and Levelland putting up handmade posters in every burger joint drive-in I could find. When the day for the show arrived, I paid the $35 rent, and they opened up the armory. I set up the folding chairs around the perimeter of the cavernous space. My folks chaperoned, as they did all my shows, and set up a pop concession. After the Sparkles arrived and set up, we went to the Green Hut Grill for a chicken-fried steak.

In those days, the price of admission was always one dollar. I sensed the excitement and demand, so I decided I would raise the admission price to two dollars! Kids from Brownfield and all the neighboring towns started arriving and lining up at the door. I was met with loud protests when they came in, and I informed them the cover was two dollars. Some kids had to go home and get another dollar, but nobody left and stayed away. The place was packed. The Sparkles were pleased when we settled up, as they hadn't anticipated my doubling the cover charge. I took $100 and gave them the balance of about $500. That was a mighty good payday for all of us at a time when gasoline was nineteen cents a gallon, a bottle of Coca-Cola was a dime, and a hamburger with fries was ninety-nine cents. Lucky and Bobby spent the night at our house, and our relationship grew closer.

But things were not perfect in the Sparkles camp. Lucky was always at odds with the guitar player, Stan Smith, a very religious teetotaller who had opinions about Lucky's drinking. Lucky had a taste and fondness for beer, and he smoked in the band car, which Stan detested. Lucky and Donnie Roberts were very competitive as

they were the ones who attracted the girls. Donnie was a very handsome fellow, but Lucky, though not so handsome, was the undisputed star of the band. In any case, they had a knock-down, drag-out
argument, and Donnie, the rhythm guitar player, quit the band.

I got a call from Bobby Smith telling me about it, and he asked
me if I would be interested in taking Donnie's place in the band!
*Oh . . . my . . . God! Was I dreaming? Could this possibly be true? I
was going to be a Sparkle?* They had a weeklong club gig booked in
Hobbs, New Mexico, not too far from Brownfield just across the
New Mexico state line, and I was to start immediately. I had never
played an electric guitar and didn't own one—or a guitar amp. I
have no idea what guitar I used. I did know the standard chords,
and by this time I was pretty familiar with their repertoire. I went
to Hobbs and did that gig with them. I was playing with the best
and most popular band in West Texas! I was feeling real good about
myself. But it was not to last. Within a few weeks, Bobby called to
tell me Donnie wanted to come back to the band. Bummer! My
dream come true came crashing down.

By that time, I had made plans to go to college at the University of Texas and had been accepted. I was undecided about what I
would pursue as a career, and the pursuit of a career in music was
unheard of. Since I was good in math and science, I was encouraged by my high school counselors to study medicine. It really didn't
appeal to me, as I always got queasy when I saw people in pain or
injured, so I chose to major in pharmacy. I already had a student
apartment booked to room with my classmate and fellow football
player Jimmy Purtell.

At that point, I received a call from Bobby Smith, and he told
me he had heard of a band in Lubbock—the Night Beats—that
needed a bass player. The Night Beats were built around a tenor sax
player from Slaton by the name of Don Caldwell. They also had
Don Baggett, who played a big, fat Gibson ES-175 guitar and was
more of a jazz-type player. Jim Turley was a senior Phi Beta Kappa

accounting major at Texas Tech who played a Wurlitzer electric piano—one of the first electric pianos developed and like the one Ray Charles played on his hit "What'd I Say." Their drummer was Jimmy Marriott, also from Slaton.

I drove over to Slaton from Brownfield to meet with Don Caldwell, who was living on a farm outside town. He was out in a huge pigpen with rubber boots up to his knees, feeding hogs! He was operating a commercial hog-breeding farm and had a bunch of Berkshire sows with litters of baby pigs. I'm thinking to myself, *What kind of band could this guy have?* Turns out he was a very talented guy and was all business when it came to his music. We talked, and he asked me to come on board with the Night Beats. Soon after, I drove out again, and we rehearsed with the whole band. I canceled my plans to go to the University of Texas and quickly enrolled at Texas Tech. I had no trouble being accepted as I had graduated at the top of my class with only a few hundredths of a grade point average behind the valedictorian.

Playing with the Night Beats was new and different and a good learning experience. We did a lot of R&B tunes that featured the saxophone. "Honky Tonk," "Night Train," that kind of stuff. I had to hunker down and learn how to "cop the groove" more in the blues and R&B styles, which are different genres and ones that required a discipline I wasn't used to. I was the only vocalist, so I stepped up and sang. By this time, I was doing a lot of Roy Orbison tunes that I had picked up from the Sparkles. Don Caldwell and I roomed together in a little shack just off University Avenue across from the Tech campus. He played in the Texas Tech band and was an outstanding tenor sax player. He'd stand in the corner and practice for hours. Don is still very much involved in the music business in Lubbock, with his own recording studio, promoting festivals for the city, and until recently he ran one of the main performance venues, The Cactus Theater, in the Depot Entertainment District on Buddy Holly Avenue.

I might sneak in here and relate the tale of how I was a "Cricket" for a weekend—as in *the* Crickets: the band that played with the great Buddy Holly.

Don Baggett taught guitar lessons in one of the music stores in Lubbock. One day in the fall of 1964, I got a call from the owner of the store, who said he had gotten a call from Jerry Allison, a drummer who had played in Buddy Holly's band. He had booked a gig in El Paso the coming weekend, and he needed a guitar player and a bass player. Would I be interested in doing the gig? "Well, hell yes! What's the deal?" I would have to drive to El Paso for two shows with the Crickets for maybe a couple of hundred dollars and expenses. Okay! Baggett and I jumped in my '57 Chevy after Thursday classes, I skipped Friday classes, which included a chemistry lab, and we drove to El Paso. We rendezvoused with Jerry Allison and his wife, the real "Peggy Sue," and a Nashville songwriter/producer by the name of Buzz Cason, who was not an original Cricket. We rehearsed in a motel room on Friday afternoon with Buzz singing vocals and playing a clavinet, a little handheld keyboard instrument that had a sound similar to a harmonica when blown into. (Later, I used the same instrument on the intro when Michael Martin Murphey cut "Cosmic Cowboy.") Allison played the drums, Baggett played guitar, and I played bass. They only had ten or twelve songs in their list, and they needed some filler material. When they asked if I could do some songs, I said yes. Baggett was familiar with what I knew, so we pulled it off.

Bobby Fuller and the Fanatics opened the show. Man, they were awesome. All good-looking guys with Beatle haircuts and powder-blue Beatle suits and black boots. They had top-of-the-line Fender guitars and blonde piggyback Showmans across the stage. They played the latest Top 40 hits: Beatles and Rolling Stones, with dance steps, lights, the works! Bobby Fuller, whose career was just taking off, died in Los Angeles under mysterious circumstances in 1966 at the time he had a Top 10 record, "I Fought the Law."[1] We went on right after they finished. We did the Cricket thing—all Buddy Holly hits, and then, they asked me if I could do something. Roy Orbison's "Pretty Woman" was a huge hit in 1964. I knew it and could do a pretty good job of it. Well, I sang "Pretty Woman," and the crowd just went wild. I think I ended up doing it three times before the night was over. Naturally, I felt pretty good about it, as it appeared that I was the star of the whole show! (I had to throw that in, as it was one of the highlights of my whole career!)

The next night, we played at Texas Western College (now UTEP), as it was called in those days. Bobby Fuller wasn't on that show, and it didn't go quite as well. After the show, Britt Pounds, a Brownfield buddy of mine who had moved to El Paso, took me across the border for some Mexican food. My first flautas—in fact my very first Mexican food! Of course, we visited one of the bars that he, being a local, was familiar with. This was my first taste of a Mexican border town . . . and, no—to answer your unasked question—I did not dabble in that forbidden fruit!

Back in Lubbock and back in class, I dove into schoolwork and spent the weekends gigging with the Night Beats. I was taking my second semester of chemistry and had a four-hour lab from 1:00 to 5:00 on Friday afternoons. I would finish up the lab and walk over to the Student Union Building (SUB) for a cup of coffee and to see who was playing at the TGIF affair they presented there Fridays at five o'clock. That's where I first saw Joe Ely, who was still in high school. He was fronting a band and doing a pretty good imitation of Mick Jagger. I knew right then that he was a talented young man who had a future in the music business. Several years later,

---

1 The song was written by Sonny Curtis, a Meadow, Texas, (just ten miles north of Brownfield) native, who was very close to the Crickets. We did the tune in the Crickets set that night and it just occurred to me that it could have been where Bobby Fuller picked it up.

I would have the opportunity to land him a record contract with MCA Records, and his long and successful career has validated my first impression. It was also one of the first occasions that I began to realize I had a natural ability to recognize genuine talent.

Jim Turley, the piano player for the Night Beats, graduated magna cum laude from Tech in accounting and departed Lubbock for law school. The Night Beats disbanded, and I found gigs playing for a couple of bands whose names and players I can't recall. I had run into a couple of kids still in high school who I thought were pretty good, and for the first time, I decided to put together my own band. I approached Louie Holt, who played a hot Telecaster, and Don Telford, who had a good singing voice and played good rhythm guitar, and asked them to join my band. I also got Jimmy Marriott, the drummer from the Night Beats, to come on board. By this time, Jimmy was enrolled at Tech and playing snare drums in the Red Raider Marching Band. I decided to name the band the Shucks. When I was in El Paso with the Crickets, Jerry Allison mentioned to me that if he ever started another band, he was going to call it the Shucks. I put down my Oklahoma credit card and stole the name fair and square!

I based the bulk of our repertoire on the Sparkles' set list. They played regularly at the Music Box, a teen club at Slide Road and the Brownfield Highway. It was the most popular place in town and was always packed when the Sparkles played. We learned most of the songs they played, and as a result, we became fairly popular and could fill up the Music Box. When the Sparkles played, and we were free, we went to see them. They had a Righteous Brothers show worked up, and to get Lucky off the drums and up front with Bobby, they would have us sit in to back them up. I would take over Bobby's bass, Jimmy would take over on the drums, and Lucky and Bobby would get up front with microphones and do "Justine," "You've Lost that Lovin' Feelin'," and so on. The fact that we knew their material would become crucial in the near future.

Lucky and Bobby were still at odds with Stan and Donnie, and when the relationship finally reached the breaking point, Stan and Donnie quit the band. With no advance notice, I got a call from Bobby informing me of the situation and asking if Louie, Jimmy Marriott, and I would be interested in joining the band. I made a few calls, and it was all settled. A new incarnation of the Sparkles was born! Sadly, there was no room for Don Telford, a really good kid, and he got left behind. I was, at last, a bona fide member of the Fabulous Sparkles!

OUR TRANSPORTATION WAS AN Oldsmobile station wagon. We put five people and all our instruments, including two drum kits (as we now had two drummers), in that car and departed Lubbock after midnight for a debutante ball in Beaumont, Texas. We drove the six hundred miles, did the show with only a "skull session" rehearsal, and then packed up and headed back to Lubbock that night. We were just outside of Slaton the next afternoon when the old Olds gave up the ghost and died. Back in those days, we rarely got hotel rooms, and when we did, we'd get one room with two double beds and a rollaway for the five of us. The deal was that if anybody ever got a girl . . . they got the rollaway! It was a good plan, but it never happened that way. We were moving too fast to take time for girls on the road. We always just played, packed up, and drove back home.

I transferred from Tech to South Plains College in Levelland for the spring semester of '66. I had traded my '57 Chevy for a little red MGB convertible. I was making piles of money, and my expenses were minimal. I commuted from a house I was living in with four architecture students, one of whom was Jeff Pemberton, a schoolmate of mine from Brownfield. Later, I moved to a rental house in

Levelland with Louie Holt, Bennie Redman, and Johnny Snyder, a couple of boys who grew up on farms in the area.

I really enjoyed my classes at South Plains (SP) because they were much smaller than at Tech, and you could get help from your professors if you needed it. The reason I went to SP in the first place was because I couldn't get a "Quant and Qual" (Analytical Chemistry) course at Tech that I needed for my pharmacy degree plan. At SP, there were only seven students in the whole school taking that course. Lectures were two hours on Tuesday and Thursday mornings, with four-hour labs on Tuesday and Thursday afternoons. We were free to do lab work on Monday and Wednesday afternoons. We had our own individual Mettler balances, total access to the stockroom, and access to our professor, who was available to help if you hit a stump and needed some guidance. It really was an ideal setup for learning the material. My schedule left Fridays off, which was perfect as I was free to travel with the Sparkles and not miss any classes.

I wrote my second song in a history class at SP. It was called "Tired of Living This Way." Tommy Allsup—whose history included having been the one who lost the coin toss for who would get on Buddy Holly's plane that fateful night in Iowa—had a studio in Odessa. He had gotten wind that I had the song, and he sent a guy to Lubbock with papers to publish the tune. I was green as a gourd when it came to any knowledge of what that all meant, so I eagerly signed the publishing contract. Tommy produced a record for a horn band out of Dallas. It was the first song I ever had published and recorded, and it actually turned out very well.

I was making $200 a week, which would be the equivalent of almost $1,500 a week in today's dollars. I bought and paid cash for any instrument my heart desired. I bought a brand new '67 Chevy Malibu and paid $2,900 cash for it. I had new clothes, money in the bank, and a motorcycle. I was pretty much rolling in dough. I blew a lot trying to impress people. I didn't know a thing about business or investing, but I did manage to save some money since I was making more than I had ever dreamed of. I had no mentor or anyone to turn to who would prevent me from letting lots of money slip through my fingers. I had to learn that the hard way—and that's a Harvard Business School education.

During this time (the fall of '65 through the spring of '67) we played all over the South Plains. We were also being booked by Charlie Hatchett, owner of the Hatchett Agency in Austin. He was originally from Lamesa and had been a member of a former incarnation of the Sparkles. Hatchett was a real businessman with his own three-piece band called the Chevelles. He practically had a monopoly on the band-booking market in Austin, and we were his top-grossing band. He booked us a lot in Austin, especially for UT Roundup, the annual fraternity rush season, debutante balls, and other good paying gigs—we made $500 a show, which was top dollar at the time, and sometimes he would book us for more than one gig a day.

On one of those trips to Austin for Roundup, we met Don Henley, who was playing drums and singing for another of Hatchett's bands out of Linden, Texas, called Felicity. We saw Jimmie Vaughan as a fifteen-year-old old guitar slinger at one of the "party barns" that used to dot the Hill Country cedar breaks around Austin. He played an old Telecaster through a Super Beatle amp. His band, The Chessmen, did Yardbirds songs and would kick the drums and throw their instruments off the stage as a finale. I will always remember a blistering guitar version of "Eleanor Rigby" from that night. It didn't take a genius to know that kid was going far.

THE SPARKLES WERE PLAYING all over the state. We had quit the Music Box in favor of a larger venue in Lubbock called The Village Swinger. They were booking touring acts, and we got to open for the Turtles and the Everly Brothers. We got to meet the Everly Brothers backstage, as well as Buddy Holly's dad and his widow, Maria Elena.

I had acquired a Farfisa organ, which was the first electronic keyboard to appear in the music stores, and for the first time, I was playing some keyboards along with rhythm guitar. James Brown was really big at the time, and Lucky had started doing a lot of his songs like "I Feel Good," "It's a Man's World," and "Please, Please, Please." Since we had an extra drummer, Lucky started getting up front with the microphone and doing a James Brown show. Lucky was "no kinda dancer," but the James Brown show went over big, and it brought him a lot of attention. He would do a lot of screaming à la James Brown (an excessive amount in my opinion), and he started letting the Roy Orbison songs that he sang so well fall by the wayside.

The Beatles, the Rolling Stones, Cream, the Yardbirds—and the whole psychedelic, fuzz-tone era—had started having a profound effect on the rock-and-roll music scene. They were way out of our league and experience, but we started trying to merge with that movement with the material we were playing. At this time, Lucky and Bobby started writing some songs. Occasionally, I was in a position to participate and had a hand in writing one called "First Forget." I eventually recorded it myself in 2000 at the urging of Lloyd Maines, who produced a CD for me titled *It's a Texas Thing*.

> Hey there, is that a tear in your eye?
> And don't try to hide it,
> It's got to come out to dry
> And I'll tell you what to do
> First forget what has made you blue.

Prior to the change in the band, the Sparkles had signed a record contract with Hickory Records, the label that Roy Orbison recorded for. Larry Parks and Jay Turnbow, who wrote the million-seller "Bread and Butter" recorded by the Newbeats, arranged that deal. The band cut a single in Tommy Allsup's studio—one side was called "The Hip" and the other "Girls, Girls, Girls." Parks and Turnbow convinced Hickory that Lucky Floyd could be another Roy Orbison. They wanted him to come to Nashville and be a featured single artist, without the Sparkles. Lucky declined. He didn't want to split with Bobby. They had grown up together in Seagraves, had been bosom buddies since childhood, and had always played together, so Hickory signed the Sparkles as a band. In that short window of time from when I had taken Donnie Roberts's spot, we cut a couple of songs at Tommy Allsup's studio in Odessa: "Jack and the Beanstalk" and "Something That You Said." I was nineteen years old, and it was my first experience in a recording studio. I discovered I was really in my element in the studio situation, and I had the opportunity to make a couple of suggestions production-wise that improved the cuts significantly. Tommy Allsup took note, looked at me, and gave me a wink and a thumbs-up. It was my first taste of producing—and without any prior experience, my very first opportunity was met with respectful approval.

On spring break, 1967, we went to Nashville in our Dodge cargo van. Hickory Records was the artist arm of Acuff–Rose publishing company, one of the most successful Nashville publishing houses—they owned the copyrights to all of Hank Williams's songs. The Acuff was Roy Acuff, the main man at the Grand Ole Opry, and the Rose part was Fred and Wesley Rose, Nashville icons in the publishing world. Hickory Records had Roy Orbison, the Newbeats (featuring Larry Henley, who sang the high part on "Bread and Butter" and later cowrote the megahit "Wind Beneath My Wings" recorded by Gary Morris and Bette Midler), and Donovan.

I recall sitting in Wesley Rose's office with Lucky. A glass-encased fiddle that had belonged to Hank Williams was hanging on the wall behind his desk. Wesley said, "I really don't see what's the big deal about this guy Donovan—I can't understand a word he's saying!" One morning we were hanging around shooting the breeze with the guys in the Newbeats, when a young man who had driven all night from Houston walked in. His name was Mickey Newbury, and he had a new song he'd written called "Just Dropped In (to See What Condition My Condition Was In)." He pitched it to us and urged us to cut it. The problem was the song was about the dangerous effects of LSD and was way too far out there for us—we didn't "get" it. So we declined. Kenny Rogers and the First Edition later cut it and had a huge hit. It was featured in the movie *The Big Lebowski* as Jeff Bridges was being depicted in a psychedelic stupor.

We went into the studio and cut four sides in a session that lasted just one day, with Don Gant, an artist and repertoire (A & R) man, producing. It was the first time we had ever worked with a designated producer. Back in those days, the A & R guy played a significant role in the recording business: It was his job to find the right songs for the right artist. Today, I don't think that role is as significant because so many artists are songwriters, and they do their own songs. The songs we cut were the ones that Lucky and Bobby had written— "No Friend of Mine," "Hipsville 29 BC," "I Want to Be Free," and "First Forget." Except for "First Forget," these songs were attempts to get "hip" with the times, so we had Louie Holt, our guitar player, do fuzz-tone guitar riffs for the first time. This was a departure from the kind of band we had always been, and we were out of our element. However, those tracks are highly prized by grunge band fanatics, and the vinyl singles are coveted collectors' items.

With the four sides cut, we set out for Pittsburgh, Pennsylvania, where the single of "Jack and the Beanstalk" was getting some significant airplay. I drove that little van all night, the whole distance, while the other guys slept with their heads leaning on each other on the bench in the back. We arrived in Pittsburgh around sunup and slept for a few hours. We were to make appearances at three "sock hops"—as they were known then—that evening. Sock hops were basically teen dances promoted by radio stations where radio DJs would spin the latest hits and a touring band would make a showcase appearance and perform. It was quite a night's work to go to the venue, set up all your gear including two sets of drums and a PA (which for us was just microphones plugged into a Fender Dual Showman amp), do a show, pack up, and do the same thing twice more in the same evening!

We were very inexperienced and had no professional guidance or direction. It was a long way from playing in West Texas to the sock-hop-record-promoting scene in Pittsburgh, Pennsylvania. But we went over pretty well! Those Yankee kids were quite amazed when Lucky got up and did his James Brown show. They had never seen anything like it—or like Lucky and Jimmy Marriott's duel drum solo simultaneously playing identical licks! The next day we piled into the van and drove straight through back to Lubbock. Each of us would drive one hour; then someone the next in line would drive while the others slept. Monday morning, I was back in class at South Plains College.

I finished out the spring semester of '67 with Quant and Qual chemistry under my belt. We continued to play around Texas that summer, but Lucky and Bobby were starting to feel we had done all we could do in and around Lubbock. They started talking about moving to California and making a legitimate attempt at "hitting the big time." Everyone in the band was married and had kids except for Louie and me, and they had deferments with the selective service. I had a student deferment as long as I stayed in school. That summer, Lucky, Bobby, and Jimmy Marriott made the decision to move. The war in Vietnam was heating up, and any young man of draftable age who didn't have a deferment was promptly drafted into the Army. I knew that if I didn't stay in school, it would be my fate as well. I informed the guys that I couldn't move to California, and I applied once again at the University of Texas and got ready to move to Austin to continue my studies in the school of pharmacy.

We had one show to do for a debutante ball at the Austin Country Club before they left. During the first break, a fellow by the name of Richard Lipscomb came up to me, chatting away, and I told him I would be moving to Austin very shortly. He asked me where I was going to live. When I told him I hadn't made any arrangements yet, he informed me that he and two other guys were moving into a brand-new apartment complex on Town Lake, and they needed one more roommate. How would I like to move in with them? Problem solved!

I wrapped things up with the Sparkles, said my goodbyes, and packed up to leave Levelland. You will recall how my dad took a teaching job in Brownfield after having been a school superintendent for many years. As the years passed, several vacancies for principals had opened up, but he was turned down for them all. Dad was all about the straight and narrow when it came to politics and lifestyle, and I had never heard him express himself publicly, except for his support of Eisenhower back in 1956. I can't help but think that because he was not a part of a clique, he was passed over for the higher jobs. In any case, when I graduated, my folks left Brownfield and moved to Iowa Park, so they could be closer to Oklahoma and all the kinfolks.

I departed Levelland, went to Iowa Park, and spent a week or so with my family before I made the move to Austin. I left the flatlands and dust storms of West Texas behind—along with the Sparkles—with a feeling of excitement and anticipation for what lay ahead.

Chapter 6

Moving to Austin

I HOOKED UP MY brand-new Chevy Malibu to a U-Haul trailer and headed to Austin for the fall semester of '67. The La Estrada Apartments we were scheduled to move into were unfinished, so they put us up in a hotel near the Capitol downtown. Richard Lipscomb and I lived there for a few weeks while getting settled into classes at UT. Richard was the classic fraternity cat. He wore the latest college Joe wardrobe with cordovan saddle oxfords or penny loafers, drove a brand-new top-of-the-line Buick Riviera, and was a member of Delta Tau Delta fraternity. He was a good-natured, easygoing fellow and very hip to the music scene, which was centered around a few clubs near campus and catered to the college crowd. He took me to the Club Saracen on San Jacinto, a couple of blocks north of Scholz Garten, which is all that's left of the street from how it was in those days. The Saracen, one of the most popular clubs in town, was run by Marie Nora, a portly Lebanese woman who was well known in her own right around the Austin music scene.

Charlie Hatchett, the law student-booking mogul, played in his three-piece band, the Chevelles. Al Stahealy, a tall, handsome fellow with beach-boy blond hair and also a law student, played bass and did all the vocals. Chuck Rogers, an electronics major, played drums.

Hatchett, who played a hot lead guitar, worked the three-piece band and took all the $300-a-show gigs, often doing two shows a day. One hundred dollars a gig was good money in those days, and with Hatchett taking all the $300-a-night gigs and booking his other bands for the other better paying gigs, he was making a fortune while going to law school.

The Chevelles had something else going that enhanced their draw—a go-go dancer! Her name was Maggie Cowart. She was tall and beautiful and wore these cool pink dancing costumes with white fringe that were sexy, but not vulgar. Maggie was Al Sta-healy's girlfriend, and they were a good-looking item around town. The Chevelles played every Friday afternoon for happy hour at the Saracen. Their repertoire consisted of all the latest rock-and-roll hits of the day—Jimi Hendrix, Eric Clapton, and the Stones, as well as old rock-and-roll and R&B standards by Sam & Dave and Wilson Pickett. The Saracen was packed every Friday afternoon with a "frat-rat" clientele, but a lot of musicians showed up there too—so did I, checking out the scene and looking to meet some other musicians. I became such a regular that Marie once put me to work as a bartender, which consisted solely of pulling beers out of the cooler, popping the tops, and putting the dollar in the register.

The Jade Room club was just south of the Saracen on San Jacinto, and was run by a grumpy, tight-fisted old lady, Marge Funk. Marge booked most of the bands in town and featured live music six nights a week. Each band had its own regular night to play, and the pay was what you could draw at the door, which often was not very much. But it did give the bands work, and having a regular gig there meant they were somebody in town. Some of the bands I recall had strange names such as Strawberry Shoemaker, The Eternal Life Corporation, New Atlantis, The Sweetarts, and the Lavender Hill Express. Lavender Hill Express played Thursdays and were by far the most popular and best-drawing band.

Rusty Wier was featured doing vocals from the drum throne, with Leonard Arnold and Layton DePenning on lead guitars, Jess Yaryan on bass, and Johnny Schwertner on organ. A little later, Ron Coleman opened the New Orleans Club at 12th and Red River, and it became a popular venue.

It didn't take me long to find a band that I wanted to play with. It was one day after I had finished an organic chemistry lab and had dropped by the Saracen to see what was happening. A band was onstage doing a really good rendition of "The Letter," a hit song by the Box Tops. The Georgetown Medical Band (GMB) members were all premed students going to preppy Southwestern University in Georgetown. I was particularly impressed with the drummer, who was also doing a good job with the vocals. Since I was a bass player, I was always on the lookout for drummers who could keep good time, "cop a groove" and stay with it, and he was the best I'd heard since I got to town. His name was Rick Cobb. The other boys were Chuck Greenwood, who played guitar and sang most of the vocals, and Bob Snyder, the bass player who actually became a doctor; I don't recall a fourth man, or even if there was one. They had a unique repertoire and even did the Supremes' tune "Stop! In the Name of Love." I was impressed by their originality and uniqueness, as most of the bands in town played the same, most popular songs.

We got together and rehearsed. I learned their material, and we added some of my tunes. We got a regular Wednesday night gig at the Jade Room and picked up weekend gigs from Charlie Hatchett—mostly keg parties at fraternity houses in the $300 range. Some of the frat boys were wilder by far than any musician I knew.

As time went by, Mike Lucas started booking the lion's share of our gigs. Mike was a disc jockey and program director at the Number One rock radio station in Austin, KNOW—"The Rock of Austin." KNOW promoted all the big acts coming through town. Mike emceed those shows, which were all done at the old Palmer Auditorium on Town Lake, so he was a well-known celebrity in town. He booked and managed us in an informal, noncontractual arrangement.

Later, the Georgetown Medical Band added the guitar genius Johnny Richardson. Johnny was a good-looking, soft-spoken young man who had incredible natural talent, especially in the blues guitar realm. He was extremely laid back, but he could bend a string like no one else in town; he nailed all the guitar classics like Freddie King's "Hide Away." I was really happy when we brought him on board. He added greatly to the band. He is still in Austin, but sadly, has been almost invisible all these years.

Amid all this, I was still a full-time student at UT in the pharmacy college, taking organic chemistry, calculus, pharmacognosy, physics, and a class called "Functions of the Human Body." Most of these classes required four-hour labs each week, which was like taking another course. I particularly liked pharmacognosy, and my professor, Dr. Sullivan, knew about my playing music and thought it was cool. I did very well in that course. I studied hard and made ninety-fives on the quizzes. I wasn't too popular—the class average on the quizzes was about sixty-five—since I would blow the curve and cause the other students to make lower grades as a result. Tough luck for them! (Pharmacy 101 was a simple orientation to pharmacy course, but you had to wear a tie to class to make an A.)

There was a duality to my existence: I was in the pharmacy school in the daytime and playing music in the clubs at night. Also—this was 1967, and the whole counterculture movement was making itself felt on campus. I'd be in the classroom wearing a tie, and anti–Vietnam War marches and Students for a Democratic Society (SDS) rallies would be happening outside the windows. Of course, long hair or beards were not tolerated if you wanted to make good grades, and since I was not inclined to buck the status quo in school, I toed the line. However—although I did my work in school, I couldn't wait to get out of a chemistry lab and get to a club where the music was happening!

During this time, Richard Lipscomb introduced me to a girl named Marcia Sleeper. Now Marcia was a character. She had a mouth on her, and she could charm her way through any situation making the most of her feminine skills. She resembled a young Barbara Stanwyck. She knew her way around both the fraternity scene and the music scene, and she ran circles around me. I tried to catch her, but she was way too wily and managed to stay just beyond my reach. She would take me to the Vulcan Gas Company, a venue on Congress Avenue at about 2nd or 3rd Street that featured Shiva's Head Band, the Conqueroo, and other far-out, so-called psychedelic bands that predated the Armadillo World Headquarters. She actually got the Georgetown Medical Band booked for a spring break trip of college kids to Acapulco. They drove our equipment to Acapulco, and we flew down on the charter flight with the tour group on a funky DC-3. We performed three shows, including in the Plaza de Toros—the bullfighting ring! How many people can honestly claim they played a gig in a bullfighting ring in Mexico?

I had one additional close encounter with destiny while on that trip. Marcia and I and another couple decided to rent a jeep and drive a few miles north to a beach known for bodysurfing. We arrived and, of course, had to indulge in the Coco Loco cocktails served in coconut shells right there on the beach. That beach, unlike Texas beaches that are flat and shallow, fell off quickly, and good-sized waves came smashing onto the beach with a great deal of force. If you failed to stay on top of the wave, you would get slammed to the ocean floor under it. The undertow would drag you back, and before you could recover, another six- to eight-foot wave would pin you to the bottom again. The undertow and backwash would once again carry you back toward the ocean. You couldn't recover in time before another wave slammed you again. That was exactly what happened to me. I got caught in a series of three waves: As soon as I could surface and gasp for a breath of air, another wall of water would slam me to the bottom. After the third wave, I had the clear impression that I was going to drown before I could get out of there. I held my breath as long as I could, and at the point I could hold it no more, I opened my mouth—miraculously, there was air. I fought desperately and managed to escape to the beach, completely exhausted. It was only by the grace of God that I survived. Forces greater than me and beyond my control had taken advantage of my stupidity and sheer foolishness. Marcia and I were no longer together when I went to California at the end of the summer of '68, and that was the end of that.

I PLAYED WITH THE Georgetown Medical Band through the fall of '67 and into the spring of '68. I found myself unable to have much influence on the direction of the band, and I wasn't thrilled about that. It was reminiscent of days in high school with the Premiers. Chuck Greenwood was not unlike Alton Nicholson in the sense that he considered the band *his* band, which it was. But I felt stymied creatively by his having to have final say on every issue that arose. It wasn't bad, but it wasn't love! I was frustrated with my inability to explore my own ideas or have any influence on the material we would do, but once again, I submitted to get along.

The spring of '68 had been momentous for the country: Martin Luther King Jr. was assassinated in April and Robert Kennedy in June. In March, I had watched on a TV in the Student Union building as Lyndon Johnson announced, "I shall not seek, and I will not accept, the nomination of my party for another term as your president."

The times they were a-changing, but to a certain extent, I was so occupied that I really didn't grasp just how much.

I decided to go to summer school in '68 to take microbiology.

The course required attendance at a three-hour lecture every day and a four-hour lab twice a week—it was a full-time load for three hours of credit. It was very demanding, but I found it very interesting. The course consisted of the basics of microorganisms, growing cultures in petri dishes, and lots of microscope work. After that, we got into the study of blood chemistry—antigen-antibody reactions, to be specific—which I found fascinating. It was the only course that I ever really got into, as opposed to just memorizing the material and regurgitating it back on the quizzes.

I stayed up all night to study for every major quiz I took in college. The subjects were very complex, but I actually "grokked" the concepts involved. *Grok* is a word from the Robert Heinlein book *Stranger in a Strange Land* that means to understand something completely. Well, I may be overstating it a bit. But it reinforced my belief in God as the creator of all things and in the microscopic-macroscopic equilibrium and perfection of all His creations—from subatomic particles to the universe as a whole. Nothing short of a higher, all-knowing power could create all things in nature with such precision and balance.

I finished up the microbiology course with a sigh of relief. I had been living with Rick Cobb, the drummer for the Georgetown Medical Band. He had neglected his studies, and I think perhaps he had flunked out of school. It might have had something to do with a hot romance he was having with his girlfriend . . . He confided in me that he was going to drop out of school and return home to Dallas, and he asked for my advice. I told him I thought that would be the best thing to do, because in my mind, I couldn't see a long-term future for the Georgetown Medical Band.[1] As far as I was concerned, that was the end of the GMB, and it triggered my decision to leave the band as well.

---

1   Rick Cobb moved back to Dallas, ended up joining a band called Bloodrock, and became a bona fide rock-and-roll star. Independently wealthy, he moved to Marin County, California, retired, and started writing poetry.

Suddenly out of the blue, who do I get a phone call from? None other than Bobby Smith, my former bandmate from the Sparkles. I had heard nothing from or about the band since we had come to a crossroads and parted ways. Bobby said the band was really doing well . . . TV shows, private parties for the Smothers Brothers, regular monthlong gigs at the Factory in Santa Monica where all the TV stars hung out, and gigs at other top venues in the Los Angeles area. But, he said, they were having problems with the two fellows they hired to replace Louie Holt and me. Same old story: Lucky and Bobby didn't get along with them. Al Perkins was a great musician and a virtual clone of Stan Smith as far as his playing went, but he didn't like Lucky's beer drinking and cigarette smoking and wouldn't tolerate it in his car. It caused a lot of friction, and that, as well as personality conflicts with the B-3 organ player, Jay Larimore, had come to a head. They wanted me to come out to California and join the band!

Wow! I was stunned, but pleasantly so. He caught me at just the right time. My head wasn't into being a pharmacist. I had been in school for sixteen years straight, and, frankly, I was exhausted with it—plus the thought of going to California was so very alluring. I made the decision on the spot in my mind. I really wanted to do it. I called my dad and told him. He responded very calmly, "Go ahead and do it, but you're going to get drafted if you do." He had a way of always being calm and nonjudgmental at critical times, leaving the decisions up to me. Or course, I ignored his advice and made immediate plans to move to California.

I PACKED MY STUFF in another U-Haul trailer, hooked it to my Chevy Malibu, and bucked a stiff wind for twenty-four hours driving straight through to Los Angeles, arriving midmorning. I made my way to where the guys were living in North Hollywood and knocked on Lucky's door. I was greeted by all of them and their wives in a joyful reunion. We got reacquainted, and they got me settled in with Jimmy Marriott and his wife, Debbie, who provided a spare room for me to bunk in until I could find my own place. I slept in all that afternoon and through the night. The next day, we went into Hollywood, where they introduced me to Mike Martin, the manager of the Pearly Gate—the guys had renamed the band to sound more timely and hip than the Sparkles. Mike Martin was a true Hollywood cat through and through. He wore designer shades and the latest in California clothes. His house was up in the hills just above Hollywood Boulevard with a nice view of the city. I thought it was all so cool, but I was painfully aware of feeling that I was a greenhorn kid who had just fallen off the turnip truck! Martin played the part of a Hollywood mover and shaker to the hilt. He talked about what all was going on and the big plans he had for the new band. They had replaced the guitar player, Al Perkins, with a Hollywood native: a singer-songwriter by the name of Jimmy Dutch.

Jimmy Dutch was nowhere near the guitar player that Al Perkins was. His background had been doing folky, singer-songwriter, Bob Dylan stuff. He put me in the mind of a Steven Fromholz as far as his size and appearance went, and he had a similar great sense of humor and outgoing nature. He played a big fat Gibson hollow body guitar that constantly "fed back," but was, for the most part, an acoustic-type player who had switched to electric. His presence, as well as mine, I'm sure, altered the nature of the Pearly Gate significantly. Al Perkins and Jay Larimore[2] may not have been able to get along with Lucky and Bobby, but they were excellent musicians,

---

2   Al Perkins went on to play steel guitar with the California-based band Shiloh, with Don Henley prior to the Eagles, and then with the Flying Burrito Brothers. Later, he became an in-demand session player in Nashville, where he remains to this day. Jay Larimore joined the Hare Krishnas.

and together they had put together a show that stayed booked in the better class of clubs in the Los Angeles area.

Mike Martin booked us at Arthur's Club, a top club on La Cienega Boulevard, and The Cave at the Ambassador Hotel (where Robert Kennedy had been murdered just weeks prior to my arrival). The Cave was the music venue-cocktail lounge just downstairs from the famous Cocoanut Grove, a Las Vegas–type showroom that featured show acts like the Four Tops, the Supremes, the Temptations, and Lou Rawls. It was *the* Las Vegas showroom in LA and a very upscale Hollywood scene. You might see people like Ann-Margret walking down the carpeted halls outside The Cave. Sometimes, I would sneak up to the Cocoanut Grove to catch a part of the show during our breaks. And many times, these acts would finish and come down to The Cave to watch our shows and hang out with us. We did a Four Tops medley, and it was a thrill to do with the Four Tops sitting in the audience!

We also played regularly at the Factory, in Santa Monica near the beach. Generally, we'd be booked into these rooms for six nights a week, for two or four weeks running. The Factory's clientele was predominantly TV and movie stars and sports celebrities. It was the every-night hangout for people like Bill Cosby; David Janssen, star of *The Fugitive*; Peter Lawford; Tommy and Dick Smothers and Pat Paulsen from *The Smothers Brothers Comedy Hour*; and Dan Rowan and Dick Martin from *Laugh-In*. They'd just be hanging out on sofas in the lounge area, and it was not uncommon for us to go sit down with them on the breaks and shoot the breeze. On one occasion, I had the opportunity to shoot a game of pool with Wilt "the Stilt" Chamberlain, known by everyone as the first seven-foot Hall of Famer in pro basketball, who played for the Los Angeles Lakers. It goes without saying that he didn't require a pool crutch to make a long, across-the-table shot. I let him win . . . When I was still in high school, in the summertime after I'd finished my paper route, I would head off to the west side of town on my scooter to Thad Risinger's Pool Hall. It opened at 7:00 a.m., about the time I would finish my route. It was surprising how many people would be there that early in the morning. Connie Vernon would usually meet me there, and we'd play "straight pool" till lunchtime. I got to be a pretty good hand at shooting pool, and snooker too—so it's not unreasonable to consider that maybe I could have beaten Wilt in a game!

The biggest night at the Factory was Halloween. On any ordinary night, everyone you saw was a recognizable star, but that night was a special occasion. The Chairman of the Board, Paul Newman, showed up! He had to be, without question, the biggest star I have ever been in a room with. He had on a beautiful suit and wore a derby hat. I was probably one hundred feet from him, but I swear, his blue eyes glowed from that distance—in a not-so-well-lighted room! There was a distinct aura about his presence, and it was easy to see why he was such a big star. I've never been the starstruck type, but I confess I was impressed, and I moved from where I was to see him closer up.

We played around in the Los Angeles area in different clubs. I had found a little house to rent off Lankersham Boulevard in North Hollywood, just a few blocks from where the Batmobile was prominently displayed. The house was owned by an animal trainer, who had barns and pens where he kept a lot of animals. He had owned and trained Francis the Talking Mule who had starred in several movies from the fifties and early sixties.

On my days off, I would take Mulholland Drive over to Hollywood and hang out at the Pussy Cat A-Go-Go trying to meet some girls. I didn't know a soul in California besides the guys in the band. I did meet a couple of girls, and I invited them to come see us play at the Ambassador. But only one actually came to see me, and that was the extent of my socializing with the opposite sex.

IN NOVEMBER 1968, WE got a four-week gig in Seattle. We drove all the way from Los Angeles, which was quite a haul, but it was beautiful driving up Highway 1 along the coast. Seattle was a cool, seaport, university town, and I enjoyed my time there. The election of '68 was going on, and Vice President Hubert Humphrey had gotten the Democratic nomination after Johnson declined to run. Richard Nixon was the Republican candidate—again—after having lost to John Kennedy in 1960. The Beatles' "White Album" was released while we were there. We did the four weeks and started the drive back to Los Angeles in that same old Dodge cargo van pulling a trailer.

It was well into the night when we reached the Mount Shasta pass on the Oregon–California border, and it was snowing like crazy. We weren't equipped to pull a trailer uphill in a snowstorm, and at one point we could go no further and found ourselves slipping off the side of the highway. "Oh, damn—what are we going to do now?" Luckily for us, some young enterprising local men with a Jeep came along and offered to pull us to the top of the pass for a price that we were more than happy to pay. Our little van's heater couldn't heat the whole space, so we were bundled up and huddled together. The little 6-cylinder engine was under a metal cover between the driver and passenger seats. I found the best thing for me was to lie on my back on the engine cover, with my head hanging off the backside and my legs hanging off the front. I stretched myself out and slept very well in that position. The heat from the engine kept me warm, and it was the best seat in the house when it was cold.

We got back to Los Angeles around the first of December, and after a brief respite, we headed out for a run in Sparks, Nevada. We rented a single cheap hotel room and, like always, it had two double beds and a rollaway for the five of us. The venue was a place called the Lemon Tree, and—like every place in Nevada—it had slot machines. The gig was for two dance sets and three show sets a night, the last show being at 3:00 a.m. It was a hard gig. Lucky did his screaming James Brown show three times a night, and it really took a toll on his voice. One night, some fellows from Harrah's Club and Casino in nearby Reno came in to see our show. They seemed to be impressed and invited us to be their guests at the show at Harrah's. We showed up at the red rope line in our blue Nehru suits and white patent leather boots. We were immediately ushered to the front of the queue and seated in great seats right in front of the stage. Unfortunately, I don't recall the name of the group, but I remember they had a long, successful run there, and the experience has stayed with me all these years. The lead singer was a great vocalist who fronted the band and played guitar. The bass player played bass with his left hand and a valve trombone with his right hand. The drummer played the drums with his right hand and a trumpet with his left. The only mics onstage were vocal mics on them. Behind them was a fifteen-piece orchestra composed of brass, saxes, and a string section. Everything was totally acoustic otherwise, and they played at incredibly low volume. The lead vocalist worked away from the mic, and you could hear his voice acoustically in the room. He only got close to the mic on low quiet notes, but for the most part it was acoustic. I swear, it was the most impressive live music I have heard in my life, and I have always dreamed of working in such an incredible professional situation. Everything a performer could ask for was there . . . a perfectly acoustic blend of the horns and strings accompanying a very accomplished three-piece front band. From our front-row seats, I felt like I was swimming in natural, acoustic stereo. That show has always remained the ultimate in what I dreamed music could be, and it impressed upon me the fact that you don't have to be loud to be good! After the show, I saw the lead singer in the casino wearing a full-length mink coat. No doubt he could afford it—he was just that damned good!

During that stint in Sparks, the University of Texas football team was scheduled to play Arkansas for the Southwest Conference Championship. On that Saturday, game day, I got up to watch the game while the other guys slept. The TV had those rabbit ears antennae, and the rabbit ears were wrapped in aluminum foil, but that did little to enhance the snowy reception. Coach Royal replaced Bill Bradley, putting James Street in for quarterback and moving Super Bill to receiver and defensive secondary—a decision that proved providential and fortuitous. (Bill Bradley was a Sparkles fan from way back, and we had known him and followed his career as the quarterback of the Texas football team.) The Longhorns beat Arkansas that day in a tremendously exciting football game.

I watched it happen, by myself, in a cold motel room in Sparks, Nevada, and it sparked a great deal of pride—and not just a little bit of homesickness in my heart. I will never forget it, and neither will anyone else in Texas. The next season, the Longhorns were undefeated, beating Arkansas in what was billed as the "Game of the Century." They were named national champions after defeating Notre Dame in the Cotton Bowl. James Street was 20–0 as a starting quarterback for Texas. I had the opportunity to visit with him in the years preceding his untimely passing in 2013. He was a fine man. Bill Bradley went on to have an All-Pro career as a safety for the Philadelphia Eagles, and then in coaching at the pro and college levels. We are still good friends and stay in touch to this day.

WHEN WE GOT BACK to Los Angeles from Nevada, I had a letter from the selective service informing me that my student deferment had been revoked. The Richard Nixon administration was going to institute a draft lottery system. Well, the gig was up, as they say. I had no alternative but to get my butt back in school, and quick. We had one more gig to play at the Ambassador Hotel; then I had to hightail it back to Texas. Rick Cobb, my bandmate from the Georgetown Medical Band, had decided on a whim to fly out and visit, not knowing I was getting ready to head back to Texas. He spent a few days, and I asked him to ride back to Texas with me. He was staying at Carroll Shelby's house down close to the LA Airport. Carroll Shelby had made his fame and fortune by designing the Ford Shelby Mustang. He was a friend of Rick's dad in Dallas, who was H. L. Hunt's private pilot. I packed my things in another U-Haul trailer, and Rick and I drove down to the Shelby place where Rick had his luggage stowed. We retrieved his bags and got on I-10 East about 3:00 a.m. We drove straight through to Dallas where I dropped Rick off, and I backtracked to Iowa Park to visit my folks. I was completely drained, but it felt good to be home and back in the bosom of the family and eat some of Mother's good cooking.

I reenrolled at Texas for the spring semester of '69, got my student deferment reinstated, and moved to Austin again. Because I was so late in arriving, housing was scarce, and it was difficult to find a place to live, but I located a room to rent in a house just off campus near the law school. I could walk to campus, eliminating the need to drive and find parking near campus. I just had one room that shared a bathroom with the room next door. I had never lived alone before, but it turned out to be the best thing for me. I settled into school and focused on my studies since there was nothing and no one to distract me. I didn't own a TV—just a thrown-together stereo system on which I would listen repeatedly to my favorite album of the day—Harry Nilsson's *Aerial Ballet*. That album contained the Fred Neil song "Everybody's Talking."

Consistent with my modus operandi, as soon as I got settled, I started looking for a gig. I had always earned all my own money and didn't want to burden my folks. It was a matter of pride in my own self-sufficiency that I immediately got out about town to scope out the scene and find a paying gig. It never occurred to me to find a "regular" working job. Austin hadn't changed a lot in the four months I had been in California. One thing that had changed was that the Lavender Hill Express had risen to the top of the town. Their popularity had increased significantly, and they were packing the Jade Room on Thursday nights, taking as much as $500 a night at the door at two dollars a head! This was a good week's pay in itself—and they still had Fridays and Saturdays available to book.

I set my sights on getting a gig with them. There was only one problem: They already had an organ player, Johnny Schwertner. I don't know how I did it, but it wasn't long before I replaced Johnny as the keyboard man. I think maybe the fact that I had a Hammond organ, could do lead vocals and harmonies, and I had a great deal more experience in general had something to do with it. In any case, once again, I had found a way to get hired by the most popular and successful band in town.

The Lavender Hill Express was a five-piece outfit that featured Rusty Wier on drums who had previously been with a popular band called the Wig. Rusty sang most of the lead vocals. The Wig had won the Aqua Festival Battle of the Bands, which was the precursor to today's SXSW Festival. The Lavender Hill Express released a single titled "Watch Out" that was one of the first records released by an Austin band besides the 13th Floor Elevators. Leonard Arnold and Layton DePenning, both excellent guitarists, played Gibson Les Pauls through Marshall stacks, but they used the less powerful fifty-watt amps, trading leads and doing things together. It was still plenty loud! Jess Yaryan played bass. He wasn't a whiz-bang bass player, but you don't need a whiz-bang bass player—just a good one—and he was good and worked well for the band. I played an M-3 Hammond organ with a Leslie cabinet speaker and did some lead vocals and harmony singing. Layton had an excellent voice and did some lead vocals and good harmony vocals. All in all, they were a really good band. They never kept really metronomic time as Rusty was constantly speeding up and slowing down, but it didn't seem to matter, because the band would speed up and slow down with him. They were all together, and it worked. It would drive me crazy because I have a clock in my head, and rushing and dragging grates on my very soul. But, like I said, it worked. Rusty had a performance style and charisma about him that was very engaging, and the rest didn't matter. I went along with the program and was happy to be playing with the "hottest band in town."

The Lavender Hill Express had attracted some financial and promotional support in the form of a new arrival from the East Coast—MacEnroe McQuade and Austin attorney John Ludlum. Neither had experience in the music business, but they saw great potential in the band and were determined to do something to help them. They went to Tyler, Texas, and cut four sides in Robin Hood Brians studio, which was regarded as one of the best in Texas. ZZ Top cut their first four albums there, and they all went platinum. James Brown, Bill Mack, Jimmie and Stevie Ray Vaughan, The Box Tops, and a host of other well-known acts cut their stuff there. I arrived after these sessions had taken place, but it was clear that the Lavender Hill gang had the greatest potential. Mac and John had established relations with International Consultants out of Phoenix, who produced concerts for big acts out of California. Steppenwolf, who were red hot at the time with "Magic Carpet Ride" and "Born to Be Wild," was their primary client. This put us in a position to open for acts that were touring through Austin, such as Steppenwolf, Mountain, Eric Burdon and the Animals, and The Beach Boys. We also opened for Janis Joplin and the Full Tilt Boogie Band at the old Gregory Gym on campus. I had an original blues song I'd written called "I've Been Down So Long (It Looks

Like Up to Me)," and I performed it that night for the first and only time. I was told after the show that Janis came out of her dressing room and stood backstage and listened to me. That's one of those little memories I have tucked away. It's not enough to brag about, but it does give me pleasure to think that Janis Joplin would leave her dressing room to listen to that song. I have completely forgotten the words except for the title, but now I'm thinking it must not have been half bad!

By this time, I was involved in my first serious relationship with a woman, Pat Barnett. She had been married and had a young daughter, so she was a lot more experienced than I was. She introduced me to the pleasures of marital bliss without the benefit of the blessings of the Church, the State, or our family and friends. I was not totally comfortable with the situation, as my mother's words and Christian upbringing kept reminding me that it was not the right way to live. But it's hard for a young man to think straight when regular sex is staring him in the face!

The summer of 1969 found the band living together in a four-bedroom wooden house not far from Memorial Stadium, near the Interregional (as I-35 was known in those days). That whole area has been demolished and replaced with fancy athletic practice facilities for the University. Leonard Arnold and his future wife, Vicki Henneger, lived there, as well as Layton DePenning; our roadie, Danny Gibson; and me. It was more or less a hippie/musician communal living arrangement, and we were trying the Brown Rice Macrobiotic Diet and turning yellow, reading Carlos Castaneda books like *A Separate Reality*, throwing the I Ching coins, and any other faddish thing that came along that was purported to be a source of cosmic knowledge and enlightenment. After living like that for a summer, I found it very difficult to get my head back into my books at the UT pharmacy school. I would tell Pat, "I can't see you tonight. I've got to study!" She would whine and moan about how I was keeping

her away from her friends (my roommates), and so I was having
difficulty finding the time to study and focus on school. I had made
all As the previous spring semester when I was living by myself, but
now I had a woman demanding my undivided attention, and I was
living in a community household full of musicians and their girlfriends. I recall one course in particular—Pharmaceutical Organic
Chemistry. The professor was a visiting German who would get
up and start writing organic chemical reactions on the blackboard
while speaking in a thick German accent—toward the blackboard!
When he filled up the front blackboard, he would go to the one on
the side of the classroom and fill it up. I'm thinking to myself, *Oh,
my God. Here I go again. This is going to be one of those extremely hard
courses under the best of conditions, and I can't understand a word this
guy is saying*. I was unaware at the time that I had suffered significant hearing loss, no doubt from the years of playing loud music—
or maybe I had inherited the deafness gene from Grandpa Tollie.
Whichever the case, it was plain to me that I could not succeed in
that environment. And frankly, my enthusiasm to stay in school
and do the hard work necessary had diminished dramatically. It was
the Texas "Summer of Love," and we were going skinny-dipping at
Windy Point every day. The environment I was living in was the
antithesis of the discipline and focus needed to do well in a scho-
lastic setting. I was coming to grips with the reality that I did not
want to be a pharmacist. Nothing against the worthy pharmaceutical profession, but it finally became clear to me that it was not what
I wanted to do with my life.

I went to Dr. Sullivan, my "pharmacog" professor and confided
in him about my dilemma. He was sympathetic and suggested that
I might try to salvage a teaching degree from my academic record.
With the courses I had already completed, I would be qualified to
teach math, physics, biology, and chemistry. I would have to immediately drop my pharmacy courses and enroll in the UT education

department. It would take a couple of semesters of education courses to graduate and qualify to be a teacher, so that's what I did.

I enrolled in the education school and was assigned to a classroom full of freshmen women education majors. I had been in the pharmacy program for five years, taking all these extremely difficult science classes, and there I was in classes with eighteen-year-old girls, most of whom were going to be elementary school teachers. It was like going back and climbing through the window of Mrs. Gatlin's first-grade class. Honestly, the education courses were like kindergarten compared to the courses I had already completed. I'm sure my parents and school-teaching relatives believed that my becoming a schoolteacher would be the best thing for me and right in line with our family tradition. But the fact is, I could no longer pretend that teaching was what I really wanted to do with my life, so I dropped my classes, quit school, and said, "Damn the consequences!"

I FELL COMPLETELY BACK into the lifestyle I had become immersed in during the previous summer—playing all over with the Lavender Hill Express, packing the Jade Room every Thursday night, and regularly appearing as the opening act for the big rock-and-roll shows coming through Austin. But things weren't perfect. Pat and her daughter, Loretta—without my approval—moved in with me in a funky "roach trap" efficiency apartment that was connected to the band house on the back. So it was like I was married and a surrogate father as well, and I wasn't prepared for either. I felt like I was falling into an abyss with no bottom in sight. I had completely lost control of that side of my life, and I felt I didn't really have any real purpose or direction. To add to that, I was having personality conflicts with some of the band members.

Mac McQuade and John Ludlum had arranged, through their

connections with Entertainment Consultants, to book us for a multiweek, six-nights-a-week stint at the Number One country and
western venue in Phoenix called JD's, which had previously featured
Waylon Jennings as its main artist. We played in the rock-and-roll
room downstairs that was reminiscent of The Cave in Los Angeles at the Ambassador Hotel. Once again, we got one room with
two doubles and a rollaway, and this time there *were* girls. Four of
us spent several sleepless nights while one of our gang, who will
remain unnamed, pounded the daylights out of some of the local
groupies who followed us.

At the end of that run in Phoenix, Pat Barnett drove out, and
we rode back to Texas in her little VW Beetle. We were somewhere
in Arizona and listening to the radio when we heard the broadcast announcing the results of the draft lottery. Three hundred and
sixty-six plastic blue capsules containing birthdays were chosen for
the Vietnam draft lottery the evening of December 1, 1969. The
first date pulled would be called for the draft first. We listened as
the dates were selected and announced. My number was 175. My
number fell in the group drafted in the first round—a first-round
draft pick; that was not funny.

THERE WAS A HIPPIE family of "merry pranksters" from the East
Coast who had come to town in Austin that year. They were a happy
bunch and always showed up at clubs and love-ins and other local
festivals that were always happening somewhere back then. They
were always bright and cheery with that hippie love vibe, and they
seemed to spread sunshine and joy wherever they went. If the truth
were known, they were probably spreading banned substances! On
December 4, my birthday, we made a somewhat triumphant return
to our Thursday gig at the Jade Room. Having been absent for a

couple of weeks, there was pent-up demand for the Lavender Hill Express, and the Jade Room was packed to the max!

In those days, the bars closed at midnight, so after the shows, it was still relatively early. We would often go to someone's house and hang out. That night, we were invited to an after-party at a friend's house in West Lake Hills. Most of the band, their girlfriends, the roadies and their girlfriends, and a few other friends gathered at an upscale two-story house owned by our host. It was a typical after-party. We were just hanging out, visiting, and generally having a good time, when in walked six or so of the aforementioned merry pranksters, bringing their peace-and-love vibes with them. They really were the nicest people. Turns out, it was also the birthday of the female member of the "family." I'll call her Nonie. Each family member was carrying two bottles of red wine. They were greeted with friendship as they moved among the people at the party and distributed the bottles of wine around the room. I recall Pat and I shared a bottle between us, and, as I finished it, I noticed some dregs of something. We were totally unaware at the time that the wine had been spiked, but we later found out that there were ten hits of Orange Sunshine LSD in each bottle!

It's hard to describe the happenings of that evening, but as time passed, things started to get strange. The psychedelic effects of the LSD started to come over us. People started saying things like, "Oh wow, look at that . . . did you see that?" As the hours drifted by, the effects become increasingly pronounced, and we were all laughing and crying and hugging and expressing our love for one another. At one point, we were saying, "Can't you see it? We are all ONE!" I truly became aware of the sensation and the vision that we were all just one swirling whirlwind of energy! Is there really a separate reality? Paisley flowers and flashes of light filled the atmosphere with spectacular displays of visual imagery! Pat and I clung to each other to prevent flying off on a tangent into the universe. We were somewhere between absolute bliss and the realization of true and cosmic love—and absolute fear and desperation. It was impossible to separate the real from the hallucinations that were triggered by anything you saw or heard, and it was impossible to keep your mind from just soaring off into a sea of colored space!

For me, the most significant part of the experience was that I had—it seemed to me—a real confrontation with what I perceived to be Satan! He came from below in the form that we have all seen him depicted: a dragon-like form with horns and scales and a long tail with an arrow-pointed tip. He was illuminated in a sickly red glow and breathing fire! He seemed to be focused on me and determined to drag me into the fiery pits of Hell. I was in a desperate struggle for my life, and if I didn't resist with all the strength and willpower I could muster, surely I would be overpowered and lost forever! Pat grabbed me and said, "Hold on to me," and with that, I was able to free myself from the grasp of Satan himself.

From that moment on, I became acutely aware of the presence of Satan. He is everywhere and constantly conspiring to separate us from God. He is easy to spot once you find out that he actually exists!

Finally we all realized that we needed to escape from this hellish place, and like soldiers caught in a dangerous position behind enemy lines, six or seven of us huddled together and forged a plan to make our escape. Everybody knew it was time to go. Our roadie Danny seemed to have possession of his faculties and took charge. It was raining when we all managed to pile in a car. The windshield was covered with raindrops, and they reflected the light from the streetlights and oncoming headlights. The reflections initiated more "light shows" and did little to help us focus on driving out of there. Getting back into Austin from West Lake Hills was a tremendous ordeal on the winding, hilly streets in the rain with the car crammed with hallucinating passengers. But we did survive and managed to get home. A couple of days later, I was still experiencing the effects: Giant iridescent paisley flowers would rise out into the air from the toilet bowl, for example. Now you know why so much of the artwork of that period depicts paisley flowers. The immediate experience had a bonding effect on Pat's and my relationship. We figured that if we survived that together, then we were meant to be together. But it was not to be.

Things returned to normal. It seemed that the experience had a profound effect on all of us, but it did more than enlighten us in a "cosmic" sense. It forced us to examine our own individual situations and decide whether we were actually content with our own lives. For me, it made me realize that, in truth, I was not at all happy with my situation—either with my relationship with Pat or my relationship with the band. I felt totally smothered and not in control of my own destiny. I was miserable. To add to my misery, I got notice from the selective service and was ordered to report to San Antonio for induction into the Army.

AROUND THAT TIME, BILL Day came into my life. I was vulnerable emotionally, and I fell under his influence. He was several years older, and I think he had been to graduate school at UT. He was very well read in ancient religion and philosophy and would lay things on me like, "The age of Jesus Christ, the Piscean Age, was only meant to last for two thousand years, and now we are entering the Age of Aquarius!" I was going through a lot of emotional turmoil, caught between my unhappy situation with Pat, the fact that the band seemed to be fracturing, and the reality that I was facing imminent induction. I was coming unglued. I felt if I didn't die from the emotional stress, that I was surely going to die in Vietnam.

I called my dad and expressed my feelings. He just said, "Go ahead and go into the Army. It will do you good." I sensed I would probably make a good soldier, but I felt a moral obligation to resist being put into a situation where I was called upon to kill other human beings.

Bill Day said, "Don't worry. You are going to be okay."

I decided I would make a last-minute appeal to my draft board to see if there were any alternatives available. The secretary of the draft board in Brownfield was none other than Imogene Nicholson, Alton Nicholson's mother. I had practically grown up in her house playing music in their living room. The Nicholsons were good friends with my parents, and we often had Sunday dinners at their house. I called her and scheduled an interview with the draft board. Bill Day accompanied me on that trip, spouting his cosmic spiel the whole way.

The interview with the board was over in less than a half hour, and they informed me that if I weren't in school, they had no other alternative but to recommend that my induction go through as ordered. The induction was supposed to happen two days later. *The gig is up. I'm a goner!* We drove back to Lubbock for some reason—probably to buy beer. A wrong turn on the way to Slaton found us on a dirt road in the middle of nowhere surrounded by section after section of cotton fields. All of sudden, in the middle of the night, in the middle of the dirt road, and miles from the nearest lake or stream, lay a very large dead fish! The symbolism was unmistakable. Bill's words about the ending of the Piscean Age surged to the front of my mind. *Is this the sign? Does this mean that the Age of Jesus Christ is really over? I am in cosmic vegetable land . . . a lost soul.*

We drove back to Austin that night and arrived in the wee hours. I was scheduled to report for a bus that was to transport a group of draftees to the San Antonio inductee center the next morning. I was resigned, and I surrendered to the reality of the situation. I reported to the bus. However, that did little to alleviate my emotional state. I had had little sleep in the days prior. The draftees arrived at the induction station and were herded into lines for physical examinations. Stripped to our shorts and supplied with little paper slippers, we shuffled in single file from one doctor to the next. I was shivering from the cold room and the anxiety that I felt. After the physical examinations, one by one, we were directed to a table manned by an Army sergeant. Next to the table was a red line about four inches wide. When a draftee crossed that line, he was officially in the service of the United States of America. *Okay*, I'm thinking, *here I go and I'll do my best*, when the sergeant blasts out, "Nunn—you failed your physical. You did not pass the hearing test and are not fit to serve in this man's army. Turn around and get your ass out of here!"

I exited the cold building out into the warmth of the sun shining on the streets of downtown San Antonio. I called Pat on a pay phone and gave her the news. I sat down and waited by one of the monuments in Alamo Plaza till she drove to San Antonio to get me. We drove back to Austin with the specter of the draft removed and life returned to its less than happy normal.

YOU WILL RECALL HOW the Lavender Hill Express was packing the Jade Room on Thursdays. Most of the other bands that played there drew small crowds and were forced to take the door receipts for their pay—which often was not enough to pay their bar tab. Then something happened that changed all our lives: The American Federation of Musicians began to organize in Austin. Most of the musicians in town joined, and we attended regular meetings of the union. The main topic of discussion was the fact that bands were playing the Jade Room and making no money, whereas the Lavender Hill Express was packing it every Thursday and walking out with big money in our pockets. A movement got started that pushed for all band members to get minimum union-scale wages for their gigs at the Jade Room. The musicians' union bowed to the complaints and issued a ban on any bands playing the Jade Room if Marge Funk didn't pay minimum union-scale (probably around $35 a man per night) to all the musicians working there. Compliance put her in a position where she lost money most nights. The Lavender Hill Express was also forced to comply or be in violation of union rules, and our gigs there came to an immediate halt. That money was our bread and butter, and losing it cost us dearly. The loss of income exacerbated our internal strife and eventually led to the demise of the band. The musicians' union's action and its negative repercussions have always left a bad taste in my mouth regarding unions. In the end, the union had the effect of helping no one and harming us greatly. The Jade Room eventually closed down. The road to disaster is often paved with the best of intentions! It certainly was here.

Around this time, Charlie Hatchett started having Sunday afternoon shows on some acreage he owned out on Howard Lane called King's Village. It was way out in the country in those days but now is smothered in housing developments. Charlie was no dummy; at one of these Sunday afternoon love-ins, I first saw ZZ Top. Man, what a band! Billy Gibbons and the boys had perfected the power-trio format and were as good then as they ever were! They were doing original material and honed in on the fusion of rhythm and blues and rock and roll, and it was no surprise they were the first and only band out of Texas from our era to attain permanent national prominence.

The shows at King's Village came to a screeching halt when one Sunday, a well-known and popular Hispanic character around town named Paco was shot and killed. This was around 1970.

The Lavender Hill Express had split up and gone our separate ways. Leonard Arnold formed a band called Blue Steel. Rusty Wier, on my advice, quit playing drums and got up front with a guitar and started doing a solo act. Jess Yaryan quit playing and merged into the private sector. Layton DePenning and I chose to stay together, and we put together another band. We still lived in the band house near the football stadium. Layton had the idea we might take a different tack and suggested we try something new. He had heard of a singer-songwriter named Richard Dean who might fit the bill. Richard was living in Denver, but somehow we got in touch with him and invited him to come to Austin to join our new band. He relocated to Austin with his new wife, Camille. They moved into the band house, and we went to work. Richard was an acoustic singer-songwriter from Oak Cliff in Dallas who grew up in the same neighborhood as Michael Murphey and Jimmie and Stevie Ray Vaughan. Influenced by Michael, Richard was in a similar songwriting genre as Steven Fromholz and Townes Van Zandt, who worked the college coffeehouse circuit. Richard had a great voice, had written several songs that we incorporated into our repertoire, and we taught him the songs we already knew and played regularly. We called the band Genesee, the name of a Colorado town just west of Denver. I thought it had a good ring to it—a combination of the words *genesis* and *Tennessee* that I deemed might have appeal—perhaps invoking illusions of Colorado. Colorado was becoming a popular "move to" destination thanks to John Denver and his idealistic depictions of the state with songs like "Rocky Mountain High." The arrival of Richard Dean proved to be a transformational point in my life.

Layton and I were, and always had been, band guys. We played loud electric guitars! Having a singer-songwriter up front was a whole new ball game. Richard collared us soon after he arrived and dragged us to the Chequered Flag, a folk club/coffeehouse on the corner of 15th and Lavaca. I had heard of it, but wasn't into that scene and had never been there. It was owned and operated by Allen Damron and Rod Kennedy, who later started the Kerrville Folk Festival, one of the premier folk festivals in America even to this day. At the Chequered Flag, I first saw Steven Fromholz and Dan

McCrimmon, who called their duo Frummox. They were onstage singing original songs from their recently released LP, *Here to There.*

Aside from my experience with the Sparkles in Nashville and Odessa, the thought of writing and singing your own songs and getting record deals was a new ball game and the beginning of a new era from my perspective! This experience introduced me to a new world of songwriting and presented a new realm of possibilities. I had written a few songs in high school—real sad songs—that I can't remember and had gotten a good response from my classmates when I got up the nerve to share them. But I had no confidence, was scared to death, and couldn't visualize the route from "here to there."

We played with Richard for a while, and then I think he and Camille realized they wanted more out of life than living in the crash-pad environment of a band house. They eventually moved back to Denver, but while he was in Austin, he pulled me over the line that separated covering hits to performing original music.

With Richard's departure, Layton and I formed another incarnation of Genesee with Chuck Rogers, former drummer for the Chevelles, and bass player Jerry Potter. I played an electric piano. I had my eye on another guitar player named John Inmon. I had first seen John play on an off night at the New Orleans Club with a band out of Temple called Plymouth Rock. He was pushing strings around reminiscent of Johnny Richardson, and it was apparent that he had extraordinary natural talent and guitar-playing ability. I said to myself that night, "If I ever get the chance, I sure would like to play in a band with John Inmon." Layton and I approached him. He asked us if we were serious about doing something other than playing the local club scene, and if so, he would be interested. Otherwise, he was content to stay where he was. We responded that we were interested in writing songs and making records. With that, he agreed to come on board. We were doing songs like the Beatles' "Hey, Bulldog" and starting to pick up on vocal harmony stuff from

Crosby, Stills & Nash and even the song from *Hair*, "Easy to Be Hard." We began to write a few songs.

Layton's sister lived in Los Angeles and worked for a record company, Uni Records. He had a new VW microbus, and one day we decided to go to California for a few days. It just so happened that Uni Records was the first American record company to license the recordings of Elton John, and while we were in there, Layton's sister got us an advance copy of Elton's first US record. I was totally blown away. *Man,* I thought, *this guy is going to be a big star!*

The New Orleans Club was where the action was, and I started learning songs from Elton's album that we ended up doing there before the record had even been released in the United States. Songs like "Take Me to the Pilot" and the giant hit "Your Song." I loved Elton John's voice, piano style, and chord progressions.

PAT BARNETT QUIT HER job as a hairdresser, and she, Loretta (whom I adored), and I moved out of the band house into a rent house just off Duval north of the University. Pat had two sisters, Jude and Donna Farar. Jude moved in with us, too. Now, I loved those girls, but all of a sudden I found myself being the sole supporter of three people besides myself! Pat was really getting into the women's lib thing and taking a hard liberal stance on all the social issues of the day. She didn't want to work anywhere that she didn't want to work, or do anything that she didn't want to do. I have an open mind, and I was willing to consider new ideas, but life was about day-to-day survival.

My income had fallen off precipitously after the demise of the Lavender Hill Express, and I became increasing uneasy about the situation I found myself in. I had to pay, but I had no say. Any attempt I made to express my concerns to her was met with stern opposition, along with lots of whining and moaning about the exploitation of women and the injustices in the world. Well . . . the injustices I felt were the ones being perpetrated on me. I felt trapped and helpless to alter my situation. I was looking for a way out, but somehow, I couldn't escape. To top it all off, we had a crazy old woman as a landlady who watched us like a hawk from her garage apartment next door. She would bang on our door and scream and holler about things—real and imagined. We finally had enough and found another house on Shoal Creek Boulevard up around Hancock Drive. Jude made other arrangements.

Things didn't improve between Pat and me. We didn't exactly break up, but we separated. I moved in with the band and the roadies in a nice, four-bedroom suburban house on Matagorda Street that was owned by Chuck and Julie Joyce. Chuck and Julie were a married duo on the fringes of the Austin music scene and were known to be close with Janis Joplin, who reportedly stayed with them when she was in Austin. But the current tenants were Layton; John; our roadies, Danny Gibson and Leroy Click; myself; and the most unlikely character, Barry Linthicum. Barry was a laid back, frat-rat sort of guy who worked at the Reynolds-Penland men's store on the Drag. He was a fan of Genesee and somehow ended up moving in with us. Leroy Click hung some sheets from the ceiling for privacy and made a bedroom out of the living room. I cleaned out the double garage and made a place for myself to sleep out there. Rent was probably $300 a month. We were paying about $50 apiece. You could live cheap in Austin in those days.

As I recall, at some point, Chuck and Julie Joyce wanted their house back, and we were forced to look for other accommodations. We had gotten wind of a nice place out on City Park Road off RR 2222, so we checked it out. It was a beautiful, four-bedroom modern home owned by Crady Bond. Red-haired Crady was tall and brawny and a skilled carpenter who was an Austin native. The house had belonged to his mother who, for some reason, had vacated it. Crady lived next door in a cool A-frame cabin he had built by hand. We arranged to rent the main house, nestled in the cedar breaks with a view of Lake Austin. Rent was $350! It had all the makings for the perfect band house where we could live together and rehearse, commune with nature, and hopefully write songs. Layton, John Inmon, Leonard Arnold, who was not in Genesee, and I, moved in with great expectations. We called it "Hill on the Moon." I didn't own a car at the time, but I did have a 650 cc Triumph motorcycle. I had a great time that summer riding the bike around the back roads of the Hill Country. Many times on the way back up City Park Road, I would turn the lights off and ride to the Hill on the Moon with the road perfectly illuminated by the moonlight and the white limestone that bordered the roadway. Crady built a stage in a clearing below the house, and we had little music fests there on Sunday afternoons.

We met a singer-songwriter and accomplished painter named Bobby Bridger around this time. Bridger was a direct descendent of the famed Jim Bridger, the mountain man who went west with the Henry expedition around 1830. Bobby was steeped in the history of that period, including the history of American Indians. He had made a couple of albums for Epic Records and was working on an epic musical/historical work that depicted the story of Jim Bridger with songs and narration. (The Lost Gonzo Band would eventually record *Seekers of the Fleece* with him, with Slim Pickens doing the narration.) At one point, Bobby arrived at Hill on the Moon with Russell Means, the American Indian activist, in tow. Russell Means was a Sioux Indian who would later be a central figure in the seventy-one-day standoff between the American Indian Movement (AIM) and the federal government in 1973 at Wounded Knee, South Dakota. Russell spent that evening with us espousing the AIM movement and the plight of the American Indian in general. We were spellbound. It made us feel like we were part of something bigger than ourselves. Magic things like that seemed to happen on a regular basis during those times.

Pat and I were not living together, but neither had we completely broken up. Hill on the Moon became a place that folks would just come in and out of, as it was such a cool place. On one occasion, Mary Egan, newly in town from Albuquerque and an excellent fiddle player, dropped by with a friend and running buddy of hers. Her friend's name was Marian Royal, daughter of Darrell Royal, the famous head football coach for the Texas Longhorns. She, like Sweet Mary, was a free spirit if there ever was one. She would come out in the afternoons, and I would cook omelets—the only thing I ever learned to cook besides bacon and eggs—and we would just hang and talk for hours. She would confide in me how hard it was to be a free spirit in Austin being the daughter of Darrell Royal, the most revered man in Texas, if not the whole country. She would talk about her brother Mack as well. She happened to mention that Mack had built a houseboat that was tied up to a dock on Lake Austin. That piqued my interest.

I said, "What's happening with that houseboat?"

She said, "Nothing. It's just sitting there empty."

Suddenly the thought of living on a houseboat on Lake Austin seemed totally exotic and desirable. I asked her if she thought that Mack would be interested in renting it to me. She told me she was certain Mack wouldn't mind if I lived there rent-free. Voila! I took the first opportunity to ride my motorcycle over to locate it. It was docked off Scenic Drive at the foot of a steep cliff overlooking the lake. A metal fence with a gate guarded the edge of the cliff. A long metal staircase provided access down one hundred feet or so to the dock where the boat was tied up. It was totally funky—handmade, with no electricity, running water, or amenities of any kind. There was an old tick mattress and that was it. Perfect! How cool is this? I can live here for nothing!

IT WAS GETTING ALONG towards the winter of 1971, and I had made a couple of trips to Colorado. Rusty Wier would go up and play as a single for a couple of weeks in a ski bar called Adolph's in Winter Park and come home with stories about how cool it was. I decided to try it. It was my first time in a ski town, the snow was incredible, and it was cool to be in an atmosphere where free-spirited ski bums skied all day and partied all night! I had never been on skis before but figured it was out of my league. I didn't perform, but I did scope out the scene and happened to hear about a ski bar/hostel called the Lift back over Berthoud Pass not far from Georgetown. I got in touch with the owner and arranged a weeklong gig there for Genesee.

We drove to Colorado in Chuck Rogers' aging Chevy cargo van and settled in for our weeklong run at the Lift. We bunked in the ski hostel and ate out of the kitchen. It was miserably cold and dreary. The band was having the same problems that had been plaguing us for so long: Layton and I were becoming more and more at odds and couldn't agree on anything. I had reached the end of my rope. One bright spot was the owner of the Lift, Tim O'Connor. He was a handsome, pugnacious former boxer from Kansas, but we shared a common love for Elton John. Late at night after the shows, we would stay up together in the kitchen listening to Elton's records and talk till the wee hours of the morning. He would turn "Yellow Brick Road" up full blast and shadowbox the air while sharing his thoughts and dreams with me. During one of those late-night sessions, I suggested that he should consider moving to Austin. I thought he would have many more opportunities to utilize his obvious music business skills and connections in Austin than in that rather isolated ski bar in Colorado. It turned out to be a prescient moment, as time would tell.

It was at the Lift in Colorado that I decided once and for all to terminate my long relationship with Layton. We had been through three bands together and always seemed to end up at the same point of mutual disagreement. I informed all the guys of my intentions as we finished out the gig there. I shaved my beard as a symbol of change and went about trying to figure out how we could settle up our mutual shares of the band, equipment, and money. I devised an algebraic formula to calculate who had what coming. With all the math, calculus, physics, and chemistry I had taken, it was the one and only time I can recall using algebra to make a calculation in real life. We divvied up the assets and separated without saying goodbye . . . a sad ending to three years of effort that had come to nothing.

The other guys had transportation home, and I was left with the equipment van to make it back to Austin. The van's heater didn't work, and the tires were slick, hardly suitable for travel on an icy road on a blustery, freezing night. I got a late start but made it to Denver and on to I-25 headed south. On the way, I witnessed a pickup lose control and run off the highway in front of me, so I stopped to see if I could help till the police and ambulances arrived. The passengers were unconscious but apparently not seriously injured.

I began to have doubts that I would be able to get that old van with slick tires back to Austin without having a wreck. On the road again, the first cougar I had ever seen ran across the highway in front of me. *Was that a sign, and if so, of what?* I made it to Raton without further incident and stopped for a burger, fuel, and coffee to go. As I departed Raton, it started to snow. Once you clear Raton Pass, the terrain is a flat plain. The roads are straight as an arrow, and there are no lights—at all. As I went farther, it began to snow harder. The road began to disappear as the snow blanketed everything. Only the occasional passing car or road sign gave me any indication that I was still on the road. I was bundled up in winter clothes, had a cowhide poncho that Barry Linthicum had given me wrapped around my legs, but I was still freezing.

The van, with its bald tires and no traction, began to slow. At one point, I ceased to move at all, and the spinning tires eased the back of the truck off the roadway. I could go no farther. *Oh, my God, I'm going to freeze to death!* I paused for a moment and, summoning up the driving skills I'd accumulated over the years, began to give the van a little gas, and little by little, the spinning tires pulled me back onto the highway. I managed to keep going the seventy miles between Raton and Clayton, New Mexico—at about twenty miles per hour the whole way. I arrived, relieved and exhausted, at about 5:00 a.m. I had been on the road for ten hours since leaving the Lift and had covered less than 200 miles. I rented a hotel room and got some much-needed sleep. Once again, I had escaped disaster unharmed.

The next day, the sun was out, and the road had cleared. With no more trouble, I arrived back in Austin late that evening. I went to the house on Shoal Creek and reunited with Pat—only to get into an immediate argument with her. My difficult journey was greeted with turmoil and disappointment rather than with open arms.

I wasn't happy with how things were going in my life, and I was in a very low place. I didn't have a single trusted friend I could turn to and share my troubles.

> There ain't nobody but me
> I'm free and I'm all alone
> I make my way through the thick and the thin
> Any place that I am is my home
> I reminisce memories, I do as I please
> I get by, ridin' high, being free
> I tote no load, I'm all I own
> There ain't nobody but me.

From the song "Nobody But Me,"
written by Rick Cardwell from my CD *Nobody But Me*.

At this point I started to seriously consider leaving Austin, taking a sabbatical, and abandoning music, or at least laying it down for a while until I could get my heart and soul back intact. The fact is, I believed I was going nowhere fast!

> I'm going nowhere fast
> I'm getting nowhere faster
> If I slow down I might make it last
> If I speed up, it's going to be a disaster
> I'm going nowhere fast
> I'm pulling off the road
> Leaving this highway behind
> I'm gonna make this town my home
> I'm going no . . . where.

───────

From the song titled "Going Nowhere Fast" by Thomas Michael Riley from my CD *Something for the Trail*. Nunn Publishing Co.

I decided to go back to Oklahoma to the ranch place my family had bought near Hanna. I thought going up there and doing some manual labor and helping my uncles with their farm and ranching work might help me get my head screwed back on. I had had a buttfull of the music business as it had led me to nothing but heartache and misery. I also wanted to separate myself from Pat, as it was apparent that we were going nowhere fast too. It was close to Christmas, 1971, as I arranged my affairs and prepared to make the move.

The word got around that Michael Murphey was booked to perform the first week in January at a recently opened venue in town. It was an old pizza parlor at 38½ and Interregional, called the Saxon Pub (no relation to the Saxon Pub of today). They had built up a pretty good business presenting singer-songwriters like Steven Fromholz, Townes Van Zandt, Three Faces West (with Ray Wylie

Hubbard, Rick Fowler, and Wayne Kidd, who had been staples for years at the Outpost in Red River, New Mexico), as well as young up-and-comers like B. W. Stevenson and Willis Alan Ramsey from Dallas. Segal Frye had come over from the closed Chequered Flag and did an excellent job as emcee.

I had my pickup packed up and was ready to go, but I decided I would stay around a few days just to see Murphey, as I had heard so much about him from Richard Dean, and lots of people were performing his songs in their shows. It turned out to be one of the most fateful decisions I have made in my life!

Chapter 7

The Murphey Era

CHRISTMAS OF 1971 AND New Year's of 1972 came to pass, and the day for Michael Murphey's much-anticipated appearance at the Saxon Pub arrived. I'd be leaving the following day for Oklahoma. Michael was booked for a six-night run, and he opened on that first Monday in January. He had Charles John Quarto with him. Charles was and is an eclectic poet-songwriter with an interesting history in his own right. He and Michael had recently collaborated on several songs, and he performed poems and songs a cappella during Michael's shows. When I arrived at the Saxon, the show was already in progress in front of a packed house. Murphey was onstage playing acoustic guitar and some piano, and the bespectacled Bob Livingston, sporting long blond hair and a bushy red beard, was accompanying him on bass.

Michael was in town from California, where he lived out on the San Andreas Fault in Wrightwood. He was pursuing a songwriting and recording career following a stint at UCLA, where he had studied classic literature. He had several notable credits under his belt, having written songs recorded by the Monkees and others—the most recent of which was a twenty-song, folk-rock concept album recorded by Kenny Rogers and the First Edition titled *The Ballad of Calico*. He had just returned from Nashville, where he recorded the basic tracks for a new album with Bob Livingston on bass. He had been signed by megaproducer Bob Johnston, a staff producer for Columbia Records, whose production credits included Simon and Garfunkel's *Sounds of Silence*, Johnny Cash's *Live at Folsom Prison*, and *Live in Berlin* by the international Canadian megastar Leonard Cohen. Johnston was a powerhouse in the industry, and the record deal he secured for Michael was with A&M Records, an LA-based record company owned by trumpeter Herb Alpert and music mogul Jerry Moss.

Michael's tunes that night were a combination of songs from *The Ballad of Calico* and cuts from the recently recorded, but yet to be completed, Nashville session, all of which was material he had written or cowritten. Wow! I was stunned—not only by the eclectic, poetic, and intellectual quality of the material but also by his singing and professional performance. It was light-years beyond anything I had ever been exposed to, especially the songwriting aspect. He was obviously a very gifted, prolific, and disciplined songwriter, the likes of which I had never seen—not up that close, anyway.

On his first break, I was standing near the back of the room, still reeling and trying to absorb what I had just witnessed, when Michael put his guitar down, stepped off the stage, and walked through the audience directly toward me. He extended his hand, cocked his head a little to one side flashing a disarming smile, and said, "Hey man, I've heard a lot about you . . . how would you like to play bass in my band?"

My life passed before my eyes. Synapses fired as my brain tried to process the words I had just heard and the implications thereof. One side of my brain was saying, *Think now, Gary P. . . . you were going to give up the music business . . . you have a pickup with a camper shell packed up in the parking lot . . . tomorrow you are going to move to the ranch and reconnect with your family, do some manual labor, and get your head together.*

But the other side was saying, *Do I go . . . or do I go around one more time? My bags are packed and my mind is made up. But this man just blew me away. He's recording original music, has a national label recording contract, can sing and write his butt off. He just walked off the stage and says he's heard good things about me. He offered me a job doing exactly what I love to do!*

At certain special times, divine providence seems to step in, and at the very last minute, offers you a guiding hand. The decision I made marked a 180-degree change in the direction my life would take. The decision came quickly—and in the affirmative! It reminded me of how I felt when I went to play with the Sparkles!

Michael went back onstage and did his second set, which was even better than the first. After the show, we began getting to know each other—I was mostly listening to him talk enthusiastically about what he'd done and what he hoped to do. It was a very exciting experience. I invited Michael to stay with me if he needed a place, and he took me up on it. Cool! We exited the club, and he followed me in a little red VW hatchback over to the house on Shoal Creek. He stayed with Pat and me for the duration of his run at the Saxon Pub and probably slept in a sleeping bag on the floor. We got better acquainted, and he played his songs for me, as I was anxious to get familiar with his material as soon as possible. I hung on his every word. Those were great days. He would do his show at the Saxon at night, and, of course, I would go to observe, which I found later intimidated Bob Livingston.[1] I know, because he's told the story so many times.

Bob and Michael lived in the mountain town of Wrightwood in the San Bernardino Mountains, where Bob had picked up the bass

---

1   Bob grew up in Lubbock, the son of parents who administered the First Methodist Church. He played football under Freddie Akers at Lubbock High, and he and his high school mates used to come to the Music Box to hear the Sparkles. He was an aspiring singer-songwriter who left "Lubbock in the rearview mirror" for California to seek his fame and fortune. That's where he became acquainted with Michael.

and started backing up Michael. Just prior to their arrival in Austin
for the Saxon Pub gig, Bob had been offered a job playing bass for
Three Faces West, which he had accepted and which was to take
effect immediately. He had given Michael notice of his intentions.
This opened up the bass-playing slot for me. Bob is writing a book
containing his own detailed account, which you should read to fill
in the blanks.

Michael and I spent the next few days seeing the sights around
Austin. I took him to Barton Springs and to Cisco's Bakery on East
6th for *migas*, introduced him to people I knew, and in general, gave
him the lay of the land. The whole time I was encouraging him to
relocate to Austin. A recent earthquake on the San Andreas Fault
had shaken him, so he was susceptible to suggestions to get out of
California. During that week at the Saxon Pub, we met a property
management guy in the restroom. Michael mentioned that he was
looking for a place to rent. The fellow responded that he had a place
that might be suitable—another chance encounter that changed
both of our lives.

The property was at 6214 North Lamar, off the street down a
narrow drive between an auto repair shop and a strip of small busi-
nesses. It was directly across Lamar Boulevard from the DPS Training Facility and about a few blocks south of Kenneth Threadgill's old
service station bar where Janis Joplin played during her Austin stint.
(It was the site where Armadillo World Headquarters' impresario
Eddie Wilson later built his first Threadgill's Restaurant.) There
were maybe a couple of acres behind the auto shop, and the property was dominated by a square rock house with a pyramid-shaped
roof! We deemed that fact significant. A story attributed to Kenneth
Threadgill, the "true godfather of Austin music," said that the house
was the site of the first radio station in Austin. Kenneth also said that
the first time Bob Wills ever played in Austin was on a live radio
broadcast from there! Wow, I get cold chills just thinking about it.

Along the right side of the property was a set of four efficiency cabins with one room, a small kitchen, and a small bathroom. Behind the main house was a garage apartment, and off to the left and behind it were a couple of old wooden sheds. The place appeared to have been a farm that was once well north of town back in the days before Austin's growth surrounded it. Being off the road and well isolated from traffic, it felt like a little country place right in the middle of town. Michael found it suitable temporarily and made a deal with the property manager to rent it with the condition that he would never go up on the $150 a month rent. The efficiency cabins rented for $50 a month and served mostly as housing for transient people living out of their cars. As time went by, they would serve as handy and inexpensive crash pads for musicians moving to Austin who were looking for cheap rent and a place to park while looking for something permanent.

Michael put his house in California up for sale and made arrangements for his wife, Diana, and their two-year-old son, Ryan, to move to Austin. Pat and I let the house on Shoal Creek go, and we moved in with Michael. A week or so later, Diana arrived, and we all settled into living together at what I would later call "Public Domain, Inc."

Michael had gigs booked on the college coffeehouse circuit, and he and I went out on weekends as a duo to do shows at places like East Texas State in Commerce, Stephen F. Austin State University in Nacogdoches, and as far away as Denver. We foolishly, as it turned out, attempted to convert one of the funky wooden sheds on the property into a recording studio. We spent a lot of time tacking egg cartons on the walls for soundproofing! It was nowhere near waterproof and subject to flooding. The other shed we hired Cosmic Carl to enclose, and it became quite serviceable as a rehearsal space, funky as it was. We shopped around in junk furniture stores up and down North Lamar and found a dozen old tumbling mats we thought might come in handy for sound baffles. Ultimately, these tumbling mats would serve another useful purpose altogether.

I was getting an education in the music business: It was not unusual for Michael to emerge from his bedroom in the morning with more than one song he had written before his first cup of coffee. He had a metal file cabinet where he kept his papers. He summoned me in one morning, opened the file cabinet, and pulled out a manila folder in which he kept his BMI royalty statements. I had never seen a BMI royalty statement and didn't know what one was. He explained to me that BMI, ASCAP, and SESAC, called "performance rights organizations," represented publishers and songwriters. He said they worked to collect performance royalties for radio airplay, television, and any other public outlets where music is performed, such as bars, restaurants, concert halls, etc., and that they distributed the funds to the songwriters and publishers (copyright owners) of published musical works. The royalty statement represented the quarterly earnings from all outlets, and BMI sent statements and corresponding checks to their songwriters and publishers. *Oh!* Then he added, "Gary P., I know you have the talent to be a great songwriter. You're going to get stacks of royalty statements like these someday!" Wow! No one had ever said anything like that to me before! The fact that he was an accomplished songwriter and someone whose opinion I had the highest regard for, made a profound and lasting impression on me. If he thought I could be a great songwriter, maybe I could be. It's funny that major turning points in my life were often based on simple declarations of other people's expectations of me—declarations about things that had never crossed my mind before. That's the reason that I have always attempted to relay to others that I had high expectations for them and to do what I could to help them fulfill those expectations. I hope I have had a positive influence on others similar to the impact Michael had on me.

THE RECORDING PROJECT FOR A&M Records was in progress, and Michael was summoned to Nashville to work on the record. We made the trip in first-class style, driving Michael's parents' Buick, and we checked into the Hall of Fame Hotel. I remember opening the door to the hotel for Loretta Lynn as we departed for the studio. The sessions were scheduled to take place at Ray Stevens' studio on Music Row. It was all so very exciting to me. This wasn't my first trip to Tennessee or my very first exposure to the storied environs of the Capital of Country Music, as I had been there with the Sparkles back in 1967, but this time, I was closer and more involved. I got to hang in the control room and observe the process from the producer's prospective. Bob Johnston had called in one of the top Nashville session drummers, Kenny Buttrey, to complete the first task at hand—overdubbing the drum tracks.

As background, Michael recorded songs live in the studio exactly the way he performed them in his shows at the Saxon Pub, with Bob Livingston on bass as the only accompaniment. Since they weren't done in metronomic time, there were lots of retardations and pauses in the performances. It was a marvel to watch the overdubbing process as Kenny Buttrey dealt with the slowdowns and pauses, which are extremely difficult to anticipate. He proved why he was one of the top drummers in town and could nail the parts after just a few passes. In a couple of days, he had completed the drums tracks. Boomer Castleman, who Michael had written songs with for *The Ballad of Calico* project, was called in for overdubs using the "Boomerizer," an innovation he had invented to allow him to bend strings on a Telecaster simulating the sounds of a steel guitar. Michael allowed me to play piano and B-3 Hammond organ on a couple of tracks, and little by little the tracks started to grow and take shape.

Michael and Charles John Quarto wrote a song subsequent to the original live session that had been inspired by a drawing by Michael's artist friend Bill Holloway. It was a picture depicting Geronimo in a top hat at the wheel of a vintage, open-air Cadillac, accompanied by three other Apaches dressed in full Indian regalia. The irony of the scene struck a chord, and the two prolific songwriters promptly knocked out a tune titled "Geronimo's Cadillac." Toward the end of that first series of sessions, Bob Johnston called in another drummer, Karl Himmel, who was the drummer for Tracy Nelson and Mother Earth, and we cut "Geronimo's Cadillac," with me playing bass on the track that would become the title track and the first single released.

We wrapped up that session and drove the Buick ten hours back to Dallas, spent the night with Michael's parents in Oak Cliff, and then made our way back to Austin to rejoin the girls and the kids at Public Domain. We were home a few weeks, did a few shows, and then it was time to go back to Nashville and complete the album. During these sessions, Leonard Cohen, Bob Johnston's Canadian artist who was a huge star in Europe and worldwide, was hanging out in the studio and observing the sessions. He was quiet and seemed rather intense, which seemed consistent with the songs he wrote.

Back at the hotel one evening after a session, he and I shared an elevator ride. I can't recall the nature of the conversation we were having, but when we reached the ground floor and he was preparing to exit, he turned to me and said, "Just remember . . . success . . . is survival." I have never forgotten those words: They have often come to mind and have served as a source of comfort at times when I was having doubts about my own success or survival.[2]

We returned to Austin without having completed the overdubbing and after a couple of weeks returned to Nashville to complete

---

2   As I am writing this, on November 7, 2016, I have just received word that Leonard Cohen has passed away.

the project. Michael mentioned he wanted to put some hot guitar on some of the tracks, so I suggested we take former Lavender Hill Express guitarist Leonard Arnold to overdub the lead guitar parts. He was a perfect choice, and he laid down some blistering tracks on "Geronimo's Cadillac." Then we overdubbed the background vocals, with me doing most of it, and wrapped up the project and returned to Austin.

Michael was focused on putting a band together. Craig Hillis, a hot guitar player in town who had played with the Eternal Life Corporation and had cowritten one of the tunes on the album *Crack Up in Las Cruces* with Michael, was an obvious candidate. He had been sitting in with Steven Fromholz, who had split from Frummox and gone solo. Craig pioneered the trend of local rock players accompanying acoustic songwriters. I got up one day and discovered he had rented one of the cabins at Public Domain. He didn't stay long: He was hooked up with Dana Strait, the daughter of Dan Strait, who owned Strait Music—the main music store in town—and they eventually got married.

TIME PASSED SINCE MICHAEL'S arrival in January of '72. We were busy and things were happening pretty fast. I persuaded Michael and Diana to make a trip to Oklahoma with me. We went to Hanna, and I introduced them to my kinfolks. We went to visit Grandma Nunn. Her home had been blown up from a gas pocket that had developed under her house, and she was living in a three-bedroom mobile home. No one had been injured seriously as the house didn't catch fire, and she and Brother escaped with a few cuts and bruises. Grandpa Tollie had died by this time. We played dominos with Brother, and Michael was amazed that weird Uncle Brother was such a killer domino player.

Uncle Joe always kept good, gentle palomino and buckskin horses for kids to ride. He would point out the older and the younger of the palomino geldings and say, "They are father and son . . . and brothers. You figure it out." We saddled up Tony, Ladd, and Smokey and rode the dirt road, backstreet section lines and made our way cross-country back to our place, which is close to the South Canadian River. An old section-line road allowed access to the river bottom and the river. On the way, we passed the old, dilapidated shack where Jack Horn, a real live hermit, had lived. When I was about fifteen, Uncle Joe would take us to see the four hundred acres of river-bottom land he owned, of which he was very proud. He had big plans for it. We would pass by Jack Horn's shack in a pickup loaded with Nunn boys up in the cab—and a pickup-bed full of kids in the back. The old hermit with his long grey beard would come out to glare at us and spit tobacco juice in our direction. Our parents used to tell us that Jack Horn would get us if we weren't good. That piece of river-bottom land would play a prominent role in my life, as I eventually purchased it.

We rode our horses down on the riverbed, which was more like a sandy beach. We stopped and built a fire and communed with nature. I think that's when Michael got the idea to write the song "Cosmic Cowboy." More than forty years later, in an interview in Steamboat Springs, Colorado, and in the presence of others, Michael looked at me and stated, "You were the real cosmic cowboy." We later wrote a rather symphonic piece called "South Canadian River Song," with Michael composing lyrics to a piano piece that I had made up.

He thought the rural scenery in and around Hanna would make an excellent backdrop for an album cover photo, so he summoned photographer and album cover designer Bill Matthews to come down for a photo shoot. Bill flew into Tulsa, rented a car, and joined up with us in Hanna. The cover shot of Michael, looking like a genuine Old West cowboy, was taken in the middle of the dirt road in front of Uncle Samuel's and Aunt Velma's house, not fifty yards from where I was standing when Velma announced we were moving to Texas back in the summer of 1957. On the inside cover was a photograph of Michael taken in what was one of several rural one-room schoolhouses that dotted the countryside back when my dad was growing up. When we were there, it served as a church house for the Muscogee–Creek Indians in the community. Later that night, we went to the bar "uptown" and mingled with the local clientele of "half-bloods," good ole boys, and "good-for-nothings," all totally drunk and juiced by the presence of outsider "celebrities"—a very rare occasion in the backwater environs of uptown Hanna. Bill Matthews was having a field day with his camera, and they were all cooperating with ridiculous, and exaggerated, drunken modeling poses. Bill was shooting away and laughing hysterically the whole time. That trip was a lot of fun.

Eventually, we made our way back to Public Domain. It was getting along toward springtime. I walked out of the house one morning and glanced over toward the cabin that sat directly opposite the back door, which I will henceforth refer to as "the groove shack," as that's how it later came to be known. Sticking his head through a crack in the door was none other than Tim O'Connor! In our absence, he had somehow found his way to renting the shack. He had taken my advice and made the move from Colorado to Austin. To this day, every time I see him, he tells me that anytime anything goes wrong in his life, he just tells whomever, "Blame it on Gary P. Nunn . . . he's responsible for me being in Austin!" I confess that I was the impetus for many people moving to Austin, several of whom became major players in the story of Austin's music scene.

Michael was still working on getting a backup band together: I was on board on bass, and Craig Hillis was standing by to step in on lead guitar. It wasn't long before Tim O'Connor had vacated the groove shack and a new tenant was occupying it, in the form of Michael

McGeary. McGeary was a drummer from California who had been
a part of the band that Three Faces West was putting together. They
had hired Bob Livingston to play bass and that's the reason he was
gone. All of a sudden, a drummer was living right next door! So we
added McGeary and started rehearsing MMM's (Michael Martin
Murphey) material, and things started rocking along.

I CAN'T RECALL THE circumstances, but Michael and I were in
Denver when I got a call from Mary Lou Sullivan, someone I've
known since she was a teenager living in Denver City. Denver City
is not too far from Brownfield, and we always played them in school
sports. She had been a big Sparkles fan and would show up from
time to time during that period and hang with me. Now Mary Lou
was consumed with a passion for music and anything related to it.
She had made her way to Austin and gravitated toward the scene
and apparently had found a job working for Tim O'Connor. She
was calling with the information that a club called Castle Creek was
interested in booking Michael.

Tim O'Connor and Doug Moyes, late of Telluride, Colorado,
had partnered up and acquired the space formerly occupied by the
old Chequered Flag, renaming the place Castle Creek. It was a
somewhat larger venue than the Saxon Pub and other folky listening rooms where we normally played, so this news represented a
step up. I put Michael on the phone with Tim, and they settled on
the earliest opportunity. We hustled back to Texas to rehearse and
prepare for our debut at Castle Creek.

The date came around, and we set up and sound checked. I
grabbed a bite at the Texas Chili Parlor just across the alley and
hurried back to Public Domain to change and freshen up. When
I arrived back at Castle Creek, I headed for the funky little band

room behind the bar for our usual preshow powwow and pep talk from MMM. When I entered, I saw that Michael, Craig, and McGeary were all there—and much to my surprise, Bob Livingston was too! Michael sat us all down to inform us that he wanted Bob to rejoin the band and that he had decided to bring him back to play bass!

Needless to say, I was shocked and dismayed. *If Bob's going to play bass, what am I going to do?* It was a rather tense moment. I felt like the odd man out and not just a little bit betrayed. I had my heart set on playing bass, I had twelve years of bass-playing and band-leading experience behind me, and I was set to fill that role. Playing bass allows you to have a significant influence on the band as a whole, because you can directly affect the very important aspects of dynamics and timekeeping. This surprise development obviously threw a monkey wrench in that deal. What are we going to do with *two* bass players? How does that work? Michael informed me that I could move to piano; but I didn't have a piano. Michael said there was a piano onstage that I could play. Yes, there was an old out-of-tune upright piano facing the back wall of the stage. I was shocked and upset. I felt like I had been demoted to the bottom rung on the ladder. *I thought I was his right-hand man!* Again, because I was versatile, I found myself in the position of having to fill a secondary, even tertiary, role. The only other alternative would have been to walk out right then and there!

Yes, I was upset, but I did what I always do . . . I swallowed my pride and went along to get along. It took me awhile to adjust to the situation, but I found that Bob was a likable guy. We had a lot in common, and we got along very well. I made the adjustment and concentrated on playing piano and organ. Besides—the *Geronimo's Cadillac* record was due for release!

We were rehearsing one day in the makeshift rehearsal space we had created in one of the old sheds on the property at Public

Domain, when none other than Jerry Jeff Walker stuck his head in the door. It was the first I'd seen of him since a sunrise serenade he had given in Greenwich Village a year or so before, when I went to New York with Jay Verholz.

Jay was a local figure acquaintance of mine in Austin who was originally from Vermont. When he asked me if I wanted to go with him to New York, I was free, and so I agreed. He had a friend who managed an apartment building in Greenwich Village with access to a vacant apartment. We could stay there for free. It turned out to be a very funky situation. There was an apartment all right, but the only stick of furniture in the place was a mattress. To add to that, the heat was turned off since the apartment was vacant. There were no sheets, pillows, or blankets—just one cheap, thin bedspread. It was wintertime and cold. I eventually caught a bad cold and spent most of my time in the apartment wrapped in that bedspread, fully clothed, trying to stay warm.

Jay would go and hang out in the Village, and I rarely saw him. One morning about sunrise, he came into the apartment and woke me up. He said he wanted me to meet somebody. I wiped the sleep out of my eyes and looked up to see Jerry Jeff Walker. He and Jay had been up drinking all night in a nearby bar. Jerry Jeff looked like the rounder-sounder-troubadour-cowboy-gypsy-songman that he is. He was going full blast at six in the morning. He had an old Gibson Roy Smeck Stage Deluxe acoustic guitar. It was there, in a cold, unfurnished apartment in Greenwich Village at the break of day, that I got my first dose of Jerry Jeff Walker. With no talk or banter to speak of, he leaned against the wall, squatted down on his haunches, and began to sing "Charlie Dunn," a tune he had written about the Austin bootmaker who had stitched leather for decades at the Capitol Saddlery—in the employment of Buck Steiner, the patriarch of Austin's Steiner cowboy clan. I was pleasantly surprised to hear a song about an Austin character in this most unlikely situation. Then Jerry Jeff sang a song about the Roy Smeck Deluxe guitar he was playing called "That Old Beat-Up Guitar."

Of course, Jerry Jeff had a six-pack under his arm. His reputation as a notorious drinker preceded him, so that was no surprise—even though it was early in the day. We chatted awhile and JJ informed us that he had written a bunch of songs and he wanted to make a record. He asked if we'd be interested in backing him up in the studio. Why, *hell yes!* We were not getting invited to play on records every day. Then he disappeared as quickly as he had appeared and left it at that for the time being.

By this time, *Geronimo's Cadillac* was scheduled for release, and A&M Records summoned Michael to Los Angeles for a showcase at the Whisky a Go Go. The club had this iconic mystery about it, and I was excited about our performing there. One of my favorite albums had always been *Johnny Rivers at the Whisky a Go Go,* and I'd driven by the club many times on my off-night, solo sojourns to Hollywood while in California with the Sparkles but had felt too out of place to go in.

We drove to California and checked in at the Tropicana Motel in Hollywood. The Tropicana was a popular place for show business people on a tight budget to hole up while pursuing their interests in town. A&M Records hosted a press reception, with Jerry Moss and other company bigwigs in attendance, along with a representative from Bob Johnston's management office in New York. He huddled up the band before the reception and cautioned us to "present a unified front." They went all out to promote their newly signed, up-and-coming artist—Michael Murphey. We got the first-class treatment. After all, he was Bob Johnston's artist, and all expectations were that he would become a big star! I was of the same opinion and determined to do everything I could to make that happen.

Doing nothing second-class, A&M had arranged for us to rehearse on the sound stage at Charlie Chaplin's former movie studio complex. When we arrived, there was a fellow named Herb Steiner already set up with a steel guitar. Herb was an old friend of Michael's from his California days, and they were both a part of a loosely knit group of Los Angeles musicians and songwriters who gravitated toward country music. The group included people like Don Henley and Richard Bowden, who had migrated west from Linden, Texas; J. D. Souther from Amarillo; Al Perkins; Linda Ronstadt; and others who eventually formed bands like Shiloh, Poco, The Flying Burrito Brothers, and the Eagles. Texans had their influence in Los Angeles!

Michael introduced us to Herb and informed us that he would be joining us for the showcase. We got busy and rehearsed the show for the next evening. Herb fit in well, and the steel added a country dimension to our sound. The next day, we spent the afternoon sound checking and going over last-minute details. I was provided with a B-3 Hammond organ.

Showtime arrived, and Michael huddled us up in the dressing room for a motivational pep talk. Then we took the stage. The room was dimly lit except for the stage lights, and the stage was elevated five or so feet above floor level. I can't recall ever seeing the audience in the room, but it was full. We did our first show to a good response and took a break. I walked off the stage and passed by a few tables against a wall oddly situated twenty feet or so directly in front of the stage. Sitting at one of the tables, I recognized none other than Robert Plant and Jimmy Page, the lead singer and guitar wizard of Led Zeppelin! As I passed their table, Robert Plant said to me in a distinct British accent, "Best f***ing band I ever heard! Best f***ing band I ever heard!" I was so taken aback that Robert Plant was speaking to me that I couldn't respond.

Thinking back, I realize what a once-in-a-lifetime opportunity I missed. I was just too green. Rick Cobb and I had seen the Led Zeppelin show at the Texas International Pop Festival on Lake

Lewisville, Texas, in August of 1969. They were awesome . . . sounding just like their records—but even better. I can't believe that we were the "best f***king band" he had ever heard, but it sure was cool to hear him say it. I think his comment said a lot about the truly original and genuine quality of Michael's music. The sensitivity and purity of the band's performance elicited an incredible response from one of the biggest rock-and-roll stars on the planet! Robert Plant has a place in the Austin area, and I have often thought that if I ever had the opportunity, I would ask him if he recalled that evening.

Everything seemed to go well that night, and the event was judged successful by all accounts. After the show, Herb Steiner invited me to his house. It was close by, in Hollywood, where he had been raised. We hung out, shared some refreshments, and began a friendship that lasts to this day. Like I was so prone to do, I told Herb he should move to Austin! (A few months after Murphey moved to Austin, Jerry Jeff Walker, late of Key West, Florida, arrived in town. He would show up at all the bars where music was going on. Michael and Bob had had previous encounters with him in California and Red River, New Mexico, and the stories of those encounters are classic Jerry Jeff Walker!)

We returned from Los Angeles with a new album on a major label, a single of "Geronimo's Cadillac" being promoted nationally, and a pretty good little band backing Michael up all the way. He was starting to draw attention and crowds at Castle Creek, and a little buzz of excitement began around town. Jerry Jeff was always close by where music was happening. Other rooms like Mother Earth, a good-sized venue that opened up at about 12th and Lamar on Shoal Creek (now the site of the Whole Earth Provision Company), booked Murphey, with Jerry Jeff opening. Jerry Jeff would invite us to back him up as well, which we were eager to do. Before long, Jerry Jeff would use us when he had gigs and Michael was open. During this time, another singer-songwriter showed up in town, sitting in at the Saxon Pub and Castle Creek: His name was Willie Nelson.

JERRY JEFF HAD WRITTEN a bunch of songs and wanted to make a record. We had played a few shows with him, and things had gone well, so he asked us to play on the record. His manager/producer, Michael Brovsky, whose office was in New York, came to Austin to oversee the project. He booked time at a studio being put together by local boy Jay Podolnick, whose dad owned all the movie theaters in town, and a local sound tech named Steve Shields. Together, they had been the first to assemble sound systems capable of doing larger shows, which led them to the next step of putting together a professional recording studio. The space was in the old Rapp's Cleaners building on West 6th Street across from the Hoffbrau Steakhouse. The studio was near completion except for one small factor: The mixing board was not ready. In multi-track recording, the signals from the microphones on the instruments and voices are fed to the mixing board, where the recording and volume levels are controlled for recording or playback, and effects such as reverb can be added. Each individual signal (instrument/voice) can be controlled individually, before it is routed to specific individual tracks on the recording machine. After the recording process, the whole track or any combination of individual tracks can be played back for over-dubbing and review.

To deal with the situation, the board was bypassed and all the microphone signals were fed directly to the tracks on the recorder. I'm not sure it was ever done before or since, but at the time it was apparently the only option.

Jerry Jeff would schedule the sessions at 10:00 p.m., with me on piano, Bob on bass, Craig Hillis on electric guitar, and Michael McGeary on drums. Harmonica player Mickey Raphael, who had been playing with B. W. Stevenson, was called in to play as well. Mickey later made a lifelong career playing with Willie Nelson. By the time we arrived at the studio, Jerry Jeff had mixed up a five-gallon water cooler of "sangria wine." Playing a mic'd acoustic guitar, Jerry Jeff would, one by one, run down the songs for us. We would play along, learning the material as we went, recording every pass live, and then we'd listen back. When JJ was satisfied, we would move to the next track.

I played piano on all the tracks, with the exception of "High Hill Country Rain," a high-energy song that called for a rock-and-roll style bass part. My rock-and-roll bass experience was called into play on more demanding tunes like that one. This set a pattern of Bob and me switching instruments whenever the song called for it. It was a formula that worked well for us in the years to come.

It's amazing how the absence of the board failed to have any significant ill effects on the recording, and the record would eventually stand up to industry standards. That's what led me to the conclusion that the essence of any good record was not as dependent on the mixing board and the engineer, as it was on the quality of the song, and the heart and soul of the performance. We always had a way of surrendering to the song and playing accordingly, which is a rare quality.

During that session, Michael came into the studio and was surprised and perhaps a tad upset to see his band backing up Jerry Jeff. He went to the sandwich shop next door to the studio and wrote the song "Alleys of Austin." We finished the tracking, and Bob and I overdubbed the background harmonies, wrapped up the project, and refocused our attention on Michael, who was booked on a promotional tour that took us to The Bitter End in New York. We did a week at Paul's Mall in Boston, opening for Seals and Crofts. They played as a duo with a backup bass player who had a bass drum pedal rigged to a tambourine for percussion. It substituted for a drum kit with great effectiveness. We played Philadelphia and other small listening venues in major markets on the East Coast. Our funky long-haired cowboy appearance and completely new and different sound apparently fascinated the Yankee audiences. We played to good crowds and were well received, picking up favorable press reviews along the way. Jerry Jeff showed up in New York and had us join him in a studio where we cut a couple of tracks. Back in Austin, the buzz was getting louder. We returned to Austin and played Castle Creek to a packed house!

Eddie Wilson, the aforementioned head honcho at the Armadillo World Headquarters, had taken notice of the rise in Murphey's popularity. He contacted Michael at Castle Creek and sounded him out about the possibility of playing the AWH! Playing the Armadillo represented a huge transition, not only for us but for the Armadillo as well, which had traditionally been a rock-and-roll venue that accommodated big-name touring rock-and-roll acts. There wasn't a hint of country music at the Armadillo World Headquarters, and the whole atmosphere was the antithesis of the traditional, conservative American culture that Nashville focused on projecting. We were the first local act to play there and . . . how shall I describe it? The first non-rock-and-roll act to ever play there! Michael's music contained a good dose of Southern Baptist and old-time gospel, so we brought that element with us, and it was a refreshing change. We were country leaning, mostly since we wore cowboy hats, but we had beards and long hair. The Armadillo was absolutely and unquestionably a "hippie" rock emporium! Our music, however, seemed to appeal to the Armadillo crowd, many of whom probably had suppressed country roots in their DNA. It's been said that our music was the catalyst that brought the hippies and the shit-kickers together at the Armadillo!

EDDIE WILSON, THE IMPRESARIO, the visionary, and driving force at the Armadillo, was working on a promotional campaign for the AWH. He was in contact with Jerry Retzloff, the head PR guy for Lone Star Beer, to have Lone Star be the principal beer image. The artwork of Jim Franklin that incorporated the image of the armadillo was also going to play a part.

In June of 1972, Herb Steiner moved to Austin and immediately joined the band. The addition of the steel guitar really fleshed us out and added a genuine country aspect to the band's sound. He knew more about country music than all of us put together. Plus, Herb brought with him his inimitable character and wonderful sense of humor. He was a welcome addition to the band and fit right in.

In August of 1972, Eddie Wilson promoted a tour called "Armadillo Country," headlining Michael Murphey with Willie Nelson opening. Willie had abandoned Nashville and relocated to Texas. Eddie booked us in Abilene, Amarillo, Lubbock, Wichita Falls, and we were to finish the weeklong tour with a grand finale at the AWH.

We were to open early in the week in Abilene in a huge concert auditorium. We arrived at the venue in the afternoon for a sound check, and someone told me Willie Nelson wanted to talk to me. He and Paul English, his "faithful sidekick" drummer, were traveling together in that old beat-up Winnebago that had *Remember Me* painted across the back. I stepped into the Winnebago and found Willie and Paul playing chess. Willie looked up from the game and said to me, "Hey man, can you play bass for me on this tour?" Well . . . I knew "Night Life" and "Funny How Time Slips Away" because I had played them since high school . . . the Ray Price version . . . and Roy Orbison's version of "Pretty Paper" (not knowing Willie had written it) . . . but other than that, I didn't have a clue about his repertoire. So I said, "Sure."

He said, "Great. I'll pay you $50 a night." I was making $75 a week with Murphey, so I could pick up a little extra cash in the bargain. That was it. He returned his attention to the chess game. No rehearsal, no nothing.

Showtime arrived, and we went onstage in an auditorium that could probably seat three thousand people. But, I swear, there couldn't have been more than ten people in the whole place! It was just Willie and Paul and me, and I didn't have a clue! His show was a medley of his songs like "Crazy," "Night Life," and "Mr. Record Man," and he would change keys between every song. Because he typically turns to the left when he plays his famous guitar—Trigger—and I was on his right, I couldn't see his hand to know what chords he was playing. For me, it was a disaster! I probably didn't hit two right notes the whole show. Willie, no doubt sensing my discomfort, walked over and said to me, "Don't worry, son. It don't mean a thing." I was relieved somewhat but still painfully aware of my mistakes.

The next night, we were in Amarillo, and there was a decidedly better crowd. I will pass on a story here told to me by Herb Steiner. Herb said that after the show, they were playing poker in the hotel room when Willie and Paul walked in with a trash bag full of pot and said, "Hey, you guys want to get high?" Willie has never made any secret of the fact that he enjoys the weed, so I don't think he'll mind me relaying that story.

We finished playing the other towns and were back in Austin for a two-night finale of the tour at the Armadillo—to a packed house both nights. We opened with Michael and brought the house down as the Austin audience was already well established. By this time, I had a handle on what Willie was doing as he did exactly the same show every night. Willie had made one previous appearance there with Greasy Wheels, but no one was familiar with him, and according to Joe Nick Potoski's book, the four hundred attendees were there to see Greasy Wheels. These two nights were different. Willie Nelson was debuting as a headline act at the Armadillo, and

I was playing bass with him and Paul! The hippies at the Armadillo loved it. He was straight out of the hard-core country music scene in Nashville, and his songs had been huge country hits, but the hippies at the Armadillo sensed, *He is one of us!* As fate would have it, I was involved in one of the most pivotal and iconic events in the history of Texas music!

After the show, backstage, Chet Flippo, a stringer covering the Austin music scene for *Rolling Stone* magazine, asked, "Gary P., do you think country music will go over at the Armadillo?"

My reply to Chet was, "The place was packed, and the crowd went crazy. The proof is in the pudding!"

Willie put his Family Band together and started working the Texas scene. As time went by, acts like Asleep at the Wheel, Commander Cody and His Lost Planet Airmen, Leon Russell, New Riders of the Purple Sage, and David Allan Coe began appearing at the Armadillo, and the cross-pollination of the two music cultures had begun to have its effect: Chet Flippo was covering it for *Rolling Stone*, so the whole country was reading about it and taking notice. It was, however, Michael Murphey, Jerry Jeff, and our band that had set the stage for it all to happen!

For the remainder of 1972 and into '73, we were technically Murphey's band, but we continued to bounce back and forth between him and Jerry Jeff. Both were gaining popularity by leaps and bounds. We opened with Michael for Elton John at the Palmer Auditorium on his first American tour. We went on like this the rest of that year making steady progress. Other singer-songwriters like B. W. Stevenson and Willis Alan Ramsey started moving to town, landing record deals, and the whole thing just kept growing. We were pretty much at the top of the heap. Little did I know what we had started or what it would lead to on that cold January night back at the Saxon Pub not that many nights before. We just kept going with the flow, riding the wave, and taking advantage of every opportunity that came our way.

It was very exciting to go from the local scene in Austin to head-lining the Armadillo, traveling around the country, playing famous venues in New York City, and promoting nationally distributed albums that I'd had a hand in creating. For sure, 1972 had been a watershed year on many levels, and as it came to an end, our story as well as the Watergate scandal were starting to gain traction. I had a new lease on life. I spent every available minute with Michael, still hanging on his every word, and soaking up lots of valuable experience and knowledge about songwriting and the music business.

As with many talented people, it was not always peaches and cream with Michael. He had a blustery Irish temper and could be a stern taskmaster. He wouldn't hesitate to dress you down in front of an audience if you made a mistake onstage. He demanded absolute loyalty. When we first got the band together, he gathered us up and told us in no uncertain terms that he would not tolerate any of us playing with anyone else in town—the notable exception being our dabblings with Jerry Jeff. He didn't seem to perceive that as a threat, and perhaps he sensed that there was, in the bigger picture, an actual benefit . . . something like . . . the whole is greater than the sum of its parts. It was obvious something good was happening.

IN THE MIDST OF all these goings on, it wasn't long before Michael, Diana, and toddler Ryan found a piece of Lake Travis property out on Comanche Trail to purchase, and they moved out of Public Domain. Theirs was a modest place built around a mobile home that probably was a funky fishing cabin by the lake in days gone by. Anyway, it was plenty adequate and a good landing place within walking distance from Windy Point that turned out to be a good investment no doubt.

My relationship with Pat Barnett was a testy one. We had been on again, off again, and I had moved in and out more than once.

This new situation with Michael seemed to take the focus off our problems. We inherited Public Domain and took over as renters. Of course, Loretta, her eight-year-old daughter—the sweetest little girl—was with us. One day, Pat's sister Donna and her husband, Dennis, came by the house for a visit as they were inclined to do. Donna came to me straightaway and said, "While we were coming over here, I had the greatest idea for a country song!"

I said, "Okay, let me hear it."

She said, "The last thing I needed, the first thing this morning, was to have you walk out on me!"

I immediately sang the line back to her in an exaggerated country style, and told her, "That's great! I want you to write the lyrics for it, bring it back to me, and I'll make a song out of it."

In a few days, she came back with some lyrics. The first verse is hers, verbatim. I thought the second verse tended to stray a bit and lose focus, so I picked it up from there. I was tuned in to the theme, so it was no trouble visualizing the story from that point. I sat at the piano and made up the second verse and the chorus while singing along. The singing part survived intact as the melody line, just like I did it the first time. This turned out to be one of the most significant events of my life![3]

Pat Barnett was one of the first women I was aware of that adhered to the philosophy of the women's liberation movement that accompanied the social and cultural tremors of that period. The movement would upend the traditional notions about women's roles in society. Now, I'm no prude, and I'm tolerant of others, but sometimes little things can create big problems. For example, one evening I was in a hurry to get to a fancy gig where I needed to wear a white shirt. I had some clean but not pressed. I asked Pat if

---

3   As I am writing, I just received word that Chris Stapleton, currently the hottest artist in country music, has recorded the song, and it's due for release on his new CD in early May 2017.

she would iron a shirt for me while I took a shower. She informed me—in no uncertain terms—that she didn't intend to iron the shirt. It seems this would violate her newfound tenets of the movement! Then I made a fatal mistake. I said to her, "My mother ironed every shirt I ever wore when I was growing up!" Oops! As soon as those irretrievable words slipped past my lips, I realized I had made a big mistake. Her reaction came in full fury in an instant. I remember her bared teeth, green eyes shooting daggers, her freckled, fair face a fiery red, and cobra-like venom spewing in my direction!

"I AM NOT YOUR MOTHER!"

I had the good sense to retreat from a war that I could not win. I dropped the matter and ironed my own shirt. This example was just one instance of how things were between us. Once again, it seemed clear to me that ours was not a match made in heaven, and it was certainly not the relationship I had envisioned with a life partner. What needed to be done, needed to get done, and we would debate the social and political ramifications of things later. But this tension kept my spirits dampened, despite the excitement I was enjoying from the success the music was having.

The winter of 1972 rolled around, and it was a cold one. It rained, it froze, it snowed. Michael had moved out to Comanche Trail. I remember driving out to Michael's house one blustery morning, when I met Shake Russell and Johnny Vandiver for the first time. They were friends of Michael's who had made their way down from Kansas City with the intent of relocating in Texas. They had both ended up spending lots of time in the early days in Houston, and they made tremendous contributions to the Texas folk scene for years. John Vandiver's life came to a tragic end, and a great artist's life was cut short. Shake Russell's path and mine would cross again.

Those cold days in January of '73 had a good effect on Michael's songwriting. He would hole up by the fire and write songs like crazy. I used to make a lot of piano pieces, and he and I had collaborated on one. Back when we lived at Public Domain, he dragged me out to the rehearsal shed, where I played that song over and over on an old upright we had moved out there. While I played, he wrote lyrics to match the melody lines of my piano tune.

He started having problems with his voice and went to Dr. Paul Burns at the Austin Ear, Nose, and Throat Clinic. Dr. Burns examined him and determined that he had nodules on his vocal cords. Michael needed laser surgery to remove the nodules, and it would require him not to speak for six weeks! This surprising news came at a particularly bad time as Michael was scheduled to go back into the studio to record his second album for A&M. This created quite a dilemma. He was writing songs as fast as he could turn them out. But how could he finish the songs and teach them to us if he weren't allowed to speak, much less sing?

Bob had moved out to Horseshoe Bend, just across Mansfield Dam and on the other side of Lake Travis—not that far from Michael's place on Comanche Trail. Michael McGeary, Herb Steiner, and I lived in Austin, which was a good hour's drive out to the Lake. Michael decided we were to have rehearsals at Bob's house, five days a week for six weeks, to prepare for the upcoming recording session; this meant we town-dwellers would have to make an eighty-mile-a-day round-trip every day. The burden fell on me to provide transportation for the three of us who lived in town. Michael had us on a $75 per week stipend. Considering the circumstances, he told us that since he couldn't work during this time, he couldn't afford to pay us, and we'd have to forego our $75. The caveat was that we would make a good sum of money playing at the recording sessions. *Hmmm* . . . we scratched our heads and said okay.

This began the most unusual period I have ever experienced in my music career. The rehearsals began: I picked up McGeary and Herb Steiner, and we headed out RR 2222. As I've said, it was an unusually cold and icy winter. The roads varied from wet and cold to ice-glazed to covered with ice and snow, and often it was tough going up and down the big winding hills between Balcones and RR 620, where we'd then have to cross the Mansfield Dam and go up Hudson Bend Road. We somehow managed to arrive safely at Bob's, where we would drink some coffee, catch up on the gossip, and listen to Herb Steiner or Bob Livingston—neither of whom lacked the gift of gab—tell stories. The lively banter and laughter was very entertaining. Eventually, I might start a jam, or we would go over some of Murphey's tunes, or anybody else's, for that matter. Those were and are the best times—when you're just playing for fun—and I had a knack for initiating some of those moments.

Eventually, Michael would walk in the back door with a strange look in his eyes. He would have a briefcase or a pile of legal pads under his arm, where the songs he had recently composed were written. He might write a few notes on his tablet if he had something he wanted to communicate to us. He would use soft guttural sounds to punctuate the syllables he was trying to indicate. When it was time to get down to business, which never took long, he used Bob as his translator or medium, for lack of better descriptive terms, between him and us. It was very strange, but the process intrigued us all, and we paid close attention. The ritual went something like this.

Michael would go to Bob's spinet piano, peck out the melody line with one finger on the keyboard, and indicate how the lyrics joined up with the melody with the eraser end of a pencil tapping the lyrics scribbled on the yellow legal pad. Bob would follow the pencil taps and try to match the lyrics with the melody line. After a few times through, the lyrics and melody lines would join up, and the song would emerge. Bob was officially the demo vocalist those six weeks that we rehearsed our way through the songs that Michael was writing. I got to take a more active role when we started rehearsing "South Canadian River Song," as I was a cowriter and piano player on a piece that was neither ordinary nor easy and was quite lengthy. The piece had three distinct movements and a wide range of dynamics approaching symphonic, as it's been described. It required everyone to know and play very distinct parts—especially me, as the song was composed for the piano. We spent five or six hours a day rehearsing until we had it down pat. The same went for all the other tunes. I don't care what any of those musicians say—rehearsal paid off, just maybe not always with money.

Toward the end of the six-week period, Jim and John Inmon came out and set up a small recording situation. We recorded all the songs, which helped us to really focus on what we were doing and tweak what needed to be tweaked. When it came time to go to Nashville, we were very well prepared.

WE WENT UP TO Nashville, got settled in, and headed once again to Ray Stevens's studio. We reunited with Bob Johnston, and the process began. We spent a lot of time tuning and getting sounds for the drum kit. The studio supplied the drums, and they had Michael McGeary in there for two solid days. "We've got to have a hit-record drum sound on this record," I recall hearing Bob Johnston say. Finally, we got started tracking the songs. Bob, Craig, Herb, Michael McGeary, and I were the session players. We started with the title track, "Cosmic Cowboy." I had looked for an instrument for the intro because the first sounds on the record needed to set the tone and create the visual image of what the record was about. In my mind, I could hear a harmonica or an accordion, neither of which I had or could play. I did, however, have a clavinet that I carried around with me. The clavinet was the instrument Buzz Cason had played back in '64 when we did the Crickets gig in El Paso. I liked to always have one with me as it served as a handy and portable substitute for an accordion or harmonica during the many

on-the-road picking sessions we had. I blew the part in the beginning, and we proceeded to cut the song live on the first take. "Alleys
of Austin" came next. It was laid back and soulful, but not difficult,
so we nailed it in no time. I played bass on that one. We were knocking out the tracks one after the other, and Michael's tracking vocals
were keepers. *Next!* I think we cut five or six tracks the first day.

The next day, it was the same thing. We cut "Blessing in Disguise" and a song titled "Country Rock and the City Rock" that I
really liked, but it ended up on the cutting room floor. We saved
"South Canadian River Song" for last, as it was definitely the
most demanding. It was written in F, relative to C major scale,
but Michael determined it was a bit too high for his voice, so he
directed that we lower the key to E-flat, relative to B-flat. I was
totally unfamiliar with the key of B-flat, so I had to get busy and
transpose it to learn it in the new key. As it turned out, we nailed
it the first take! Voilà! We'd been in the studio less than two full
days and were finished!

Sadly, a misunderstanding developed that resulted in the band
leaving Michael, returning to Texas, and joining Jerry Jeff. I elected
to stay.

The next day, Michael, Bob Johnston, and I were back in the
studio working on finishing up overdubs. The studio had acquired a
synthesizer keyboard—the first I had ever seen. Remember, this was
in the seminal days of digital technology when digital keyboards
were just beginning to appear. I had some ideas about adding strings
and horns to the track. Michael and Bob gave me the go-ahead, and
I experimented with various sounds available on the synthesizer.
I overdubbed cello and French horn parts that proved to be quite
effective in adding another dimension to the track. I was thrilled
to have the opportunity to be creative, and to have the confidence
of Michael and Bob. During that experience I felt, even for a brief

time, that I was working as a co-equal in the production process with two highly respectable professionals in the music business. My work was met with enthusiastic approval by both. I was happy and felt a sense of pride and accomplishment.

When we finished with the overdubs, Michael and I drove back to Texas. He was in a funk, as you might imagine. But it wasn't long before he got word that arrangements were in the works for him to go to England. Marty Machat, Bob Johnston's attorney and a powerful and influential mogul in the musical industry with offices in New York and London, had secured a deal with EMI Records, one of the biggest record companies in Europe and worldwide. They wanted him in London to promote his signing with EMI. Michael invited me to go along for "services rendered." I was thrilled to have my first opportunity to go overseas.

Michael's wife, Diana, was British and had been living in London at the time the Beatles were breaking out. She was acquainted with Brian Epstein, the Beatles' manager. I will tell the story as she once related it to me: She got a phone call one day from a frantic Brian Epstein, whose phone was ringing off the hook with business pouring in for the Beatles. He was in desperate need of an assistant to help him handle it. She went to work for him and was right in the middle of that whole scene in '63 and '64. She spent a lot of time with the Beatles, mostly with George and Ringo during downtimes, as John and Paul, being the leaders, were blowing and going. She also mentioned a fellow named Derek Taylor,[4] who was quite often around during that time. She was with the Beatles when they made their first tour of the United States in 1964. Some years later, she immigrated to the United States and settled in Los Angeles, where she got a job with A&M Records. That was where Michael met her while he was shopping around for a record deal.

---

4   Derek Taylor was the Beatles' press officer and often called "The Fifth Beatle."

Diana's parents lived in the Midlands in England in a town called Atherstone. We flew into London and made our way north to her parents' home. Dennis Vero, her dad, owned a hat factory. They were fairly well off and lived in a nice two-story home they called The Croft, with a tennis court in the backyard. Naturally, they were delighted to have their daughter home and to see their two-year-old grandson, Ryan, for the first time. They made me feel very much at home. They showed us the sights around the English countryside and entertained us in fine fashion. We made day trips to Nottingham and Sherwood Forest, of which there is very little forest left.

We wrote several songs together during that time: "Rye by-the-Sea," "Nothing's Your Own," and "Night Patrol." Michael was in the writer's seat with lyrics and melody lines, and I rode shotgun, making contributions with chord progressions and minor parts as I was able. We stayed at the Veros' home about a week, and then went back to London leaving Ryan with his grandparents. Michael and Diana stayed in a hotel and put me up with Diana's brother, who lived with three others in Montague Square in a fashionable, two-story, four-bedroom flat just off Oxford Street near Hyde Park. I was afforded a couch in the living room to sleep on. Diana's brother was an insurance broker, one roommate was a stockbroker, one was Swiss, and the fourth was a very nice and handsome fellow from El Paso, Texas, who was studying at the London School of Economics. All being young professionals and bachelors, they didn't spend much time in the flat except for a few evenings, so I saw very little of them. I spent a lot of my time alone over a period of three weeks.

Early on, Michael came by and we went out to see the sights in the neighborhood. We walked down Piccadilly Circus and visited the famous luxury store Harrods. As we were walking along we looked up and saw directly ahead was the Royal Albert Hall! Cool. On the big marquee in front of the building was a sign that read TONIGHT THE EAGLES. Michael and I looked at each other and grinned. The Eagles were in London recording their *Desperado* album. We walked around to the back of the building to the loading area, and since there was no security or anyone to prevent us from doing so, we walked into the backstage area of the Royal Albert Hall.

We made our way toward the stage, and as we walked around the stage curtain, we ran smack dab into the familiar face of Tommy Nixon. Tommy had been the drummer for the Chevelle Five out of Abilene, another Charlie Hatchett band. We had been friends since back in the Sparkles days. He was now the road manager for the Eagles. We had a joyful reunion, hugging and slapping each other and both surprised to run into each other at the Royal Albert Hall after all these years. Soon, Don Henley appeared, and we all greeted each other warmly. Don and I had crossed paths several times back when we were doing Roundup gigs in Austin when he was with a band out of Linden, Texas, called Felicity, and I was with the Sparkles. He and Michael knew each other from Los Angeles, and they paired off catching up on old times. I also met a fellow from California by the name of David Jackson, who was backing up J. D. Souther on bass. J. D. was hanging with and opening shows for the Eagles and had also written hits for them. They were all busy preparing for the show that night, so our visit was cut short, but we did exchange phone numbers and made plans to get together again.

EMI had arranged a showcase/press reception to promote Michael's signing at a club whose name I can't recall. We had planned to do it as a duo, but Michael invited Don Henley to come sit in with us for the showcase, which he did. I have an old Kodak snapshot somewhere in my boxes of stuff of Don Henley playing drums with us at that showcase. After that, Michael and Don spent time together. I hooked up with David Jackson, and we bonded and got along very well. It was good to have someone to hang with. Michael and Diana took day trips to places like England's southern coast, in addition to his doing various PR things. One night, he got invited to go to a reception for Paul McCartney. Paul McCartney was my idol and my main influence as a bass player. I'm not the jealous type, but I must admit, I was envious of Michael's having the opportunity to meet him.

Bob Johnston was also in London, having flown over earlier and overdubbed the London Philharmonic Orchestra on a song from *Cosmic Cowboy* titled "Blessing in Disguise." He had booked time in Abbey Road Studios to mix down and master the track, which they planned to release in England and Europe as a single on EMI. I did get invited to tag along for that! Walking into the studio where the Beatles cut their records was like entering a sacred temple. It was rather plain in décor, nothing fancy about it. The mixing board was the same board used by the Beatles. It was rather plain with huge knobs—nothing like today's spaceship-looking consoles. Over on the left side were the four sliders where the final mixes went down. They cut their songs on four separate tracks and then mixed the four tracks down for the final mix.

While I was observing the process of mastering "Blessing in Disguise," I met a very interesting fellow named Mike Collier, who had a tremendous influence on me. We were sitting and talking on a couch off to the right of the console while the others were busy with the song. He told me that he was in the music publishing business. He may have been bragging, but he told me that he had published ninety of the top one hundred songs on the British hit parade during the past week! Wow! At the time, I wasn't hip to the publishing business except for the little Michael had shared with me. He asked about me, and what I did, and I told him I played bass and worked with Michael. He asked if I had written any songs, to which I said that I had written some. Then he asked me if I would like to come to his office the next day to play him what I had written. "Sure, I'd be glad to."

The next day, I caught a London taxi to his office. He was a very outgoing fellow who told me stories about songs he'd published and about the songwriters he'd had to bail out of jail on a regular basis. Then he invited me to sing some of my songs. I sang "The Last Thing I Needed, First Thing This Morning." He bolted out of his seat and started jumping up and down and clapping his hands. "It's a hit! It's a bloody hit! It's a bloody *monster* hit! It could be a smash for Loretta Lynn! I'm calling Loretta Lynn right now!" He got on the phone but was unable to get through because it was still early morning in Nashville.

We concluded the meeting, and I was pretty stoked by his enthusiasm. I think it was right there that I realized the significance of the publishing aspect of the music business and that I may have had an aptitude for it. I could relate to the stories about his role, and it inspired me to start focusing my attention in that direction. I never saw or spoke to Mike Collier again, but I think about him often, and wish I could shake his hand and thank him for planting the thought in my head.

IN THE DAYS THAT followed, I found myself alone in the flat on Montague Square. I filled my days watching BBC, including the daily horse hurdle races, and sleeping just to pass the time. The fellows I was staying with kept nothing in the house to eat, so I couldn't pilfer anything there. I had very little money; just a one-hundred-dollar bill that I was clinging to, swearing not to break except in the direst of circumstances. The flat was cold, as the heat went off every morning at 6:00 a.m. and didn't come back on until 6:00 p.m. I would walk to Oxford Street and wander around in Hyde Park, then usually descend into the Marble Arch tube station to get a croissant and a cup of coffee. I people watched and listened to the buskers playing for tips. I was wearing my cowboy hat and boots, and that attracted a lot of attention. Comments like "Hey cowboy, where's your 'orse?" or "Look, it's John Wayne" or "There's bloody J. R.!" were tossed in my direction. The English sense of humor . . . I felt very vulnerable and homesick.

I was walking around the flat one day with my guitar in my hand—the same one I had bought in Mexico back in 1962—looking out the window down into the park that the apartment buildings bordered. It was one of those classic, stereotypical, drizzly, foggy, and cold London days, and I just sang out:

> Well, it's cold over here, and I swear, I wish they would turn
> the heat on.

I had met a girl at a dinner party, and we had agreed to meet, but she never showed up. The next line out of my mouth was:

> And where in the world, is that English girl
> I promised I would meet on the third floor?

From there, I thought I would just play with it, so I made a game of mixing British phrases with Texas phrases, and the lines started falling into place.

> London Bridge has fallen down
> And moved to Arizona
> Now I know why
> Those limey eyes, they were eyeing the prize
> Some people call manly footwear

That line was a reference to the Merle Haggard song "Okie From Muscogee."

Well I decided that I get my cowboy hat
And go down to Marble Arch Station

And so it went. I had plenty of time to fool around with it without distraction and was able to come up with three verses. The chorus just wrote itself:

I wanna go home with the Armadillos.

Armadillos was the term I used to characterize the folks of the counterculture scene happening in Austin. I wasn't specifically referring to the Armadillo World Headquarters. To me, it was just an exercise in writing a song. I never imagined at the time that anything would ever come of it!

The last week we were in London, I continued passing my days alone in the cold flat on Montague Square watching three-year-old thoroughbreds run the hurdles and sleeping. One day during one of those sleeping sessions, I began to have a series of dreams. In the dreams, and in chronological sequence, I would be back at the places I had lived: in Oklahoma, at Eram, then Olney, and finally, at Bradley. In my dreams I was grown, but all the people I remember from those places were the same age as when I knew them. We'd be back in the schoolyard playing Work-Up, bidding on our favorite girl's pie at a pie supper, or collecting our paper bags of candy and nuts at Christmastime. At the end of each dream, I would wake up, ponder the dream, and then go back to sleep. In the last dream of the sequence, I saw my father die in a barn lot after feeding the horses at Grandma Nunn's house. This upset me terribly as you might imagine.

Back in the late sixties, my dad took summer jobs in Belvidere, Illinois, supervising a dorm where young workers who worked summer jobs in the fields for the Green Giant produce company were housed. He was driving to Davenport, Iowa, to visit my sister

Judy, who lived there with her husband and newly adopted infant son. In a thick fog, Dad ran into a chain-reaction pileup but was not injured. Before he could get out of his car, another car crashed into him from behind, and he *was* seriously injured. He spent about a month in the hospital recovering from broken limbs and surgeries for a ruptured spleen and to remove a portion of his intestines. He had always been an active and vigorous man, but this really knocked him down. He never fully recovered from that awful wreck. He had to return to work teaching school in Iowa Park before he should have, and from that point on, he began to develop heart trouble. This was a time before heart bypass and advanced heart surgery had been developed. The only therapy available was the nitroglycerin medication, and he took it often to relieve the onset of potential heart attacks.

That was the context in which I woke up from the final dream. Understandably, I was suddenly filled with fear that my dad would die before I got to see him again. I wasn't really doing anything of any consequence in London, and I felt the terrible urge to go home. I told Michael of my dreams and my urgent wish to return to the United States. But Michael had planned for us to travel to Amsterdam and Paris before returning to Texas, and he urged me to just settle down. "It was just a dream; don't take it seriously." But I wouldn't relent and insisted he arrange for me to return home immediately. Finally, he did. I went to the palatial offices of Marty Machat in ritzy Grosvenor Square, and he gave me the plane ticket home.

I HADN'T MADE ANY money since arriving in England and was flat broke except for that one-hundred-dollar bill I had hoarded in my wallet. I flew from London to New York, where I had about an eighteen-hour layover. I had three large bags and a guitar with me. That's when I learned to never travel with more than you can carry yourself. I couldn't afford a skycap to assist me, so I had to move the bags two at a time several feet, then retreat, and retrieve the other two. I finally got the bags to the sidewalk. I had called a friend who mercifully offered to let me stay over. So I hailed a shuttle van to take me into Manhattan and made arrangements to be picked up and taken to the airport the next day. I arrived wired from the trip itself, feeling anxiety over my dad's health and my own precarious situation: It had cost me $45 one-way for the shuttle. When I finally got to the apartment, which was just under the 59th Street Bridge, I pulled out my guitar and nervous energy took over. I began banging away an up-tempo R&B-style riff and made up the song "People Will Dance."

> People will dance, if you give 'em half a chance
> People will dance, if you give 'em half a chance
> You got to be a dancer if you want to play drums in the band.

———————

From *Lost Gonzo Band* LP, MCA Records, 1975

How that song came out of that situation I can't explain. I later recorded it on the first Lost Gonzo Band album.

The next morning, I caught the shuttle to the airport and flew back to Austin—exhausted, relieved, and literally without a penny in my pocket! Pat met me at the airport and drove me to Public Domain where I picked up my truck. I followed her to a house she had rented in Cedar Park. She sat me down and informed me that in my absence she had become involved with another man. I was a bit shocked but too tired to respond with anything but resignation. I had been looking for a way to terminate our relationship, and she had opened the door. I took my leave and went home to an empty Public Domain. The next morning, I drove to Iowa Park to be with my dad.

I found my dad laid up with his heart condition. He was having periodic chest pains and would grab his nitroglycerin pills for relief. Sometimes, it was touch and go, and I didn't know if he would make it through a spell. Oddly enough, my mother and dad did not sleep on pillows. I can't imagine why, except they probably believed—as with coffee or tobacco or alcohol—they were not good for you. (I told you they followed the straight and narrow.) Dad was lying in his bed, without a pillow, studying a world atlas, which he did quite often. We talked about the happenings in the world using the atlas for reference.

He also talked to me about what he perceived as the decline in morality in the country, particularly the decline he had observed in the education system. He said he was glad he wasn't going to be around long enough to witness what he expected to be the decline of America if things didn't turn around. He was so concerned about the effect it was going to have on kids going through school, and he feared they wouldn't have the tools necessary to succeed in life and become productive citizens. "Productive citizens" was a phrase often used in our family and was defined simply as being self-sufficient. To be a productive citizen, any able-bodied person must, first, provide for his or her own welfare and not be a burden on the family or the community. That was the bottom line. It's funny that in his last days, his concerns were about his school students. I think he was trying to pass his final thoughts on to me as if he knew his days were numbered. I spent every available minute by his side for a week. Then the time came for me to return to Austin. I hugged his whiskered face and said my farewells, knowing this might be the last time. I made my way back to Public Domain.

IN MAY OF 1973, Michael and I went back to Nashville to record his third LP for A&M Records. We recorded the songs that we had written in England and others that Michael had never recorded. The themes of some of these songs were rather out there, more on the order of the Beatles' "I Am the Walrus" than "Cosmic Cowboy." Songs with titles like "Daredevils," "Dead Cat on the Line," "Nothing's Your Own," and "Deadheads and Suckers" dominated. It was very eclectic, edgy, and a bit strange. I'm not sure if it was my influence on Michael or his influence on me, but it seemed we tested the limits when we wrote and worked together. A&M saw fit not to release it.

One morning toward the end of that session, the phone rang in my hotel room. On the line was Cherry Brown, my brother Steve's girlfriend. She informed me she was calling for Steve to tell me that our father had passed away. Steve was too upset to talk to me. Dad had died in Hanna after working all day setting corner posts on a fence he was trying to get completed. After finishing, he had gone to Grandma Nunn's house to feed the horses. My dream had unfortunately come true. I flew to Tulsa. Tollie Boy picked me up and drove me to Hanna to attend the service. My dad's middle name was Ulysses, and he would frequently use the self-deprecating term "Useless" to describe himself in a humorous fashion. During the eulogy, the country minister mispronounced his name and said, "William Useless Nunn." It wasn't funny. I played one of Michael's songs, "Waking Up," on the piano at the First Baptist Church, and we buried him among his family there in the Hanna Cemetery.

I was at Public Domain alone one evening when Michael

walked through the door. He, Diana, and Bob Livingston had made a trip to a Hopi reservation near the Four Corners area. He told me a story about how he had met the holy man Lama Govinda and had invited him to their campsite. He was obviously very moved by the whole experience because he had this faraway look in his eyes, as if he had ascended a few steps up the spiritual ladder. I listened to his story intently, and as I did, I felt myself sharing his experience vicariously, and I felt somewhat elevated as well. Eventually, he played a song he had written during that time called "Southwestern Pilgrimage."

> I ain't gonna drink your muddy water, babe
> Sleep in a hollow log
> I'm gonna take up with a stranger
> And find myself a fast-moving dog.

This was the first indication I had that something might be amiss in his relationship with Diana. It wasn't long before he shared that they were breaking up their marriage. It was coming springtime in Texas, and as you might imagine, this situation threw Michael into a total funk. I felt so sorry for him as he was suffering terribly. I stuck by his side every available minute and tried my best to be a supportive friend. The good news was that he dove deep into himself and wrote a flurry of great songs that would eventually appear on his future albums with Epic and Columbia Records.

We had no band that summer, so as a special project, he conceived of the idea of putting together a show based on the tunes from the *Cosmic Cowboy Souvenir* LP. He wanted some string players for the project, and I was familiar with a group called the Avalard String Quartet that had been performing around town and in the Armadillo Beer Garden. It consisted of the exotic, Jean Harlow look-alike

Linda Weatherby on viola, and three others whose names I didn't know. I approached her to sound her out about any possible interest. She said she would be very interested and could probably persuade the other members to join in.

I hadn't read any music for years and had *never* written a single note of music on paper: I volunteered to write the string charts. I approached Doug Harmon, a B-3 organ player in town who also played cello, to see if he would be interested in participating in the ensemble and assisting me in writing the charts. He was well versed in written music, and he agreed. I started spending my days at his house on West 5th Street. I would peck out the parts on the piano, and he would write the charts for two violins, viola, and cello. We spent a good deal of time writing the charts and rehearsing the ensemble with me on bass. The "South Canadian River Song" that Michael and I had written together was the showpiece, as it had three movements and featured brass and strings, especially the cello. Michael managed to book two concerts featuring the "Cosmic Cowboy Orchestra"—one at the Armadillo World Headquarters and one at the McFarlin Auditorium on the SMU campus in Dallas. Both shows sold well and were critically acclaimed. It was a very rewarding experience for me, because I had taken on the challenge of writing the charts just by believing I could.

Around August of '73, I heard that Tim O'Connor had opened another bar in town. It was a tiny little place called The Squeeze Inn located on 19th Street (Martin Luther King Jr. Boulevard now) on the south side of the street where Guadalupe takes a quick turn there on the south side of the campus. It was a hot summer day about happy hour time, and the place was elbow to elbow. *Man, Tim O'Connor really knows how to run a bar. He just opened, and the place is packed.* I squeezed my way in, made my way to the bar, and ran into Jerry Jeff Walker, who was in a merry mood. He grabbed me and said he wanted to talk to me. He started going on about how he wanted to make another record, but he didn't want to do it in a studio. "You can't capture the magic in a studio. I just want someone to follow me around with a Niagara cassette recorder and record me when I'm in the mood. That's when the magic happens."

"Sounds like a good idea, Jerry Jeff," I replied. Then he proceeded to tell me about a funky little place in the Hill Country out west by Fredericksburg he'd discovered that might be the ideal place for what he had in mind. The name of the place was Luckenbach!

"There's a real character in Luckenbach, and he has some magic about him. I think I'd like to cut a record there. It just feels right!"

The name of the character he was referring to was Hondo Crouch.

Jerry Jeff said, "I know you're playing with Murphey, but I'd like to have you come down and play piano on it."

"Sure, Jerry Jeff. Great!" He asked me if I knew anyone who played fiddle that we could get to come play.

I said, "I think I do know someone."

The person I had in mind was Mary Egan (Mary Hattersley). I had gotten to know "Sweet Mary" a bit when she and Marian Royal would come out to Hill on the Moon. I had seen her playing around town and had taken note that she had a really smooth touch and a sensitive approach to the way she played. I sensed that her style would suit Jerry Jeff's project perfectly.

When the date for the recording project in Luckenbach rolled around, we arrived one by one. It was my first time there, and I was enchanted by the place. I met Hondo Crouch and was equally enchanted by him. The cast of characters included Bob Livingston, Craig Hillis, Michael McGeary, Herb Steiner, Mary Egan, Mickey Raphael, Joanne Vent (a vocalist friend of Jerry Jeff's from New York), Kelly Dunn (a killer organ and keyboard player-friend of Michael McGeary's from San Diego), and me.

We began the set-up process when Michael Brovsky, Jerry Jeff's manager/producer from New York, realized we needed some baffling for the instruments. I knew it was haying season, so I suggested we use hay bales. We asked around and arranged to acquire some from a nearby farm. Michael and I headed out to the hayfield and loaded my pickup full of square bales. It was a sight to see Michael—dressed in polyester pants and shirt and wearing platform shoes—sweating like crazy. I couldn't help but compare him to Uncle Brother bucking bales back when I was a kid. We took the load back to the Luckenbach Dance Hall and proceeded to arrange the instruments in a square on the dance floor in front of the stage, baffling the amps with the hay bales. We put McGeary's drums on the stage and stacked hay bales around his kit. Jerry Jeff's vocal and acoustic guitar mics were situated in the center of the square. The make-do studio arrangement proved to work quite well.

We spent most of the day finalizing sounds for Dale Ashby's New York mobile recording bus that was parked just outside the building. By the time evening rolled around, we were ready to start cutting tracks.

We were staying at the Peach Tree Inn in Fredericksburg. The normal routine was to get up and have breakfast and then mosey out to Luckenbach, arriving about twelve. Normally, we would sit around under the big oak trees and pass around a few tunes. Then we would gravitate to the instruments, maybe jam a bit, and wait for Jerry Jeff to arrive. I don't think Jerry Jeff slept the whole time we were there, but eventually he would arrive and say, "Let's do 'Gettin' By' or 'Backslider's Wine,'" or whatever he was in the mood for. We would cut well into the night, then break it off, relax, and listen back. Those afterhours were some of the most memorable, as we often gathered around Hondo under the trees behind the beer joint/post office. We listened to him tell stories and recite poems he had written about Luckenbach.

Nothing much happened in Luckenbach this month
Except the potata chip man came by.
Then, there was the moon
We try to tell who come to look at our town
What a big moon we have, but nobody will listen
They can't believe we have such a big moon
For such a small town.[5]

———

From "Luckenbach Moon" by Hondo Crouch

We would listen in total silence, enchanted, as his words floated in the cool night air. This was our routine as we made our way through the songs. He made it seem as though Luckenbach was a fairy-tale kingdom, and he was the magic prince of this Hill Country wonderland. His vibe set the tone for the whole week of recording.

One day toward the end of the week, people started discussing the album cover photo. One picture in particular was being considered. It was a photo of the handbill that had been printed and distributed around the Hill Country announcing that Jerry Jeff Walker would be performing a live concert at the Luckenbach Dance Hall on the coming Saturday. The handbill had been tacked on the barnwood door of the dance hall. In the photo, Hondo's hand was pointing to the handbill. Also in the photo was a ¡VIVA TERLINGUA! bumper sticker, a permanent fixture on the door. I happened to be present when Michael Brovsky and the photographer, Jim McGuire, discussed their concern about what could be done about the bumper sticker that inadvertently showed up in the photo. I suggested simply leaving the bumper sticker in the picture and titling the album *¡Viva Terlingua!* And that's how the album came to be titled. Little things have big consequences.

———

5   I highly recommend the book *Hondo, My Father* by Becky Crouch Patterson.

The admission price for the concert was $1. Hundreds of people showed up. They were sitting in the open windows and hanging off the rafters (not literally) of that rustic, old German dance hall. We played the songs that we recorded as well as other songs from Jerry Jeff's repertoire like "Mr. Bojangles." We cut Ray Wylie Hubbard's "Up Against the Wall Redneck Mother," which the crowd loved. Toward the end of the show, Jerry Jeff looked over to me and said, "Do that song about London I heard you singing this afternoon." Well, we had never played or rehearsed the song before. I had sung it for Bob, and he was familiar with the chord progression, but he was the only one. I was a little apprehensive about whether we could pull it off, but I sang it, and the crowd went absolutely wild! It's very unusual to get a response like that for a song no one has ever heard before. Suddenly, Michael Brovsky ran in from the recording bus and said, "You've got to cut it again! We weren't ready, and we didn't get it! Do it again!" Wow! We'd just done the song to a thunderous response, and he wanted me to do it *again*?

I gathered myself and we started it once more. JJ was strumming the acoustic guitar rhythm, Mickey Raphael was blowing a little harp, and that's when I said, "Let me see if I can put myself back in that place again." I was referring to going back to the beginning of the song, but most people thought I was referring to putting myself back in London again. It worked both ways. We did the song again, and I was so nervous that at one point for a whole section, I was hitting a wrong chord on the piano. I realized it as it was happening, but I just kept playing the wrong chord. No one ever seemed to notice but me. I can't help but remember the line Jerry Jeff would often say: "When you're screwing up, don't flinch." Jerry Jeff had a lot of good lines like that.

We finished the tune, and once again, the crowd went crazy! I can say, without reservation, that it was the greatest response I had ever gotten for myself—or for one of my songs. I was happy to have been lucky enough to be in that spot at that time, and I was feeling pretty good about myself. The show ended and the evening wound down. Michael Brovsky searched me out and pulled me aside. He said, "Listen Gary P., your song was one of the highlights of this whole recording session. I want to include it on this record, and we want you to rejoin the band."

Chapter 8

Jerry Jeff Era

WHEN I GOT BACK to Austin from Luckenbach, I went out to Comanche Trail to inform Michael of my decision to move over to Jerry Jeff. We took a walk down to Windy Point as I broke the news. He wasn't happy about it. Now his whole band had left him for Jerry Jeff. I'm sure he felt abandoned and betrayed. I explained that I was sorry to have to go but the move would be such an important opportunity for me, and I couldn't afford to turn it down.

The self-titled *Jerry Jeff Walker* album that we had recorded for him was out and getting attention. MCA Records had released the Guy Clark song "L.A. Freeway" as a single, and it was starting to take off, especially in California. He had signed with Athena Booking Agency out of Denver, and they were keeping him busy up and down the West Coast and booking him not only in Texas but on the East Coast as well. My song on his new record presented a real opportunity for me to get my name out there and dramatically increase my income. I can live on almost nothing if I have to, but . . .

So I moved over, and we hit the ground running. John Inmon was brought in to fill the guitar slot. Craig Hillis joined back with Michael Murphey, as did Herb Steiner.

MCA expedited the release of the *¡Viva Terlingua!* album, and it was in the stores in a few short weeks. MCA promoted it hard to the radio stations, and the response was overwhelming! The album was full of magic, but the two most popular songs to emerge were "London Homesick Blues" and Ray Wylie Hubbard's "Up Against the Wall Redneck Mother." Jerry Jeff's timing couldn't have been better. Whatever was going on out in the country seemed to create a situation that made it all come together for him. NASA played "Redneck Mother" to wake up the astronauts on an Apollo space flight, and that got national news coverage. Anybody who heard that song and had the tiniest bit of a sense of humor got a kick out of it!

National focus began to turn in our direction. Something was going on down here in Texas. The country was ready for something new and different, and this record apparently satisfied that mood.

Everywhere we went, it seemed like the audience had spent the whole day drinking in preparation. When Jerry Jeff would open with "Hi, Buckaroos" (my contribution, from Buffalo Bob on the *Howdy Doody* show) from his tune "Getting By," it was more or less bedlam from that point on. He didn't have to win 'em over. They were already primed!

They branded us outlaws, and people love outlaws. Jerry Jeff had the reputation of being a "semi wild man"—contrary to an ordinary wild man—always living on the edge, pushing the envelope, and being a notorious drinker. I think a lot of people came to see if he would get drunk and fall off the stage! They were pleasantly surprised when he put on a good show, which he did 99 percent of the time—but they wouldn't have been disappointed if he *had* fallen off the stage! Jerry Jeff had a measure of charisma and charm about him that allowed him to say and do the most outrageous things—things that always ended up being remembered as hilarious stories to tell. Regardless of what condition he was in, he seemed to always be fully aware of where the edge of the cliff was, and he was careful not to go off it! Besides—the band was always there to catch him if he started to stumble.

We'd go out for two or three weeks at a time, always flying commercial and renting three cars. It's a wonder we didn't have wrecks getting to the venues. Sometimes Jerry Jeff drove the lead car, and we'd try to follow him on the freeways. He'd be weaving in and out of traffic on flyovers and crossing three lanes to make an exit without considering that he had two other cars following him in rush-hour traffic. It's amazing we survived, but somehow, we managed to avoid getting "killed or caught"!

One time, we were following the promoter when we lost him in traffic. We had no address or information about where to go. We were driving along without a clue of what we were going to do next when, on the side of the street, we saw a hand-painted sign with an arrow that said, "THIS WAY JERRY JEFF"! Things like that were always happening. We laughed a lot and pressed onward through the fog.

When the band first left Michael and went with Jerry Jeff, Bob Livingston—who knew JJW's ways better than the rest of us—made him promise to stay away from hard liquor and to only drink beer, as he was known to have a fondness for Johnny Walker Red. For the most part, Jerry Jeff stuck to that promise and confined himself to Budweiser, which he always drank from a cup, claiming that drinking from a can always made him burp! When we were on the road, he never went to bed as far as I ever witnessed and would drink beer straight through, with the help of whatever it was besides natural energy that kept him up.

Bob and I always roomed together, and more than once, Jerry Jeff would bang on our door at four in the morning and wake us up, yelling, "You guys wake up! You're sleeping your lives away!" That was pretty much the norm for the three years I worked with him.

In December of 1973, Jerry Jeff asked if I'd like to go with him to the National Finals Rodeo (NFR), which was held in Oklahoma

City before it moved to Las Vegas. He rented a small plane, and we flew to OKC for the final evening's performance. We checked into the Sheraton Hotel, where all the rodeo cowboys were headquartered. We hooked up with Bud Shrake and "Jap" (Gary) Cartwright, who were covering the rodeo for *Sports Illustrated*.

We had encountered Bud and Jap at other big rodeos in Denver, Cheyenne, and Calgary that year, as we were booked in those cities to coincide with the rodeos. They were covering Larry Mahan's trail as he sought the All-Around Cowboy Championship. Bud and Jap seemed to appreciate Jerry Jeff's unorthodox way of making music, and they apparently shared his "semi gonzo" artistic approach in their own writings. In any case, we always hung together during those big rodeos.

The highlight of the NFR is always the bull-riding championship. That night, Bobby Steiner cinched the world championship bull-riding title. Bobby was an Austin-raised boy whose dad, Tommy Steiner, was a top rodeo contractor who supplied rodeo stock for the biggest rodeos. He was the grandson of Buck Steiner, the aforementioned patriarch of the Steiner Ranch family.

Jerry Jeff was popular on the rodeo circuit, and the cowboys were aware of the connection between him, the song, and the Steiners. After the rodeo with Bobby winning the "world," there was quite a bit of celebrating going on at the Sheraton Hotel. Jerry Jeff and I did some picking in our jam-packed hotel room full of cowboys, all drinking and partying and enjoying the little show. Larry Mahan was there, as was James Caan, who was the on-air TV commentator for the network covering the finals. After some time, we wound down and the room emptied out, leaving just Bud Shrake and me. Every inch of surface area in that room was covered with empty beer cans and all manner of party debris.

Now Bud Shrake and Jap Cartwright were part of a loose circle of people who called themselves "Mad Dogs Incorporated." Just to indicate the group's basic philosophy, their motto was, "Anything that's not a complete mystery, is just guesswork!" They had taken to writing weird song lyrics and showing them to Bob Livingston and me with the hopes that we could turn them into songs. We used the pseudonym M. D. Shafter. Bud pulled out a piece of paper where he had written some lyrics. I had a guitar in my hand, and as I read the words for the first time, I sang and played a tune. It was as simple as that. No editing, no revisions. One time through, and the song was done. I love it when it happens that way. The title of the song was "Reality, So Long."

It went like this:

> I felt the watchman's night stick
> So sticky on my mind
> I woke up apologizing
> For the waste of time
> I spent the fall in El Reno
> And then I wrote this song for you
> One morning in the courtroom
> The judge looked down at me
> He said, Son, for your own good
> Don't mess with reality
> It's the freedom of really knowing
> Of what can never be
> Reality, reality—so long
> When I reflect the pleasures, reflections offer me
> I know the thing I cannot count on is reality
> It's the freedom of really knowing what can never be
> Reality, reality—so long
> With time so short, the gates of heaven
> Are looking good to me
> Reality, reality

The gates of heaven are looking good to me
Reality, reality—so long
It's sobering what a drink will do
There's nothing higher than the truth
I'm scattered up and wondering
How it might have been
Loving you and knowing I could know real love again
My mind is my own mystery
I never did belong
Reality, reality—so long

———

By Bud Shrake and Gary P. Nunn under the pseudonym M. D. Shafter.
Performed by Gary on the *Lost Gonzo Band* MCA record, 1975.

I told you they were weird songs. But they do seem to contain food for thought and reflection, and I think there is deep emotion and creative expression in there. I could relate to many of the lines myself.

While all of this was going on, Jerry Jeff was wandering the corridors of Cowboy Central, and at this point, I will tell you a story as related to me by former World Champion Bronc Rider Monty "Hawkeye" Henson, whom I ran into recently on a trail ride. I was telling him about the story, and he said, "I was there, and I saw the whole thing!" According to Hawkeye, Jerry Jeff was meandering down the hallway in the hotel alone with a guitar in his hand, when a couple of cowboys grabbed him and physically ushered him into the suite where Bobby Steiner was holding court. They more or less insisted that he sing "Charlie Dunn" for Bobby and his entourage.

Well, it's not Jerry Jeff's nature to be coerced into doing anything he doesn't want to do. According to Hawkeye, Jerry Jeff sang the song but inserted some choice improvised lyrics that were not complimentary to Buck Steiner, Bobby's grandfather. That's when Bobby Steiner bolted and laid a few good punches on Jerry Jeff!

When Jerry Jeff walked into the room where Bud Shrake and I were hanging, it was apparent something bad had happened. His face was bruised and swollen, his shirttail was hanging half out, and he looked pretty much "rode hard and put up wet"! He mumbled something about those @#$%ing cowboys and proceeded to clear the tabletops with broad sweeps of his hands and arms, scattering half-filled drink cups, beer cans, and whisky bottles across the room while spewing undecipherable epithets at invisible cowboys! Bud Shrake looked at me, shrugged his shoulders, and calmly said, "See, Gary P., that's what I'm talkin' about: Reality, reality—so long!"

We were the hot item in Texas going into 1974, headlining the shows and festivals popping up around the state. We'd be in Dallas, and the Dallas Cowboys would show up and hang out backstage; in Santa Monica, it would be movie stars. It was always a big party when Jerry Jeff Walker and band were in town. We'd go to New York and play weeklong engagements at Kenny's Castaways when it was way uptown around 92nd Street. We'd sell out at least two shows every night.

Harry Belafonte, Kris Kristofferson, and Rita Coolidge would show up and hang out backstage. One night, Bonnie Bramlett of Delaney & Bonnie fame came by, and we jammed with her backstage. Another night, it was an unknown, curly-haired girl with round glasses dressed in denim jeans and jacket named Phoebe Snow.

We made the rounds on the East Coast, playing out on Long Island at My Father's Place with Larry Coryell, at Jonathan Swifts in Boston, and in Bryn Mawr, the college town near Philadelphia. Everywhere we went, it was the same: packed, enthusiastic audiences ready to hear the songs from his records and see what these fun-loving cowboys from Texas were all about. We seemed to be a breath of fresh air. We'd stay out for as much as three weekends in a row and come back to Austin to recover. We'd maybe do a show in Dallas or at the Armadillo World Headquarters or Castle Creek, and then it was back out again. It was fun, and we were making good money relative to what we had ever known. I was living cheap and saving most of what I made.

Tim O'Connor from Castle Creek had hooked up with Willie Nelson doing promotions and organized the 4th of July Picnic at the Texas World Speedway south of College Station. Things were really starting to roll—not only for Jerry Jeff but for Willie as well as other Texas artists. The word got out big time and it seemed the whole Texas music scene converged on College Station. Leon Russell gravitated toward Willie, and he ended up being the de facto master of ceremonies, for which he was uniquely suited. The whole picnic was being filmed and recorded for a movie.

Jerry Jeff was one of the top acts. When it was time for his show, it was well into the evening, and we kicked off with "Hi, Buckaroos" and proceeded to do a couple more tunes. He would always have me do "London Homesick Blues" early in the show to get it out of the way. I performed it to what had become the usual rousing response. By this time, all inhibitions were long gone. The consumption of tractor-trailer loads of Lone Star Beer and whatever other libertine stimulants had been consumed since early in the day was having its effect on the audience. Topless women wearing only misshapen cowboy hats and cutoff jeans were sitting atop the shoulders of drunken hippie/cowboys clutching cans of Lone Star Beer. This was the norm rather than the exception.

Right after I finished "London Homesick Blues," a drunken, wrinkled old lady approached the stage. She began demanding Jerry Jeff's attention before he could get another song under way. She began hollering to him in a hoarse, whisky-and-cigarette voice, "'Ere's been a deah!"

Jerry Jeff shouted back, "What?"

"'Ere's been a deah . . .'ere's been a deah!"

Finally, through some sort of beer-soaked translation, Jerry Jeff divined that she was saying, "There's been a death!" Well, naturally, this was cause for alarm, and all attention was focused on trying to locate the source of such a revelation. The result was that her ravings ruined the rest of Jerry Jeff's show, and by the time it was discovered that there was no such death, it was time for the next act to come on. The bottom line was that the bulk of Jerry Jeff's show just didn't happen. Consequently, he missed the opportunity to have his performance included in the movie that was being made.

However, my song did survive, and it was included in the film *A Willie Nelson 4th of July*.

SOME MONTHS LATER, POODIE Locke, Willie's lifelong roadie, called to inform me that the debut screening of the movie was to happen at a theater in Los Angeles, so I made arrangements to fly out. I'm pleased to report that after my song played in the film, the audience rose to its feet and gave it a standing ovation! After the screening, we went to a get-together at the Troubadour in Hollywood. Willie did a short set, and later I got to hang out with him; Tom Waits; and the Troubadour's famous owner, Doug Weston. That was quite an experience.

I was feeling pretty good about everything and thinking, *This might be my chance to be recognized as more than a backup musician and be one of those "Texas guys."* As it turned out, the film was canned. Damn again! I'm speculating here, but I think certain managers probably wouldn't grant permission for their acts to be shown without the payment of exorbitant fees. The movie has been acquired by other parties, is being remastered and upgraded to digital quality, and is expected to be released at some point in the future. It's been forty-two years—what's the rush?!

One night, we were playing a show at Mother Blues in Dallas

when I spied a tall, attractive young girl playing foosball. She was lively and full of humor and had the gift of gab. I found a way to engage her in conversation and discovered she played the guitar and wanted to be a singer and write songs. She was also a horsewoman who rode for Rex Cauble at his training facility near Denton. Her name was Karen Brooks. Rex Cauble owned the famous champion cutting horse Cutter Bill. *Hmmm,* I said to myself, *here's a tall, beautiful girl who likes music and is a hand with horses!*

My dad had always told me to marry a woman who was tall, intelligent, and dark complexioned. "I don't want any short, sunburned, freckled-faced grandkids running around here!" I took that to mean he didn't want any grandkids who looked like me! I understood what he meant, it didn't hurt my feelings, and I usually took his advice to heart.

I dubbed Karen "Dallas Alice." At first glance, she appeared to be a candidate for a wife that my dad would approve of. Over the next weeks and months, I pursued her with vigor and finally won her over. She moved to Austin and in with me at Public Domain, arriving in a silver 1964 Lincoln Continental with "suicide doors." She plunged right into the music scene and even started doing sit-ins and opening acts at Castle Creek. She made a point to get in with the crowd close to Jerry Jeff and Willie's circle. That practice would eventually lead to both desirable and undesirable results.

THE JERRY JEFF WALKER train was moving with a full head of steam by now. We went back into the studio and cut another record titled *Walker's Collectibles.* Jerry Jeff brought on organist Kelly Dunn, as well as the incredible sax player Tomas Ramirez. We did a live show at Castle Creek with a trombone player and a trumpet player that was recorded to supplement the *Walker's Collectibles* project.

The band did an opening show that was recorded and included one of my songs, "Rock Me, Roll Me," which was a full-blown rocker that I wrote on a train trip from Oklahoma City to Austin. He also included a studio cut of "Well of the Blues" on the album. The album didn't attract the same level of attention as *¡Viva Terlingua!* or produce any hits, but it contained a lot of good tunes that went over well with Jerry Jeff's hardcore fan base.

Events like these became our routine as time passed. We were touring one minute—and then we'd be back. The band was growing into an entity of its own, and we were writing songs and doing local gigs. We'd eat *migas* at Cisco's Bakery on East 6th Street or *huevos rancheros* with two pork chops at Hernandez Café. We'd go to Castle Creek and see Steve Goodman, or Steve Miller, and the James Cotton Blues Band . . . with Bonnie Raitt dropping by and sitting in. We'd check out the other acts who were making names for themselves. We saw Ray Charles at the Armadillo. We'd socialize. The clubs closed at midnight, so we'd go to Terry and Kathy Dubose's house and pick and write songs and hang out with Bud Shrake and Jap Cartwright. We'd spend afternoons at Jerry Jeff's house . . . one time, he threw his TV into the swimming pool . . .

Austin was such a cool little college town, and the University of Texas always had a winning football team. Rent and beer were cheap. The times were a-changing, and we seemed to be in the eye of the firestorm of change going on in Texas—ignited by the "improbable rise of redneck rock." (That's a reference to a book of that title by Austin writer Jan Reid.) I had a unique vantage point of the whole movement from Day One.

The band had changed somewhat over the months. As I mentioned, after *¡Viva Terlingua!* John Inmon came in. Michael McGeary and Jerry Jeff had gotten crossways, so Donny Dolan, a former band mate of John's from Temple, was brought in to play drums. Kelly Dunn and Tomas Ramirez became regulars in what had come to be known as the Lost Gonzo Band. This added the big B-3 Hammond organ and tenor-sax dynamic to the sound. Both were well schooled in R&B and jazz and both were outstanding players; plus, they had great senses of humor—Kelly's West Coast/San Diego perspective, and Tomas's south coast/Corpus Christi Hispanic take on things. Mix that in with Jerry Jeff's upstate New York rascal persona and Bob Livingston's easygoing but slightly scattered bundle of West Texas soul and good humor, and you had the makings for some fine entertainment. There was a constant stream of hilarious repartee going down. Donny, John, and I, being the least loquacious of the lot, generally sat back and enjoyed the show.

> Didn't we have us a ball
> We can now say that we've done it all
> We rode tall in the saddle, we answered the call
> Didn't we have us a ball

———

By Luke Reed. Performed by Gary P. Nunn on the CD
One Way or Another, Guacamole/Campfire Records, 2012

Before we knew it, Jerry Jeff was due another record for MCA. I was getting more and more focused on the songwriting and publishing side of the business. It seemed I had a knack for recognizing a good song and what artist it would suit—sort of a natural A & R guy. I was constantly on the lookout for songs. It became a hobby with me—if not a passion. It gives me much pleasure to discover a good song that otherwise might likely go unnoticed.

Michael Murphey taught me about writing songs, but Jerry Jeff taught me to keep an eye out for good songs. He always had his ears open for the next "keeper" to come along—whether we wrote it or not. Consequently, we were writing and attracting good songs and had a good collection gathered up when it was time to go back into the studio. Of course, the song list was up to Jerry Jeff's discretion, and he made the choice of what he wanted to record.

This time we were going to record in Nashville and use Nashville pickers for a rhythm section. We booked in Quad Studios whose "A-Team" rhythm section was the same Kenny Buttrey from the Murphey sessions on drums, Norbert Putnam on bass, and David Briggs, who had played for Elvis, on piano. Weldon Myrick was on steel, and fiddle overdubs were done by the master, Johnny Gimble.

John played guitar, and Kelly and Tomas were called in when they were needed. Bob, John, and I sang all the background vocals. I also went into the studio and ran down the songs for the session players. Michael Brovsky and Jerry Jeff always gave me free rein to do that, and I quietly took a great deal of satisfaction in being able to operate in that capacity. It gave me the opportunity to convey not only what I thought Jerry Jeff wanted but also to interject some ideas of my own about the production. I felt like I was hitting on all cylinders and hitting my stride in my natural element.

The album was called *Ridin' High,* and it's my favorite Jerry Jeff record. The song selection was excellent, with tunes written by me and Bob, John Inmon, Willie, Guy Clark, Michael Burton, Jessie Winchester, and Chuck Pyle. I also brought in a Bill Callery song from my publishing company called "Pot Can't Call the Kettle Black." The album ended with the quintessential Jerry Jeff Walker offering titled "Pissin' in the Wind"!

> Pissin' in the wind, bettin' on a losing friend
> Makin' the same mistakes we swore we'd never make again
> Pissin' in the wind, but it's blowing on all of our friends
> We're gonna sit and grin and tell our grandchildren

———

By Jerry Jeff Walker from the MCA LP *Ridin' High,* 1975

We were "shore nuff ridin' high" about this time.

Michael Brovsky negotiated a record contract for the Lost Gonzo Band with MCA Records. We went to Starday Studios outside of Nashville to record the first Lost Gonzo Band album. We gathered up the best of the songs we had written over the years, and Bob, John, and I shared the spotlight with each of us being featured individually.

That first record turned out good, I thought—we were compared to The Band. Jimmy Buffett dropped by Public Domain, and he gave it a listen and a thumbs-up. It was a departure from the Jerry Jeff thing, for sure. We had come out of the Beatles era and had been very much influenced by them, even though that era was winding down. We were always adaptable and could go wherever the music led. That was the great thing about the Lost Gonzo Band (LGB). Jerry Jeff was working a lot, and we were flying private planes to all our shows. The LGB had a record deal, and songwriting and publishing royalties were starting to come in. Things were pretty good.

KAREN AND I WERE still living at Public Domain, and my crazy cousin Milton X. Nunn was living in the groove shack. Milton was an unbelievable character—another book in himself. He substituted the T (for Tolliver) in his middle name with an X, as in Malcolm X. He fancied himself a Yancy Derringer–style Mississippi riverboat gambler, but he behaved more like a caricature of one. It's too bad Milton didn't live to see the age of reality TV. He would have been a superstar in the world we live in today. He was hilarious, but he caused me a lot of grief. He was always getting into trouble, and I was always the one who had to get him out. I won't say any more about him, but anybody who ever encountered him would not be likely to forget him and would be likely to have some outrageous Milton X. story of their own to tell.

Willie Nelson bought the old Terrace Motel on Academy just off South Congress Avenue and opened it as the Austin Opry House in early 1975, with Tim O'Connor managing and promoting shows there. Tim booked Jerry Jeff for the opener, and JJ had us all wearing these powder-blue tuxedos. Oh, what a sight! Here we all are, a bearded and long-haired mob with all manner of cowboy hats, wearing powder-blue tuxes with ruffled shirts and cummerbunds. There's a photo of us from that night in Jan Reid's book, *The Improbable Rise of Redneck Rock*. We looked like the Beverly Hillbilly Band on prom night!

Tim O'Connor, who was always on the cutting edge when it came to bringing talent to town, went all out at the Opry House. He brought in the Eagles, Boz Skaggs, Emmy Lou Harris, Waylon Jennings, David Crosby, and all manner of big-name acts. Of course, it was Willie's home base, and he played whenever he pleased. Waylon cut the hit record "Bob Wills Is Still the King" at a live performance there.

Austin had moved up in the music world since the days of the Club Saracen, the Jade Room, and the Saxon Pub. The Armadillo World Headquarters was going strong with big-time acts on a regular basis just a few blocks from the Opry House. Jerry Jeff Walker and the Lost Gonzo Band were right up there on top with all the other major acts.

Karen and I used to go up to the family ranch in Oklahoma and ride the horses my dad had bought for all us siblings prior to his passing. We brought two or three down to Austin and boarded them out at Manor Downs, where we would go almost every day and ride. It so happened that Frances Carr, an heiress from the Farenthold family, had acquired the old "brush track" racing facility and began upgrading it. She teamed up with Sam Cutler, the British former manager of the Grateful Dead noted for promoting the ill-fated Altamont Music Festival, and they were developing Manor Downs together. Sam Cutler had come to one of our shows, introduced himself, and invited me out to see what they were doing. We became acquainted, and he offered to let me keep horses in their stables.

Sam was quite a character with quite a history. It was a great experience listening to him tell stories of his early childhood when the Nazis were bombing London during the war, plus his many other interesting tales about his experiences with the Grateful Dead and the Rolling Stones. It was also really convenient to have horses to ride without driving all the way to Oklahoma.

Then one day, Karen informed me she was expecting! Honestly, we hadn't been getting along that well, but I made the commitment to dedicate myself to the relationship and to do my best to make it work. We got married at the Travis County Courthouse, and then went to Cisco's Bakery, where we ate almost every morning, for *migas*. I had found out quickly that Karen was not exactly the domestic type: We ate out 90 percent of the time. But we were in a family way together, and I was thrilled at the thought of having a child!

Toward the end of 1975, we went back to Nashville to make another recording, employing the same formula we'd used on the *Ridin' High* album and using the "A-Team" from Quad Studios again. Bob and I brought in songs we had written for consideration, and JJ was picking up others he liked by writers like Tom Waits, Lee Clayton, Billy Joe Shaver, and Keith Sykes. Bob brought in a Butch Hancock song and wrote "Head Full of Nothin'" as well as the title tune, "It's a Good Night for Singin'." I brought "Dear John Letter Lounge" by Rick Cardwell, the Bill Callery tune "Leroy," and a tune that I had cowritten with Karen called "Couldn't Do Nothin' Right." That song had originally been covered by Tracy Nelson and would later be Rosanne Cash's first single. *It's a Good Night for Singin'* was in the same vein as Jerry Jeff's previous records and every tune suited his style.

All the records subsequent to *¡Viva Terlingua!*, which had passed the million mark, were selling in the 350,000 to 400,000 range. Not million-sellers but not too bad. I was getting a taste for making decent royalties from both songwriting and publishing.

We were touring extensively throughout the United States in two private twin-engine Piper Navajos—from Los Angeles to Vancouver, BC, on the West Coast; from Jacksonville to Portland, Maine, on the East Coast; and all points in between. Bob and I always flew with JJ and his wife, Susan, who traveled with us a lot. The rest of the band and the road crew flew in the second plane.

We were running pretty hard, and Jerry Jeff was still not sleeping. If we were anywhere in the Southeast, he would take the plane immediately after the show and fly to New Orleans, stay up all night, and catch up with us the following morning in time to fly to the next gig. He'd get pretty stretched out and the more he did, the rougher he would be. He could be a real SOB! But Bob and I had a way of smoothing the rough edges, and most of the time it was fun. We would often fly to the next town after the shows and then sleep there. We'd play dominos and laugh and tell stories from liftoff till touchdown, with oxygen masks strapped to our faces for extra energy.

In 1975, Willie went to Dallas to cut a concept album called *Red Headed Stranger*. This was the record Nashville panned saying, "We make better demos than this." Obviously, Nashville didn't comprehend what Willie was all about or realize his potential and ability to connect with a mass audience if given the chance. He covered an old gospel song written way back when by Fred Rose called "Blue Eyes Crying in the Rain." It was recorded originally in 1947 by Roy Acuff and had been covered numerous times by country artists. It was a stroke of genius. The song was released as a single and went and stayed at the top of the charts.

The album went platinum, and Willie was on top from that point on. I confess that I didn't recognize his massive appeal either when I played those shows with him back in '72. Nevertheless, I did have the good fortune to benefit from it because he had included the Bill Callery song that I published called "Hands on the Wheel." My publishing credits were beginning to grow.

Our good friend Bobby Bridger, a great singer-songwriter and historian, had written an epic work about the beaver-trapping mountain men who pioneered the Rocky Mountain West in the early 1830s. Bobby is a direct descendant of Jim Bridger, who joined the Henry Expedition as a young man and went on to discover the Great Salt Lake. The work consisted of the historical narration libretto and a body of songs. Bobby wanted to record the project, so he enlisted the famous cowboy actor Slim Pickens to recite the narration and the Lost Gonzo Band for the musical tracks and background vocals. We went to Denver in the summer of 1975 to do the project.

Bobby knew a real-live mountain man from Gillette, Wyoming, named Timber Jack Joe and invited him to join us for atmosphere and authenticity. Timber Jack Joe set up a teepee in an isolated spot outside of Aurora and filled it with beaver pelts and other furs. We would record in a studio not too far distant until all hours. Then we would retreat to the teepee, where we would pass around a gallon jug of white lightning and listen to Slim Pickens and Timber Jack Joe tell incredible stories. It was quite an inspirational project, and it turned out very well. We were paid in beaver pelts!

Bobby has just recently remastered, digitalized, and rereleased the project, which is called *Seekers of the Fleece*. It's a most timely release considering the popularity of the film *The Revenant*, starring Leonardo DiCaprio, which very accurately portrays the very story contained in Bobby Bridger's work.

LIFE FOR ME WAS a blur of activity that centered around Jerry Jeff's whirlwind of nationwide touring, the sidebar projects with the Lost Gonzo Band, and my relationship with Karen.

Karen and I lived a Spartan existence at Public Domain. We

had no air-conditioning and slept on the living room floor under a ceiling fan on a pallet made out of one of the tumbling mats Michael Murphey and I had bought back in '72. It was actually one of the most comfortable beds I've ever slept on. Karen progressed in her pregnancy, and that was a thrilling experience. But it was becoming clear that she and I did not see eye to eye about much of anything.

It was also clear that she was intent on having her own career and that mine represented a barrier to hers. That fact was the basis for the ultimate conflict that was to come. But we did make it through the pregnancy, and that happy day in March finally arrived. Lukin was born at Seton Hospital. I was as happy and proud as any father ever was!

The day after, I decided to get a 35 mm camera so I could take pictures of his growing up. I went to my good friend Scott Newton to ask for advice about what kind of camera to buy, as he was starting out as a professional photographer. He advised me to get a Canon Sure Shot 35 mm. It was a simple camera that didn't require all the knowledge of apertures and f-stops that some cameras did. Just point and shoot. He also advised me to use 400 black-and-white film. It would give me the best chance to get good photos in most situations, particularly low-light ones. I took his advice and bought one. The first roll of film I have in my extensive photo file is of Lukin in the baby basket the day we brought him home from the hospital. That was the beginning of my photography career—which I intend to follow up on as soon as I finish this book!

Scott Newton did all my processing and printing for years and helped me in many ways. Universally recognized as one of the top photographers in Austin, he was selected from Day One as the official photographer of *Austin City Limits*. His catalogue of every artist who ever played on that stage is second to none.

I started carrying that camera and taking pictures of everyone I ran into from that point in 1976. It's quite a collection, if I do say so myself—a very good photo document of the people and places I encountered during that period. The Bicentennial Year of 1976 was highlighted not only by the birth of Lukin Tolliver Nunn, but also by the Fourth of July celebration of the two hundredth year since the signing of that most inspired document, the Declaration of Independence.

We were booked to headline a show at the Superdome in New Orleans, where Jerry Jeff was always a big draw because of "Mr. Bojangles," which he wrote. We were also booked for Willie's 4th of July Picnic, which was to be held in a pasture near Gonzales, Texas. Jerry Jeff hired an extra plane, and all the wives and girlfriends came as well. We opened Willie's picnic at 9:00 a.m. I had my little camera with me, and I was shooting away.

Showtime arrived, and no sooner had I sat down at the piano than I heard a voice in my ear. "Hey man, mind if I sit in on piano?" I looked up to see Leon Russell.

"Be my guest," I said, as I relinquished the piano stool to him.

I grabbed the little guitar I always carried with me and danced around onstage singing backup harmony during Jerry Jeff's show.

There is an excellent Scott Newton photo that depicts the scene. You'd be amazed how much of a party atmosphere can be generated at 9:00 a.m. at a Willie Nelson Bicentennial 4th of July Picnic!

We finished the show, hopped back on the planes, and flew to New Orleans. Jerry Jeff had gone all out and hired Kenny Buttrey and Norbert Putnam to come down and play drums and bass. He booked us all into nice rooms at the top-of-the-line La Louisiane in the French Quarter. Everyone ate oysters (except me, as I am allergic to them) for lunch, laid about the hotel pool, and chilled out waiting for showtime.

John Sebastian, formerly of The Lovin' Spoonful, and, I think, Charlie Daniels were openers. When we started our show, the huge electronic message display in the Superdome was flashing: "JERRY JEFF WALKER—JERRY JEFF WALKER—JERRY JEFF WALKER" was spinning around the dome. Suddenly, someone started dropping lit packages of fireworks off the upper level. There was popping and flashing and smoke descending toward the floor! Immediately, the digital message display started flashing: "WARN-ING—DANGER—JERRY JEFF WALKER—WARNING—DANGER" as we were up on the stage doing "Hi, Buckaroos." It was crazy! Jerry Jeff had a way of bringing out the natural "savage beast" in people.

The Gonzo Band went back to Nashville and cut another record that was called *Thrills*. Again, it was a collection of tunes that Bob, John, and I had written. Each of us was featured on our own tunes. I included for my part a tune by Roger Bartlett and a Walter Hyatt love ballad called "I'll Come Knockin'," that was covered by Lyle Lovett some thirty years later. I also cut my first version of "The Last Thing I Needed."

Analyzing MCA's promotional efforts in hindsight shows that because the focus was spread among Bob, John Inmon, and me, it was difficult for the record company to know how to promote the product. Jerry Jeff decided for his next record project that he would go back to Luckenbach and try to recapture the magic achieved with *¡Viva Terlingua!*

Just as the mud daubers return to Luckenbach, we descended again on the tiny Hill Country hamlet.

Using the same formula that had worked so well in the past, JJ gathered up a group of good songs from a wide range of sources, including Rusty Wier, Rodney Crowell, Bob Dylan, Paul Siebel, "live" re-dos of "Mr. Bojangles" and "L.A. Freeway," and other songs he had written. Once again, he picked a song by Rick Cardwell out of my publishing company called "The Old Rockin' Chair," plus David Gilstrap's "Ro-deo-deo-Cowboy," and a song Bob and I had cowritten called "Roll on Down the Road." Charles John Quarto wrote and recited a couple of touching poems about Hondo. Jerry Jeff titled the project *A Man Must Carry On.*

The record opened with a song called "Stereo Chickens." One evening, we were sitting under the big oak tree behind the beer joint/post office. The resident Luckenbach chickens were going to roost and cackling in the limbs above our heads. It brought the musical *The Music Man* to my mind: There was a song that likened chickens clucking to women's gossipy chatter. It had a lot of repetition of the words "pick a little" and "talk a little" and "cheep-cheep-cheep" as the bed of the song. On top of it was the tune we all know:

> Good night, ladies,
> Good night, ladies,
> Good night, ladies,
> We're going to leave you now.

I taught the pick a little, talk a little part to Bob and we started singing it. On top of that, Jerry Jeff and the others chimed in with the "Good night, ladies" part. We were having a ball with it and so were the onlookers.

Fortunately, there were a couple of microphones hanging in the trees that fed the signal to the recording truck, and the whole thing was recorded live and it became the album opener! That was a classic example of how unconventional the whole Jerry Jeff Walker thing was. People loved it!

Karen and I didn't stay in town at the Peach Tree Inn with the group, but instead, we camped in my Tyson (developed by Ian Tyson) teepee across Grape Creek with Lukin, who was about six months old. I thought it was earthy and cool; I'm not sure how Karen felt about camping out in a teepee, but she didn't complain.

She did have a detached, faraway look about her the whole time we were there. She sang harmony on some of the tracks.

A quick review of my photo file reminds me of the cast of musical characters who were present while we were doing these recordings. In addition to the band—which included Bob Livingston, John Inmon, Kelly Dunn, Donny Dolan, and Jerry Jeff and Susan Walker—was producer Michael Brovsky; audio engineers Dale Ashby and father; our faithful roadie, Jack, "the miserable Pud" Borders; Patterson Barrett; Bill Callery; Milton Carroll; David Gilstrap; Frank Hill; Kent Finley; Rex Foster; Lee McCullough; Kathy Morgan; and of course, our beloved Hondo Crouch!

The morning after the project wrapped up, Luckenbach was abandoned and quiet. I packed up and loaded the teepee in the pickup, and we walked across the bridge over Grape Creek to say our goodbyes. Only Kathy Morgan, Hondo's partner, was there. We told her we were going to mosey on.

Kathy said, "No, you can't go yet. Hondo just called from town, and he wants you to wait till he gets back before you leave!" Hondo was always partial to Lukin, partly because of his name. He would brag about him being named after Luckenbach.

It wasn't long before Hondo returned with a gift for Lukin. It was a little train engineer's outfit complete with overalls, a red bandana, and a little engineer's cap. We dressed him in it, and I took photographs of him and Hondo. I just happened to have been shooting color slides that day, but I have inexplicably lost track of them. I knew exactly where they were until I went to look for them.

I gave some of the slides I had taken of Hondo to Charles Phillip Vaughn, the noted pencil artist, whose realistic drawings of Willie, John Wayne, and the Alamo are well known. He also did one of me. Two of his drawings of Hondo were done from those slides. One was the classic of Hondo in his sheepish pose with his hand over his mouth, and the other was the last picture I took of Hondo. He was standing in the doorway of the Luckenbach bar. He had a sad look in his eyes, his right hand lifted, with his fingertips signaling a final goodbye. It was the last time I saw Hondo.

A week after we left, The Grand Imagineer, the Clown Prince of Luckenbach, the Enchanter of Children of all Ages, was gone. His spirit will always remain.

WE WERE BACK ON the planes and blowing and going again, and Jerry Jeff continued his drinking and staying up all night. It was beginning to wear on everybody.

We did another East Coast tour highlighted by an appearance at Carnegie Hall! Doug Sahm opened, and the show was sold out. I'm not sure Carnegie Hall had ever experienced anything like Jerry Jeff Walker and the Lost Gonzo Band—just about as far from classical music as you can get! We did the show and went downtown to Kenny's Castaways, as Kenny had moved his venue from uptown down to the Village. We entered the bar like a hurricane with JJ leading the way. He was "roaring," no doubt. An old man sitting at the bar said to Jerry Jeff, "Young feller, you better slow down or you're not going to last too long!"

Jerry Jeff retorted without a moment's hesitation, "Old man, you may be older than me, but I've been awake more than you have!"

One morning that fall, we were packing up to head for the planes, but Jerry Jeff was nowhere to be found. When we got to the airfield, we found him asleep in the copilot's seat. We learned from our pilot that the night before, the police had gotten after him, and he managed to get to the airfield without being apprehended. He was in rough shape. His wife, Susan, was pissed! We were all aggravated.

As we got under way and up to cruising altitude, he would rouse and try to make light of the situation. But no one was buying it. After a few unsuccessful attempts at humor to ease the tension, Jerry Jeff grabbed the wheel and put the plane into a hard right turn! Our pilot quickly recovered and got us leveled out, but for me, the damage was done. The second plane always followed ours at the same altitude and not too far back. It occurred to me that we could have had a midair collision of both planes, and we would've all been dead!

We reached our destination in Memphis. I gathered the band together and informed them that in light of that incident, it was my intention to leave Jerry Jeff after the New Year's Eve show coming up. Everyone agreed it was all getting out of hand. The whole crew joined in the impending exodus!

It broke my heart because I loved Jerry Jeff. I loved his creativity, his music, and his humor. I even appreciated his rascally nature, although it was totally contrary to my own. Most certainly I appreciated the opportunities he afforded me to be creative and productive in a professional setting. I felt like I was leaving a part of myself behind.

To cap off the whole journey, we played a huge show at the Summit in Houston for New Year's Eve with Willie and a host of other big-name acts—none of whom were big-name acts when we started this thing back in '72.

Here's a note Jerry Jeff wrote for me many years later . . .

Nov 26, 1997

Gary P. Nunn's talent was at the core of the Lost Gonzo Band I used on my first three or four albums in Texas.

Without Gary's artistic vision and musical leadership, I would not have enjoyed the same amount of success that I have.

Thanks, buddy,
Signed
Jerry Jeff Walker

Thank you, Jerry Jeff! Didn't we have us a ball?

Chapter 9

Lost Gonzo Band

THE DEPARTURE FROM THE Jerry Jeff whirlwind represented a significant setback in the fortunes of the Lost Gonzo Band. No longer were we flying around in private planes, staying in the best hotels, or earning $700 a week. Instead, we purchased an oversized cargo van that was outfitted to carry most of the band and our roadies in the cab. We also had a new Oldsmobile station wagon in which Bob and I usually traveled.

We had the record deal with MCA with a production budget of $100,000 per record. They subsidized some of the touring that took us to the East and West Coasts, and we played many of the same rooms we had worked in the early days with Jerry Jeff. But the excitement created by the combination of JJ and the Lost Gonzo Band did not follow us.

MCA's efforts to promote our record left a lot to be desired. We found ourselves playing to half-filled rooms on tour. In Austin, we played in local clubs like Castle Creek and George and Carlyne Majewski's Soap Creek Saloon, which was in a party barn building in the cedar breaks outside Austin to the southwest.

That was the same building where I had first seen sixteen-year-old Jimmie Vaughan and the Chessmen back in '66 when I was with the Sparkles. It was the favorite watering hole for Austin "heads," and featured Alvin Crow, Greasy Wheels, Freda and the Firedogs with Marcia Ball, and Doug Sahm, when he wanted to play locally. We had a loyal local following and drew good crowds, but we were back at a place that was not a great deal farther along than we had been before the "Cosmic Cowboy Scare," as Steven Fromholz characterized the movement.

Michael Brovsky relocated his offices from New York to Austin and started producing records for Guy Clark, Marcia Ball, the LGB, and Jerry Jeff and his new group called the Bandito Band.

I had a regular routine (run ten "klicks" around Town Lake; swim the length of Barton Springs pool twice; have brunch at Cisco's Bakery) after which I would drop by his office to visit and talk business.

One day, he sat me down and said, "I want to talk to you. Gary P., I have more to do than I can handle here at Free Flow Productions, and I need some help. I was wondering if you would be interested to come on board as staff producer. I think you have what it takes to be a great producer."

Wow! There was a man with a bona fide production company and a proven and successful track record offering me the job I'd always wanted. I was flattered. I was thrilled. I was happy.

"Here's what I am proposing," he said. "You find the acts that you would like to produce. You produce the records, and I will get the record deals."

I was totally jazzed and thought this might be the road to get me where I'd like to be. One small step in a journey of steps.

Although I had had no official designated role, Michael and I had always worked quietly in tandem on the Jerry Jeff project. I did what I could to keep Jerry Jeff "between the ditches" while on the road. I took a leadership role within the band and did my best to make sure we did the best shows possible—regardless of what condition JJ was in. Michael recognized my contributions along those lines. He also encouraged my bringing in good songs and gave me a free rein in the studio to test my production skills. I had always made it my business to get around and see who was drawing good crowds and creating excitement and writing good songs. I didn't rush in, but I waited for an act that had real star potential to appear. I'm sure this all contributed to his offering to take me on as a producer.

One Sunday afternoon in Houston, I had the opportunity to check out an act that I was hearing about. This fellow and his acoustic band, The Ewing Street Times, were playing for a packed house, 90 percent of which were pretty Houston hippie girls who didn't shave their legs! Most of them were in some kind of enchanted state. They were dancing and had in hand aluminum cans and glass jars partially filled with dry pinto beans. When they shook the jars, they made effective homemade percussion instruments. *Shake . . . shake . . . shake.*

The star of the band was demure and handsome, with Paul McCartney-ish features, who like Paul McCartney, played guitar left-handed. He had a sexy, slightly raspy voice and great hair. His songs were sweet, beautifully written, and innocently romantic. It was obvious every girl in the place had a crush on him. His name was Shake Russell. I hadn't seen him since that morning back in '72 when he and Johnny Vandiver had arrived at Michael Murphey's house on Comanche Trail.

When I got back to Austin, I immediately went to Michael Brovsky's office to inform him I had found the act I wanted to produce. I had picked up an album Shake had made called *Songs on the Radio,* a live recording made on a Houston radio station, plus a cassette of unreleased studio demos. I played the music for Michael and described the scene I had witnessed in Houston, including the incredible excitement he created, especially with his female audience.

My concept was to rerecord what he had done to get better quality recordings. Emulating Bob Johnston, whom I had observed closely during the Murphey sessions, I viewed my role as one where I would make him comfortable and give him his creative head. He had already demonstrated he could make good recordings. They just needed to be upgraded to a quality that could compete in the national marketplace.

I was convinced that he had real star potential. I envisioned a full-blown promotional campaign with him touring in major markets and his picture being posted all over New York, Boston, Philadelphia, and other major cities. I envisioned him appearing on the Johnny Carson show and me doing everything possible to get him in front of a mass audience. If only people could see and hear him, I had no doubt they would fall in love with him. Where the women go, the men will follow. Michael agreed and said, "Let's do it!"

I contacted Shake and asked him for a meeting in Austin. We met at Cisco's Bakery for breakfast, and I gave him my pitch. His manager, John Moss, was with him. I said, "I have been retained as producer for Free Flow Productions, and I want to make a record for you. I'll produce the album and Michael Brovsky will get you a contract with a major record company."

They received the news with interest but quiet reserve, and I arranged to have a meeting with Michael at their earliest convenience. We met with them at Michael's studio in the Rapp's Cleaners location on 6th Street in Austin. Michael repeated the proposal I had presented. They responded that they were interested, but wanted to include Dana Cooper in the project and make a Shake Russell/Dana Cooper Band record!

This was a shock to me, as I hadn't seen or heard of Dana Cooper except for his harmony vocals on the live *Songs on the Radio* album. Michael looked at me with a puzzled look on his face and said, "What's this deal with Dana Cooper?" I replied that I didn't know.

John Moss took charge, and he was adamant that they wouldn't consider any alternative except to have Dana Cooper sharing equal billing with Shake. *Wow!* I was thinking. *Who does this guy represent? Shake Russell, who's standing right here . . . or the unseen Dana Cooper?*

Both Michael and I were dumbfounded. That put a monkey wrench in the whole concept of the project! My idea was to use Shake's picture on bills plastered all over Manhattan. His boyish good looks would be a major selling point in promoting him. I had nothing against Dana Cooper, but adding another face to the picture would totally distract from the image I had in mind, and one not as likely to succeed, in my opinion.

I made an alternate proposal: "How about we make a Shake Russell album, and then cut a record for Dana Cooper? Dana can sing on it if you like. Instead of cutting something in half, why not double it?"

No, that wasn't acceptable. It had to be Shake Russell/Dana Cooper. Apparently Dana had some powerful, controlling influence on both Shake and John Moss. I was disappointed and not nearly as enthusiastic about that scenario, but we reluctantly acquiesced and agreed to move forward.

The Lost Gonzo Band was scheduled to tour the East Coast. We played The Bitter End in New York and Jonathan Swifts in Boston, and other not so memorable gigs. We had added former Sparkle Bobby Smith to play bass. I was interested to shed the bass and be more of an up-front guy, and Bob was of the same mind. It was a mistake to give up the bass, since to a great degree, it meant giving up control of the rhythm section and the dynamics and the groove, which were never the same afterward. Donny Dolan was tired of traveling so much, so he dropped off the wagon, and we replaced him with Michael Holleman, a good kid with lots of licks.

When we returned from that trip, I discovered that Shake and Dana had gone into the studio and recorded the record in my absence! I was pissed, big time. This was my project, and they had done it behind my back! How could this happen? I felt disrespected.

I had been totally up front with them about my position. When I confronted Michael about it, he was rather evasive about how it all went down.

I calmed down after I heard the record, but the Shake Russell sound I had heard was nowhere to be found. It was a total departure from what I had in mind and didn't come close to the original recordings. Certainly, it didn't meet my standards. I felt that a huge opportunity had been squandered, but I was more disappointed for Shake's sake than for my own.

IT WAS APPARENT THAT my focus was starting to extend beyond just playing with the Lost Gonzo Band. I was writing more and pursuing my publishing company interests. Other writers were starting to attract my interest. I had published tunes by Rick Cardwell, Bill Callery, and David Gilstrap, that Jerry Jeff had recorded, and a Roger Bartlett tune that appeared in the hit horror movie *Texas Chainsaw Massacre*. I didn't have any more opportunities to place tunes with JJW since our "bailing out of the airplane." Instead, I focused on songs that I might pitch to other artists, or that suited me in the LGB.

I started looking for another act to produce. I had been very interested in Shake Russell's writing, but that was put on the back burner in light of the recent project gone south. It wasn't long before another opportunity presented itself. A former MCA record promoter turned A & R man named Jack Parker was coming to Austin. He contacted me and wanted to meet, so he came by Public Domain. He informed me that he had been authorized by MCA to sign five artists from Texas! This indicated just how hot the Texas music scene was becoming as a result of all the artists "breaking out" from here. He asked for my advice and who I would recommend.

The artists at the top of my list were Shake Russell, but he was already gone; Eliza Gilkyson, whom I had become aware of on my trips to Santa Fe; and last but not least, Joe Ely, from Lubbock. Joe had been cutting some tracks in Don Caldwell's Studio in Lubbock on Avenue Q , with Lloyd Maines engineering. This was the same building where Harrods Music store was located when I was a kid.

Fellow Lubbockite Bob Livingston had acquired some of those tapes and passed them on to me. I was very impressed by what I heard. I told Jack Parker that all these performers were great songwriters and singers, but in my opinion, Joe Ely was the one with the most immediately realizable potential. He had a working band and his Texas "flatlander" music fit squarely in with what was going on in Texas.

"He's got what it takes, and he's ready to go right now!" I told him.

I informed Jack about my relationship with Free Flow Productions, and my condition was that I be the producer if a deal could be struck. He gave his approval.

I met with Joe and his manager, Johnny Hughes, in Lubbock and relayed the information.

Once again, I laid it out for them: "I can get you a record deal with MCA, and I will be the producer. Are you interested?"

"Oh yeah, we are very interested!"

I relayed the news to Michael Brovsky. When I played him the tapes, he was enthusiastic about taking on the project. I put Michael in touch with them and Jack Parker. A few months go by. I was not overly concerned. I figured Michael Brovsky was working the Joe Ely project through the MCA assembly line. Next thing I knew, Joe Ely had released an album on MCA produced by Chip Young! Once again, it's "What the hell?"

And once again, I ended up on the cutting room floor. Invisible. Out of the picture.

I hadn't bothered to draw up written agreements with Michael, Shake, or Joe, so I was left with a handful of nothing. And there was nothing I could do about it but chalk it up as a learning experience. Blow by blow, I was getting an education. I have no hard feelings whatsoever about either of these incidents, and it has been my pleasure to watch these acts become successful. I'm not the least bit surprised, after all. I just want to set the record straight.

Needless to say, I brought no more acts to Free Flow with the expectation of producing. Later on, I did guide Eliza Gilkyson in, but I had nothing to do with the project Michael did for her. Another act had shown up in Austin that was attracting my attention. They were introduced to us via Willis Alan Ramsey, who described them as the "Bluegrass Beatles." They called themselves Uncle Walt's Band.

Uncle Walt's Band consisted of three handsome young men out of Spartanburg, South Carolina, who like pioneers of old, had made their way to Tennessee, before seeking their destinies in Texas (hoping not to end up in the Alamo). They were Walter Hyatt, who played acoustic guitar; DeChamps ("Champ") Hood, who played acoustic guitar and fiddle; and David Ball, who played bass fiddle. When one sang lead, he was backed up by the other two on harmonies. They were new and different and brought touches of Appalachian traditional bluegrass and jazz influences with them. It was a different and more refreshing sound than we were used to in Texas. They sang in beautiful, three-part harmony topped off by David Ball's natural high tenor voice. They, also, were a hit with the ladies. They wrote great songs that went straight to the heart—to my heart, anyway.

I was fascinated and delighted by them, not only for their wonderful music, but also for the fact that they were just the nicest and most pleasant people. They all spoke with that soft western South Carolina drawl. I was listening and scrutinizing their repertoire for songs that I could record myself and hopefully place with other artists. I ended up recording several.

This is typical of where my head was at that time. My creative head, anyway. In the real world, it was a different story.

MY RELATIONSHIPS WERE BEGINNING to deteriorate. It seemed that everyone I was involved with, personally and professionally, had developed an adversarial attitude toward me, with the notable exception of Michael Brovsky. Karen and I couldn't agree about the time of day. She was visibly disappointed that we had separated from Jerry Jeff, and my leaving took us out of the circle of stars—the circle she made a point of being part of.

When I returned home from road trips with the LGB, I'd hear stories about how she'd been out on the town with the in-crowd. When I'd come home, she'd say, "I'm so tired of staying home. You keep Lukin tonight. I've got to get out of this house, or I'm going to go crazy!" She would leave about sundown and come home about sunup and sleep till afternoon.

One day, I had had enough and confronted her.

"When are you going to get out of that bed?"

Well, that was the punk that blew up the fireworks factory! There was no putting anything back together after the confrontation that ensued.

She took Lukin and left, never to return.

For the longest time, there was a knot in my gut. Again, I was an emotional wreck.

To compound this, it seemed the guys in the LGB were starting to pull away, challenging me on even the most trivial of issues. There was a leadership vacuum. I should have been the natural leader, as I was the oldest and most experienced and it was the role I was used to, but my attempts to assume that role were being met with greater and greater resistance.

They were unaware of the fact that the record deal we had with MCA was one that Michael Brovsky had secured for me as a single artist! I had chosen to share it with them but kept that fact to myself. I did it because I loved and believed in them and wanted them to have the opportunity as well. We had always worked so well together before. It was tough enduring the resistance, knowing what I knew. It only added to my emotional turmoil.

During this time, I made a few trips to Santa Fe. They were good therapy, and I could get relief from the stress of my situation in Austin. I ran into and befriended a group of people in and around the budding music scene in the area. Among them were the Jackson sisters! These girls—Sally, Kelly, and Polly—were full-of-fun migrants from Midland, Texas, and had taken to the Santa Fe lifestyle. They took me arm in arm and gave me the "green chili" grand tour from Madrid to Tesuque, all the while imparting to me the Nirvana-seeking philosophy of life in Santa Fe. They were the ones who introduced me to Eliza (then Lisa) Gilkyson. Like the State of New Mexico, I was "enchanted" by the whole experience.

At one point, Sally said, "Gary P., I think I'm interested in learning about the music business. Would you be interested in taking me on as an intern?" This was prior to my breakup with Karen, and I gave it some thought, considering the possible effects of bringing another female into the mix, but I decided that the potential benefits outweighed the risks. It would be very helpful to have someone to cover me in my absence, help me keep track of my publishing business, and just be someone I could depend on for assistance. It would be simple to teach her the basics of the music business as we went along.

I contacted Sally and told her to "come on down." She arrived the very day Karen and I had our blowup. I'm sure she was thinking,

What in the world have I gotten myself into? Actually, it was all over and done with quickly, and Sally wasn't exposed to it directly, so it wasn't much of an issue with her. I put her up in Public Domain, and I took up residence in Milton's vacated groove shack. Milton had skipped town and gone out to Malibu before the law could lay hands on him. His lengthy rap sheet of petty crimes and misdemeanors had finally caught up with him.

Karen was gone. I knew in my heart that the day was going to come, so I didn't expect the heartache I was experiencing. My sternum had turned to stone. I couldn't sleep. I couldn't eat. A lot of it was the loss I felt from having Lukin taken away from me. He was a year old, and I had bonded with him during our times alone together.

My main concern was what was going to become of him. I had visions of teaching him how to play ball, helping him with his school lessons, and just being a dad to be around to watch him grow up. Hopefully I could give him some guidance and direction that would be beneficial to him in life. Now, that was all up in the air. *Had I lost my son?* Those thoughts plagued my mind and haunted my dreams.

As it turned out, Karen was only too happy to let me keep Lukin at every opportunity, so I had him for quite lengthy stretches until he became of school age. Sally Jackson was invaluable during that time as she cheerfully took on the task of caring for him when I needed her, for which I will always be eternally grateful.

During that time, I was playing hurt, but I kept on playing. I managed to maintain a delicate balance with my emotions and my relationship with the Gonzos. We dropped our record deal with MCA, and Michael Brovsky got us signed with Capitol Records. Capitol was the epitome of the record industry, having had the Beatles on their label and with their circular corporate offices in Hollywood resembling a stack of records. Perhaps now, we would get something happening.

We recorded in Michael Brovsky's newly named Pecan Street Studio. I had written a few songs, mostly about my feelings about Karen, and had selected tunes from my publishing company by Michael Burton, Walter Hyatt, and Mike Acklin that portrayed accurately how I was feeling at the time.

My philosophy about making records is not unlike how I imagine visual artists or painters might view their work: "How can I best communicate what I am feeling through this medium?" I never approached it from the standpoint of "I'm going to make a hit record and be a big star!" My philosophy was "Take this audio expression, hang it on the wall, and sell it if you can. I'm moving on to the next song." This illustrated how my head was more into the songwriting/publishing/producing aspect than it was into the performance side.

Certainly on the performance side, if you do get a hit record, you spend the rest of your life singing the same song! Creatively, this is stifling. Picasso didn't have to repaint the same picture for an audience every night. He'd paint another picture. In contrast, I viewed my role as a would-be producer as doing my best to cut a hit record and make somebody else a star. Unfortunately, my efforts in that area seemed to have been blocked from all memory but my own.

We recorded the album for Capitol Records in early 1978. When it was due for release and we were slated to tour to promote it, I took it on myself to fly to Los Angeles for a meeting with Capitol and representatives from Athena Artists, our booking agents now operating out of California. I met with our agent, George Carroll, from Athena Artists, and the Capitol rep in charge of our project at Capitol's headquarters. My purpose was to make sure that the record company and the booking agent were on the same page so we could maximize the effect of our tour.

"Okay, George," I said to the agent, "here is the person in charge of promotion for this upcoming tour."

To the Capitol promotion guy, I said, "Mr. Head of Promotions, here is the guy in charge of booking the tour. Now that you know each other, it would be so nice if you would coordinate your efforts, so that when Mr. Agent books a show, Capitol Records is in town with a full-blown promotional blitz!"

They both seemed to be in complete agreement. I left the meeting feeling good about our prospects.

Karen was living in Los Angeles with her mother and scouting for opportunities for herself in the Los Angeles music scene. One of the first things she did was to find out where the Eagles ate Mexican food. I got in touch with her and arranged to pick up Lukin so I could spend some time with him. We went out to Malibu and hooked up with Cousin Milton. We stayed with him and his new lady, the daughter of a famous movie producer, who had built a house on a large piece of property overlooking the Pacific Ocean up the coast a bit from Malibu above Trancas, California.

Milton always made it a point to hook up with wealthy women. Erin Murphy was the classic "earth mother." She had a house full of kids of her own, the children of her deceased sister that she had adopted, plus a baby girl, Sarah, whom she had with Milton. Sarah was my own blood kin. Erin owned a vacant beachfront lot, so we went down there a lot and played with the kids on the beach. I have many good photos of that lovely day. The kids were blissfully naked. After all, it was California.

I was staying in Hollywood with my friend Joy Houck Jr., another past resident at Public Domain, who had shown up on my doorstep one day. Joy's father owned a chain of theaters throughout the South and was a heavy hitter in the movie industry. We were invited to join him for lunch at an exclusive, private club. When we approached the entrance of the club, we couldn't help but notice the beautiful brand-new Rolls Royce parked in front. We were escorted by the maître d' to Joy Houck Sr.'s table. He was having lunch with the famous cowboy movie actor Ben Johnson. We were totally in awe, and though we were grown men, we both felt like little boys in the presence of these two giants in the movie business.

I had also gotten in touch with a California lady, Jan Smithers, I had met through Bob Livingston. They had had a touch-and-go relationship while he lived in California, and we had run into her a couple of times while on the road with the band out there. She and I had become acquainted, strictly on a friendly basis. Jan had just landed a starring role in a brand-new sitcom called *WKRP in Cincinnati.* She was busy one day with a promotional photo shoot with the cast of the show, but she said, "We're going to all have lunch together after the photo shoot. Why don't you join us?" I replied that I had my two-year-old son Lukin with me. She told me to bring him along. So Lukin and I had lunch with the cast of *WKRP* and were welcomed with open arms. Very cool!

All in all, it was an exciting, spur-of-the-moment excursion to Hollywood. I had gotten to spend some quality time with Lukin, see Cousin Milton and his baby daughter, have lunch with Ben Johnson, have another lunch with the cast of *WKRP*, and I was optimistic about the meeting I had at Capitol Records. I flew home feeling pretty good about myself.

THE CAPITOL RECORD WAS called *Signs of Life* and was due for release. It contained a list of good songs, and we had made a good record. One problem was that by this time, the world was looking for party songs. Our songs were heartfelt, reflective, and sensitive expressions, probably more suited to the mid-sixties than the late seventies. Timing is critical, but promotion is everything.

When the time came to hit the road for the record promotion tour, there was a major issue: There were only two shows on the itinerary! The first was in Eugene, Oregon, and the second in Vancouver, BC! *What the hell?* We're supposed to drive all that way for two shows? How stupid is this? This was not at all what I had envisioned when I had the meeting with George Carroll and Mr. Capitol Records Promotion Man.

The tour money was budgeted, so we rationalized we should go through with it. We hit the road with the band and roadie guys in the outfitted van, and Bob and I drove the Olds station wagon. We got an early start and drove nonstop, arriving in Las Vegas around midnight the second night. I recall that they served free breakfasts in the casinos, so we stopped and grazed on the breakfast buffet, climbed back in the vehicles, and started driving again. I think we stopped again and slept at some point, and then drove through to Eugene and went to bed.

The next morning, we got up and went to scout the university area, the venue, and the record shops, looking for signs of promotion of our show and the new record. The only indication of either was a small sign on the marquee at the venue that said, simply, The Lost Gonzo Band. A search of the local rag revealed no ads for our show. There were no bills posted anywhere. There were no records or promotional materials in any of the record shops in the area!

Unbelievable! We drove 1,700 miles for this? I got on the phone to try to find out where the Capitol Records promotion man was. Oh, he's vacationing in Hawaii. Damn! They send us from Austin, Texas, to Eugene, Oregon, and they go on vacation! The realization was staggering: We were not at the bottom of the list of priorities at Capitol Records—we were not even *on* the list of priorities! We did the show, of which I have no recollection whatsoever. We packed up and drove to Vancouver, where we were booked at the famous old Commodore Ballroom for a rerun of the same horror movie.

I don't remember anything about that show either. I think my mind was blown and so incapable of recalling such unpleasant memories. I do recall that we had a little incident at the US–Canadian border where we were delayed briefly over an issue about some bird-seed found in the crease of the car seat. I explained to the female

Canadian border patrol agent that we had just been to a carwash and had gone through it with a fine-tooth comb.

"I can't understand how this could happen," I said.

She seemed to find humor in the situation, and with a wink and nod she informed us that we were free to "get the hell out of Canada!"

We made the 1,900-mile trip back to Austin with our heads down and our tails between our legs. At least that's the way it felt for me. We had been totally let down by our agent and our record company. It was as if we didn't exist. It didn't feel good. I was forced to accept the fact that something was dreadfully wrong in my life. I hit the hike and bike trails running and started swimming in Barton Springs, hoping to ease the pain in my soul and wash the dust from my brain. I got to have Lukin for the summer.

I was a bachelor now. Sort of. Karen had filed for divorce but had never followed through. She was bouncing back and forth, living between California and Nashville. At one point, I heard she and Lukin were living in Northern California and hanging with the Doobie Brothers. Bobby Smith left the band, and we picked up another bass player, Steve Mendell. Paul Pearcy had come on board on drums following Michael Holleman's departure to New York to play in the Broadway musical *The Best Little Whorehouse in Texas*.

Replacing band members, especially rhythm section personnel, made it impossible to gain any traction, and we seemed to be spinning our wheels. When 1979 rolled around, we had to make another record to satisfy our two-record deal with Capitol. At that point, I made a proposal to the band.

"Look, it's plain as day that Capitol Records has zero interest in the Lost Gonzo Band. How about we get together ten or twelve songs, go into the studio, cut them live, do a rough mix, and turn it over to Capitol. They're not going to do anything anyway. Capitol will probably throw it in the trash!"

We had a $100,000 production budget. We could spend the

minimum, give Michael his share, divide the balance between us, and be done with it.

Oh, no! My suggestion was met with a tidal wave of opposition.

"How can you be so negative?"

So we went into the studio and started recording.

Any suggestion I had was vetoed.

"How about we try this?" I would say.

"No, don't like that."

"What do you think we should do?"

"I don't know."

It went on like that to a point where I said, "Okay, my presence here is pointless. I'm going to cut my songs. Then I will get out of your way, and you can cut your songs to suit yourselves." I cut the songs I had lined up to do. It took about three days to finish my stuff, and I left the studio and never went back. Michael Brovsky was shaking his head as I made my exit.

They stayed in the studio until the budget was exhausted. I never heard the finished product. The only evidence that the session even took place are rough board mixes that I have of the things I did. I heard from Bob that when Michael turned in the masters to Capitol, the guy listened to about thirty seconds, reached up, turned off the tape player, and said, "I hate it!" The tapes probably did go in the trash.

For all practical purposes as far as my participation, the era of the Lost Gonzo Band had come to a sad end. I hit bottom from a long, precipitous fall, but I was relieved to be free of the stress and heartache.

IT WASN'T LONG BEFORE Michael Brovsky approached me.

"I have an idea of how we can salvage the Lost Gonzo Band deal with Capitol," he said. "How about we go back in the studio and cut a Gary P. Nunn record? I think I can sell the idea to Capitol." And he did.

All our record deals had been done with the Los Angeles branch of Capitol. They were winding down their production of progressive country artists and turning over that aspect to the Nashville office. Their main focus was rock and pop. They informed us that they didn't want anything resembling country music. "No cowboy hats, no boots, and no cactus," was the way it was put to me.

Well, I was not particularly country at that time anyway, so I looked around for songs that would suit me best and accurately portray my state of mind. I put together a list, all of which I had my eye on to publish and a couple that I had written. The list was comprised of songs by Shake Russell, Walter Hyatt, Charles John Quarto, Frank Wood, Wally Stopher, Bobby Bridger, Sid Hausman, Carrie Williams (a great young songwriter who had taken up residence at Public Domain), plus an old Roy Orbison song from my youth called "Shahdaroba," a mystical tune that conjured up images of Egypt.

I had verbal agreements with the writers to publish all the tunes, except for "Shahdaroba," which was written by the great Cindy Walker.

There was a rather melancholy theme running through most of the songs, and they all were excellent expressions of how I was feeling at the time. A couple had uplifting and hopeful themes, but the overall message I was trying to communicate was that despite the heartaches and disappointments in life, I still believed that I would someday emerge from the gloom, and that someday, the light would shine on me.

> All alone in a world that's overcrowded
> I can walk down the street
> And the people that I meet all turn away
> To know the truth and at the same time doubt it
> But I don't doubt someday the truth will set me free

Then light will shine on me
But there's no sunshine in my life
Guess I was born to sing the blues
I try but I can't see the light
There is no sunshine in my life.

———

"No Sunshine in My Life." Unreleased. Gary P. Nunn. Nunn Publishing Co.

Michael gathered up the best studio musicians in town to play. Bassist Roscoe Beck, drummer Steve Medders, keyboardist Reese Wynans, and guitarist John Staehely were brought in to play on the tracks. Former Gonzo Band member Tomas Ramirez came in to overdub tenor sax on a couple of them. Artistically, it was the best thing I have ever done. Emotionally, I was still on the edge. But I became a true artist, and I sang my broken heart out. All the live basic tracks and vocal performances were as good as could possibly be expected and survived throughout the process.

Prior to our going into the studio, I had made arrangements to go to the Chihuahuan Desert in the Terlingua area of Texas on a thirty-day trek arranged by Bobby Bridger. He had told me once that everyone should be able to take a monthlong break at least once in their life. This was a monthlong backpacking trip to both sides of the Rio Grande called Desert Dance.

I was scheduled to depart for Terlingua before we had completely finished the recording. All that remained were the background vocals. I asked Michael to have Shake Russell come in and sing on his songs "You've Got a Lover" and "Deep in the West," and to have Uncle Walt's Band guys sing harmony on Walter Hyatt's "Smokey Night Life." I instructed Michael to put on the harmony parts, go ahead and mix it down, and turn it in.

I had full faith that I would be pleased with his final mixes. Michael probably thought I had completely gone over the edge. I admit I was pretty close, but I left him in charge and departed for Terlingua. I plan to release those unmixed live basic tracks that I have in my files. They are excellent artistic expressions of the state I was in at that very low period in my life.

There were five men and five women on the Desert Dance trip besides the guides, David Sleeper and his female partner, Tracy Lynch. David and Tracy had been to the desert to view the Comet Kohoutek, and they were steeped in survivalist methods and New Age philosophy.

We slept in gravel beds, carried what we ate, climbed, rappelled up and down canyon walls, and did two twenty-four-hour solo fasts and one forty-eight-hour solo fast. Try spending forty-eight hours alone in the wilderness with only two liters of water for sustenance. The trip was designed to remove you from any connection to the modern world and to make you focus on "being here now," while leaving no evidence that we had been there. It was also designed to overcome fear. The lesson was that your fear sends out messages that the natural world senses. It creates a corresponding fear response in animals.

Take rattlesnakes, for instance, or wasps. If you do not send out fear vibes, then the animals sense no fear and, therefore, will refrain from biting or stinging you. We had several opportunities to test this lesson. In every case, it proved to be true. Of course, if a rattle-snake does feel threatened, you better watch out! Four weeks in an environment like that will have lifelong effects on you—at least it did on me.

When I returned to Austin, I felt like I had gone through a time portal. The vibrations generated by electricity and neon lights, and the constant hum of motors was excruciatingly noticeable in contrast to the silence of the desert. It was also apparent that your body tenses in response to these vibrations, which prevents complete relaxation, even while you are sleeping. Could it be that this constant bombardment of artificial stimuli is the source of the emotional and health problems we experience in the modern world we live in? I think probably so.

Michael had turned the masters into Capitol, and I waited for their response. I had never heard the final mixes. Capitol transferred my project to the country division in Nashville, and their response was, "This is not a country record!" They shelved the album.

That was the last dealings I ever had with a record company, and I vowed never to have any again. Subsequently, two of the Shake Russell tunes I recorded were charted. Waylon Jennings recorded "Deep in the West" and Ricky Skaggs had a Number One hit with "You've Got a Lover." My instincts were ultimately validated regarding the quality of songs I had chosen.

Chapter 10

Gary P. Solo

AT THIS POINT, I was out of a job and completely on my own. My fragile confidence-level was at an all-time low. The words of one of my relatives kept ringing in my ears.

"None of the Nunns are ever going to amount to anything."

Some members of my family seemed to be of a mind that none of us could ever aspire to have a profession other than schoolteacher or farmer. Don't misunderstand me: Those are admittedly noble callings, and I would have enjoyed being either.

I recall an incident when my dad and I were in Lubbock when I was in high school. Lunchtime found us in the upscale Dunlaps Department Store. There was a restaurant on the second floor, and we decided to have lunch. It was a classier restaurant than we had ever been in, as we always ate in cafes and hamburger joints. I could visibly tell that my dad was uncomfortable. He actually felt that he didn't belong in such a nice place.

That made a lasting impression on me, and I vowed right then that I would never feel inferior. As long as I was trustworthy, didn't make promises I couldn't keep, and paid my own way, there was no reason I should feel inferior to anyone, regardless of my humble beginnings. Still, it was difficult to overcome a lifetime of programming that told us we were born unworthy of success.

I picked my acoustic guitar and myself up by the bootstraps and started learning songs to build a repertoire. I hoped I could get some jobs performing solo. I was scared to death and excruciatingly aware of what I thought were my inadequacies, but I managed to build the repertoire. I had been performing for years as a bass player or piano player, but always in a backup role or as a part of a band. It's a different ball game to get up in front of an audience and have their attention fixed on you alone.

I had been going to the Kerrville Folk Festival for years as a fan. One day Rod Kennedy, the festival head honcho, asked me, "When is Gary P. Nunn going to perform at the Kerrville Folk Festival?"

"As soon as Gary P. Nunn is invited," I replied.

At the next opportunity, I did perform at Kerrville, and much to my relief, I was received with an overwhelmingly positive response. I used my rock-and-roll experience to get the audience up dancing, which had never happened at Kerrville.

I set up my Tyson teepee in the "Spirit Camp" and stayed there from the opening of the festival till the close. I would pick and sing around the campfire during the days and after the main stage evening performances, and a crowd would gather round. At the time, it was unheard of for the headline performers to venture into the camps and mingle, much less, camp. They would always stay secluded backstage and retreat to the hotels in town, maintaining their star status, I suppose. But the fun was in the camps.

Since then, many of the main stage performers have hosted "campfire" picking sessions, and it has become a main attraction at the festival. I'm proud to say that I was the first to do it, and it has now become a tradition that attracts hundreds to the campgrounds every night. I was still taking pictures during these days, and my collection from the Kerrville Folk Festival is the one I prize the most. I plan to do a show of those photos someday.

PUBLIC DOMAIN HAD BECOME a well-known spot for any musician—or anyone else for that matter—who had come to Austin to stop over and stay till they got their affairs in order. Alan Lazarus, who was married to my cousin Bonita, crashed there till he found a job and a place to live. He became a well-known and highly regarded chef and restaurateur in Austin. His Italian restaurant, Vespaio, is recognized as one of the best in town. Karen Brooks, making her grand-entry return to Austin in first-class style, pulled up in a limo one day and walked in the front door with the Doobie Brothers in tow.

I could go on and on listing the people for whom the place was an oasis to park and get organized. I did my best to entertain them and show them around town. I'd take them to Trim and Swim Spa for steams and saunas, to Barton Springs for a cold plunge, and of course, to Cisco's Bakery. Some of them did just park and party, but none of those ever amounted to much. I officially christened the place, "Public Domain, Incorporated. My home for Runaway Fathers." Many guests were just that.

Sally Jackson stayed about a year, and her service and assistance were invaluable to me. She eventually returned to Santa Fe and became a successful casting agent for movie projects going on there. *Silverado* was one of her numerous credits.

Nancy ("J. J.") Levy, whom I had never met, appeared on my doorstep one day and offered to fill the spot vacated by Sally. Nancy was a Jewish girl from Los Angeles who had converted to the Hindu religion. She had a pleasant and agreeable disposition and a strong desire to serve, perhaps founded in her adopted religion. I was pleased that she had appeared, and we carried on.

Along about that time, another runaway father showed up at Public Domain. His name was Benford Standley, and he was a banker's son from Cleburne. His claim to fame was that he had been instrumental in creating the Governor's Hotline for Teen-age Runaways. He had traveled extensively in Central and South America and had been a follower of the Grateful Dead. He was into all sorts of social issues and was somewhat of an activist, I would say. He was quite the talker and seemed to be consumed with all the ills of the modern world.

Now I considered myself to be a rather "in touch with nature" sort of guy. I owned a beautiful riverside piece of property in Okla-homa, where I dreamed of having a "kids' farm," if my ship ever came in. I read *The Findhorn Garden*, subscribed to *Mother Earth News* and *Organic Gardening* magazine, and grew a garden every year at Public Domain. I had made my home a sanctuary for adult runaways, so I was susceptible, and Benford's line of BS (for lack of a better term) appealed to me.

He flattered me with his opinion of my role in the Texas music scene. He cited the fact that "London Homesick Blues" had been the theme song for the award-winning PBS music show *Austin City Limits* since its inception in 1974 and was generally recognized as the unofficial anthem of Texas! Benford Standley became a fixture at Public Domain and my constant companion. He was a natural promoter and set himself busy in efforts to do that.

In the fall of 1979, I was living on what little I could make doing single gigs and the royalties I was earning from the songs that Karen and I had written and published. Rosanne Cash, who Karen was running with, had recorded our song "Couldn't Do Nothin' Right" and released it as her first single. It was paying pretty good money and gave me some breathing room. As always, I was living on the barest of essentials and saving most of what I earned.

One morning the phone rang, and a young man from the Phoenix area named Mike Hardwick was on the line. He informed me that he played guitar and steel and asked if I needed a band, to which I replied that I did need a band—very much. He said the band he was working with would be interested in working for me, and he made a trip to Austin to meet with me and scope out the scene. I told him at the time that I could pay no more than $50 a show. He agreed and returned to Phoenix to prepare. His bandmates were drummer Billy Sink and bass player Paul Goad. Mike and Paul were newly married. They opted to move to Amarillo rather than to Austin, but somehow, we managed to get started and worked while living five hundred miles apart.

I named the band "Gary P. Nunn and the Sons of the Bunk-house," the first band ever with my name up front. The guys were rather inexperienced but had good musical instincts and were gentle souls. I credit them with saving my professional life and making it possible for me to jump-start the career that I enjoy today. We would travel from Austin to Lubbock and Amarillo to Santa Fe and back for $300 a night, which was just enough to pay them $50, buy hotel rooms, and put gas in my little Chevy 6-cylinder (with standard shift and two gas tanks) that we traveled in. This was my situation as 1979 came to an end.

Somehow, I got the big idea that I wanted to tour California, so I got on the phone to my contacts in Santa Fe. I knew Phoenix mega-producer Danny Zelisko, the manager of the Palomino in North Hollywood, and the legendary radio pioneer Larry Yurdin, who was at KFAT in Gilroy, California. Larry assisted with contacts in Santa Cruz and up the coast.

With their cooperation and support, I put together a tour of dates. We booked shows with Eliza Gilkyson in Santa Fe and Taos. Danny Zelisko put us on as the opening act for rock-and-roller George Thorogood at the Dooley's venues in Tucson and Phoenix. I managed to secure dates at the Palomino Club—somewhere in Santa Cruz—and at a room in Palo Alto called the Townhouse.

On Feb. 12, 1980, I departed Austin and headed for Amarillo to pick up the band guys. Benford was riding shotgun and began a journal of poetry and writings with the purpose of documenting our adventure. We traveled in my little 6-cylinder Chevy truck that I had nicknamed "Puppy Dog," as it was my habit to drive in the slipstream of the big eighteen-wheelers to conserve fuel. Gas was $1.14 a gallon.

We took a copy of *The Grapes of Wrath* and read it aloud along the way, comparing our trip to that of the Okies who went to California to escape the Dust Bowl of the 1930s. Benford scribbled down quotes by John Steinbeck as we rolled along. We arrived in Amarillo and spent the night. A blue norther blew in, and when we got up the next morning, the flat landscape of the Texas Panhandle was covered with a coat of sleet and ice. We had breakfast and coffee, and finally the time came to load up.

The bed of my little truck was covered with a small camper shell and was already half full of equipment. The guys grabbed their bags and bedrolls, tossed them in the back, and started to load in around the equipment with no complaints. I took one look at the situation and decided I couldn't do that: I couldn't ask the guys to take a three-thousand-mile trip lying or sitting in a pickup bed full of musical instruments, although they seemed perfectly willing.

I had an idea. I went to the nearest horse trailer dealer and located a all-enclosed two-horse trailer. I called my banker in Austin and arranged a loan. I purchased the trailer, hooked it up, and went back to the house where the band was waiting. We removed the instruments and bags out of the truck and loaded them in the horse trailer, leaving nothing in the bed but one of those tumbling mats that I had brought along. It fit perfectly and made a nice, firm mattress in the truck bed.

The guys threw in their bedrolls and pillows, and the combination of the tumbling mat and the bedrolls made a rather cozy situation where they could ride and sleep in relative comfort. This probably appeared to be paradise compared to riding while lying down with no headroom among drum cases and Fender amplifiers. We would later use the horse trailer for a dressing room.

We headed west on I-40 (old Route 66) and began our "Southwestern Pilgrimage" to California, more like *The Muppets Go to Hollywood* than the Okies from *The Grapes of Wrath*!

I was resolved to drive the whole way, which I did. I felt I had a better idea than the others of how to get the most out of my underpowered pickup. Pulling a loaded trailer requires some planning ahead. For example, you never park on the uphill side, but always on the top or the downhill side. That little truck might not be able to pull you to the top of a hill from a standing start. We arrived in Santa Fe, reconnected with Sally Jackson, and did our shows. We spent some quality time in the adobe backwater town of Cerrillos, New Mexico where Eliza was recording in a studio built by her partner, Baird Banner.

After a quick run up to a ski area in Colorado, we came back through Santa Fe for a couple of days and then headed for Tucson. Mike, Billy, and Paul seemed to be comfortable and content in the back. Benford and I were in the cab philosophizing, making up poems inspired by the scenery, mulling over headlines in the newspapers like "THREE MILE ISLAND CITIZENS SAID TO BE TERROR STRICKEN," "SOVIETS USING BLUE-GRAY GAS IN AFGHANISTAN," "SADAT GREETS FRAIL SHAH, TREATMENT SET," and reading passages from Steinbeck's *The Grapes of Wrath*.[1]

We had an afternoon show, opening for George Thorogood. Now our little four-piece band appeared in stark contrast to the "balls to the wall," power guitar, rock and roll of George Thorogood—and the audience was there to see *him*. We were inexperienced, and my

---

1   Benford put together a funky little book of writings and photographs of this adventure and printed a few copies, one of which I have in my collection of memorabilia.

repertoire consisted of several "bluesy" ballads and zero high-energy rockers. At one point during the show, someone in the audience yelled out, "ROCK AND ROLL, MOTHER F***ER!!"

I responded, "George Thorogood will be out here in a few minutes . . . in the meantime, you'll have to put up with me." It was tough to endure the humiliation, deal with my emotions, and finish the show. I was painfully aware that I was way out of my league in that situation. We played Phoenix the next day, and it was much the same. I was so grateful to Danny Zelisko for booking those dates for me as they were the cornerstone of the whole tour . . . Onward to Los Angeles.

WE DROVE STRAIGHT TO the Pacific Ocean. I walked down to the beach and touched the water to symbolize the completion of that part of the journey. So far, it had been quite an adventure. I picked up Lukin from Karen, who was living with her mother in Los Angeles, and we headed up the coast to Trancas Beach and Erin Murphy's place, where we holed up for a few days until our show at the Palomino. The guys in the band slept in sleeping bags on the porch. I didn't buy a single hotel room on the whole trip. Someone always volunteered to put us up in their home, and the guys would make their beds on the living room floor without complaint.

We did the show at the Palomino to a good crowd. I couldn't help but recall the wild shows we had done there with Jerry Jeff. Karen and Eliza were both present, and that created a bit of tension. When I got Eliza onstage to sing, it didn't go over too well with Karen's mom. She walked in front of the stage and gave me the thumbs-down while Eliza was singing.

The following is a note from Benford's journal.

March 3, 1980

Time finds us now heading North on Highway 1. Green
hills meet the Pacific. Fields of yellow flowers and blue
skies adorn our travel North to Palo Alto. We pass fields of
artichokes. A light flashes on the distant shore, a warning
to those at sea. The beauty offered us by Mother Nature
and God above is a blessing to the soul. We gain energy
from seeing and living in the presence of their gifts. The
Pacific coast . . . the end of man's western migration. Gary
says, "The ocean . . . something about the sea is calling
me." Lonely Highway 1 and the Pacific rain falls.

We did the show in Palo Alto and departed for Texas. I made
a slight detour so we could have the opportunity to visit Yosemite
National Park and spend time among the giant sequoia trees—true
testaments of God's blessings to mankind. I later wrote a song in
which I used lines inspired by that experience.

Think I'll go to Malibu, maybe I'll see me a whale or two
Come back through Yosemite, find the biggest tree
Get down on my knees, find a seed and take it home with me
Think I'll go to Mexico, Guatemala, I don't know
I just go as the wind blows, scattering seeds, gathering seeds
Sowing a few wild oats.

———
"Think I'll Go to Mexico" by Gary P. Nunn
from the Campfire Records CD *Border States*, 1986

Our route home took us back through Flagstaff and Santa Fe,
where we stopped over, ate some *huevos rancheros* with green chil-
ies to recharge, and then made our way back to Amarillo. Then

it was on to Austin. Our southwestern pilgrimage had come full circle. We had been on the road for eighteen days. It was good to be home.

Benford Standley had some tricks up his sleeve, and he started making arrangements for me to go to Guatemala. He had been there on several occasions and had some contacts, and he booked me a couple of shows as a single. In the meantime, we did some shows around Texas. One in particular bears noting.

We had a three-night stint in Denton at a place called the Broke Spoke.

They didn't supply a PA for the band, so we set up a funky little Cerwin-Vega outfit that Paul Goad owned. While we were setting up, I couldn't help but notice that the venue had a monster sound system. Large speakers and high-end horns were mounted on the ceiling directly above the dance floor. Before the show, the manager pulled me aside and instructed me in no uncertain terms, that he expected me to play strictly country and Texas music. Not a problem. We did the first set and were virtually ignored by the audience. At the break, the DJ started playing Michael Jackson's "Billie Jean" and other similar songs on the sound system with the volume cranked to the max! My sound system was one-tenth the quality and capacity of theirs. I was severely outgunned, and there was no way I could compete for the audience's attention.

I started drinking margaritas and became more and more frustrated with being reduced to nothing by the house system. I continued to drink, and by the end of the evening I was toasted and angry. *He wanted me to play country music and yet he was blowing me away with Michael Jackson on the breaks?* Give me a break.

He approached me after the show and said, "You're fired. Pack your s**t and get out!"

"Fine," I say. "Pay me for the three nights I'm booked, and I'm out of here."

"I ain't paying you s**t. Pack up your stuff and get out!"

Tequila took over.

I had a margarita glass in my hand—one of those thick and heavy numbers. A beautiful jukebox was sitting just off the dance floor. Without waiting to assess the consequences of my actions, I threw that heavy glass as hard as I could toward the jukebox! Before I heard the glass shatter, one of several bouncers, who looked like he could have been a linebacker on the North Texas football team, coldcocked me in the temple and knocked me unconscious!

I woke up sometime later after the bar was closed, sitting on a concrete step just outside the back door. The guys in the band were tending to me. They were speechless except to inform me that after I was out cold in the middle of the dance floor, the bouncers had continued to kick the s**t out of me.

"Man, Gary P., you really smashed that jukebox!"

Small consolation.

It was the one and only time I'd done anything like that. Clearly, I wasn't making much progress.

Benford went to Guatemala to arrange for our trip, and Cousin Milton and Erin Murphy made plans to meet us there. Billy Sink, my drummer, decided he would like to make the trip as well. I had no illusions that the trip would enhance my career, but how many times do you get the opportunity to go to Guatemala? Billy and I flew out of Houston to Guatemala City, caught a bus ride to Pana-jachel, and met up with Benford, Milton, and Erin at the five-star Lake Atitlan Hotel on the shores of the lake that bears the same name. It was colorful and very exotic.

The crystal-blue waters of the lake are situated in the five-mile-wide mouth of a volcano, surrounded by more volcanoes. You couldn't help but sense the geo-thermal energy bubbling all around—*ay, ay, ay*. Native women dressed in colorful traditional garb and sur-rounded by small children were omnipresent on the beach fronting the hotel. The women were selling their bright woven wares while the little girls were engaged in weaving the same.

Guatemalan villages were positioned at various points around the lake. One day, we caught the boat that delivers tourists to the villages. We met Lorie, an American girl living in one of villages, and she volunteered to be our guide and translator. She hung out with us, and we became friends and stayed in touch for several years. She filled us in on the culture and traditions of the Guatemalan people and shared stories about the goings-on—the anti-government guerilla activity, for example, which was informative and enlightening.

One of the stories Lorie told concerned the changes that modern technology was having on native culture. Traditionally, women carried water in pottery jars that they would balance on their heads. Part of the courting ritual involved these jars. It seemed that a young girl of marriageable age, to indicate her preference in a husband, would deliberately drop and break the water jar in front of him, signaling for all to see that he was her choice. As time went by, the pottery jars were replaced by factory-made jars that were unbreakable. This had the effect of destroying the courting ritual.

My shows in Panajachel left a lot to be desired. Benford had booked me in the lounge of the hotel. A busload of newly arrived German tourists was my audience, so you can imagine the response I got from them. They engaged in loud, lively conversation in German and couldn't have been more oblivious to me. Oh well, it paid for our accommodations.

Sometimes we would venture into the neighboring village to soak up the local culture. Large communal gardens by the lakeside supplied vegetables and fruits to the villagers and were tended by men wearing locally woven palm hats. In the evenings, we would dine in local restaurants that were notable for their lack of electricity. All the light was provided solely by candles.

On our walks back to the hotel past the homes, we could hear the murmur of family chatter inside and feel the warmth of the kiva-like adobe ovens adjacent to the dirt street. My Guatemalan experience, like the Desert Dance trip, made a profound impression on me, and again, as with Desert Dance, the return to Houston revealed to me the intense presence of the electrical and mechanical buzz. I felt like I had been plugged into a low-volt electric socket. Sadly, we become numb to it, but I don't think the body can tune it out completely. That's one reason I have always preferred living in a rural setting.

BACK IN AUSTIN, THE spring of 1980 was in full bloom. When the bluebonnets and Indian paintbrushes light up Central and South Texas, and Memorial Day approaches, music lovers' thoughts turn toward the Hill Country and the Kerrville Folk Festival for a week of peace, love, and music. I took my Tyson teepee and set it up in the "Energy Camp," which was beginning to make a name for itself.

The days began with the rekindling of the campfire and of friendships with those who dropped by. Daniel Huff, a young free spirit from Santa Fe who had hitched a ride in my "outfit," designated himself chief *cocinero* and busied himself with the preparation of breakfast for the beautiful people assembled in the shade of giant live oak trees.

The air was filled with laughter and the telling of stories of the night before. Tony Wilson, the originator of the camp, would be getting his long hair braided by his beautiful blonde Indian-princess-looking wife who was a master at fine leather and beadwork. Veteran pickers like Mike Williams would drop by and barter for breakfast with a song on his twelve-string. I would be snapping away with my little Canon Sure Shot, desperate to preserve the feeling of the whole scene on film. The lineup for that evening's performances was:

ROBERT SHAW—blues and barrelhouse piano maestro

ALLEN DAMRON—Rod Kennedy's partner and staple KFF performer

GARY P. NUNN—just happy to be there

CAROLYN HESTER—classic folk mistress and friend of Bob Dylan

TOWNES VAN ZANDT—poet of the dark places most fear to tread

SHAKE RUSSELL & DANA COOPER BAND—the ladies' favorite

B. W. STEVENSON—mountain man with a golden voice

GUY CLARK—the songwriter we would all like to be

It was here at the Kerrville Folk Festival where I saw a young lady who caught my eye. She was sitting on a stump in the Energy Camp with a sketchpad, penciling a drawing of me. She had long black hair, a dark complexion, and was wearing a long orange "Hare Krishna" skirt. She had the appearance of an American Indian, but it turns out she was of pure Polish extraction. I found her very attractive and made her acquaintance.

Michelle Moraczewski was an architecture student at UT from Houston and transferred that fall to Rice. I made a point of getting her phone number and contacted her the next time I was in Houston. She was the oldest of nine children—seven in a row of which were girls. The two youngest were boys. Their mother had been training to be a nun, and her father to be a priest when they met, fell in love, married, and proceeded to have nine children in quick succession. It was a Catholic family in the truest sense, although her parents by that time were divorced.

Michelle was highly motivated and had fixed ideas about most subjects you cared to discuss. I would say that she was a devotee of the philosophy of Ayn Rand and lived her life more or less along the pattern of Howard Roark, the architect-hero of Rand's novel *The Fountainhead*.

If I may paraphrase the philosophy she espoused, it was that individuals should do whatever they can to be the very best they can be, and their fellow citizens should do the same or they will be left behind. This was a new and different philosophy from what I was used to. I had always leaned toward the idea that we should be more concerned with the welfare of others, and that putting our own individual wants, desires, and ambitions on the back burner was the nobler alternative.

It was intellectually stimulating to listen to this twenty-year-old discussing issues that would have been suitable subjects in the graduate schools of the best universities. I was fascinated—rather enchanted—and drawn to her. She introduced this country boy to the world of art, dance, museums, and theatre. Surprisingly, her ideas manifested themselves as a very conservative philosophy, rather than a liberal one.

She adhered strictly to the tenets of her very Polish, Catholic upbringing as she worked her way through architecture school at Rice University, where she finished up her studies at the top of her class. Our relationship was romantic, but platonic, as she kept me at arm's distance; and out of respect for her religious convictions, it didn't bother me. This relationship continued for the next three years.

The rest of 1980 was spent doing as many shows as I could book myself. I wouldn't have a booking agent for the next twenty-five years with only a single exception. I made another trip to Santa Fe and fell in love with northern New Mexico all over again. I would gig at the Line Camp in Tesuque, the St. Bernard Hotel in Taos Ski Valley, the Sagebrush Inn in Ranchos de Taos, and at the Mother-lode in Red River, forging friendships that last to this day. I went back to the late summer edition at Kerrville, "48 Hours in Kerrville," and made a couple of trips to the ranch in Hanna. I took Michelle and two or three of her siblings. We'd saddle up the horses and ride down on the Canadian River. These kids had never been on horseback. I always enjoyed sharing the thrill of riding with city kids, and they ate it up.

Once we were back in Austin and back in the saddle, we made our weekend runs to all parts of the state. One night, at a place called Coldwater Canyon in Lubbock, I ran into an old friend and classmate of mine who dabbled in the racehorse business. His name was Troy Noel. We were visiting after the show when he said, "Gary P., why don't you make a record?"

I replied that I didn't have a record deal.

"Well, why don't you make your own record?" *Hmmm*, the thought had never occurred to me.

I replied, "Even if I wanted to, I don't have the money."

"Hell's bells son. I can sell a horse and get you the money. How much would it take?" he asked.

Having no idea of what it would cost, I popped off and said, "I think I can make a record for $10,000."

"Let's do it," he said. "I'll get with Nancy (his sister, and my first girlfriend in Brownfield) and Junior Knox (his brother-in-law), and we'll get you the money!"

Wow! What an intriguing proposition. At that time, no one produced their own records. If you didn't have a record deal with a major label, you didn't make records. It was unheard of. I thought, *What the heck? Why not?* When I got home, I pondered the situation.

I contacted Baird Banner, who owned the studio in Cerrillos, New Mexico, and quizzed him about the cost of studio time. I called a record-pressing company in Dallas about the cost of mastering and pressing. I contacted noted photographer Lisa Law in Santa Fe about using a photo she had taken of me for a cover shot. I put pencil to paper and concluded that I could produce one thousand albums for $10,000.

For a list of songs to consider, I reviewed my list of favorites from my fledgling publishing company, and reached out to Eliza

Gilkyson, Shake Russell, and Walter Hyatt and made agreements to publish tunes they had written. I called Baird Banner and booked studio time. Benford and I drove to Amarillo and picked up Mike, Billy, and Paul. They climbed into the back of the pickup, and we headed for New Mexico and set up camp in funky Cerrillos. With no rehearsal, we went into the studio and started cutting.

None of the guys had any experience, but that didn't matter. We were going to make a record. We cut most of the stuff with our four pieces. I played electric guitar with a chorus pedal, even though I had very little experience playing electric guitar myself. We brought in a couple of players to overdub and enlisted Eliza to help with vocal harmonies.

In five or six days, we had it recorded and mixed down on budget. I dropped the guys off in Amarillo, delivered the master to the pressing plant in Dallas, and secured a target date for when the product would be delivered.

Back in Austin, I contacted Eddie Wilson at the Armadillo World Headquarters and asked him if I could do a record release there. He was gracious and cooperative and gave me a date a couple of weeks past our expected delivery date for the product. Everything seemed to be going according to plan until I got a call from the pressing plant in Dallas. They informed me that their equipment had broken down, and they had subbed out my project to a company in California.

I immediately got in touch with that company to inform them that I had a cut-in-stone target date because of my booking at the Armadillo for the record release. They replied that they were confident they could deliver the product in time. As we got closer to my release date, I was in constant contact with them.

"Is it going to be ready, is it going to be ready?"

Well, they were running a bit behind but still confident. I was starting to sweat bullets.

Three days before the release and there was no record. Two days. Then one. I'm on the phone having a panic attack.

"Okay," the fellow says. "We're finishing it up tonight, and we'll put them on a plane tomorrow morning. They'll be there by 1:00 p.m. tomorrow." Damn, that's cutting it close! I went to the old Mueller Airport to meet the plane—which was delayed. I started praying. Finally, about four o'clock it arrived and the records with it! I loaded fifty boxes of albums and rushed to Public Domain to unload them. It was 5:30 p.m. I had a show at the Armadillo at nine, and I was exhausted and totally stressed out!

I had a friend who owned a spa and float tank business. Float (sensory deprivation) tanks are oversized wooden, casket-looking boxes containing supersaturated salt water. They are big enough to recline in and float. When the lid is closed, all stimuli, light, and sound are eliminated. You are even relieved of the effects of gravity. Floating in the salt water and being relieved of all stimuli for an hour has the effect of allowing your body to relax completely, going into what is called the alpha state. An hour in this state is very effective in rejuvenating the cells, and you come out feeling totally energized and refreshed. That was precisely what I needed to get me through that evening.

We did the show, and all went well, although I had narrowly escaped disaster. There is an AWH poster surviving today from that evening with me on it. A copy of it recently sold at auction for $1,300.

"A raw and unpretentious work" was how the reviewers described the record.

"The best collection of country songs I've heard this year," wrote music writer Townsend Miller for the *Austin American-Statesman*, who nominated it for a CMA Award.

So . . . I produced my own album. As far as I know, I was the first in Austin to do that. I'm a songwriter, a performing artist, a record producer, a music publisher, and I own a record label with

one product in its catalogue. I am a microcosm of the music industry, a jack-of-all-trades, and the master of none.

I began to zone in on exactly what my destiny might be. If I
could establish legitimate, survivable music business entities, perhaps I could set an example for others to follow, and we could begin
the work of creating a viable music industry in Texas!

> I'm the jack of all trades, I'm the master of none
> I play the rhythm, the bass, the piano, and the drums
> I've got everything going, but I get nothing done
> I'm the jack of all trades, I'm the master of none
> Well you know that I'm not perfect,
> but you know I'm not that bad
> And now and then, I might have been,
> the best you've ever had
> I fumble and I stumble, sometimes I get it right
> If I didn't make you proud, it's not because I didn't try
> If there's anything you need, I will make you a hand
> I will write you song, put together you a band
> I'm many things to many people, but I'm nothing to some
> I'm the jack of all trades, I'm the master of none.

"Jack of All Trades" by Gary P. Nunn from the *Under My Hat* CD,
Campfire Records, 1996

I also made a trip to Nashville to see Lukin, who was four by
then. I stayed with Karen and her new cowboy husband on a nice
horse farm near Franklin, Tennessee. Karen had landed a recording contract with Warner Bros. Records and was being touted as
the new sensation. She was driving a brand-new Mercedes 350 XL
convertible and seemed to be on her way.

I got in touch with my old friend Mary Lou Sullivan, who had
married and had a daughter with Walter Hyatt. They subsequently

divorced. Mary Lou had worked her way up from scratch in Waylon Jennings's office to being the office manager and Waylon's right-hand girl. Seemed like everyone was moving up but me.

On the way back, I stopped by and visited some old friends in Fayetteville, Arkansas. They were celebrating the "rites of life" on a farm in the Ozarks and were enjoying the bounty of the annual harvest—always a celebrated event in northwest Arkansas.

The eventful year that had taken the Bunkhouse Boys and me on a horse-trailer tour of California, to Guatemala, to Kerrville, to Santa Fe, to the sands of the South Canadian, to Nashville, and to the Ozarks and back, was winding down.

After a long and storied run, the Armadillo World Headquarters was scheduled for closing on New Year's Eve, 1980. Eddie Wilson invited me and the Sons of the Bunkhouse to open the show called "Last Dance at the Dillo" on a bill that included Commander Cody and the Lost Planet Airmen, Ray Benson and Asleep at the Wheel (with Lucky Oceans, Chris O'Connell, and Danny Levin), Maria Mauldaur, Bill Kirchen and the Moonlighters, and Jerry Jeff Walker and the Lost Gonzo Band.

I had the honor of joining my former bandmates and Jerry Jeff to close out the show with another rousing rendition of "Home with the Armadillo," aka "London Homesick Blues." I've closed down a lot of venues in my time. Many years later, I closed down the Astro-dome. But the Armadillo was one of the most notable of my career.

BACK AT PUBLIC DOMAIN, we settled into the new year. We decided to build a stage on the back of the stone pyramid-roofed house and started doing Sunday afternoon picking sessions. We called it "The Zone." Quite a few folks would drop by to hear Uncle Walt's Band and Shake Russell, or Bobby Bridger, and we would have our own private musical love-ins all bundled up against the cold and sitting on picnic tables in the back yard. J. J. Levy would fix up some Indian food to nibble on. It was a great photo op.

Daryl Perriman, a friend of Benford's from Muscle Shoals, Alabama, showed up and took up residence. Daryl was a Vietnam vet who aspired to be a writer and offered his services to do whatever to help out. Eddie Wilson, who owned a residence just across the back fence from Public Domain, offered to let us use his vacant house for an office. We moved in and set up shop.

It was funny, because we really had very few clues as to what to do. Things you *can* do cost money, and I was the only source of any and didn't have much to speculate with. We did cook up a couple of shows with Shake Russell and Dana Cooper that turned out good for them, but it was just breakeven for me after putting out a lot of effort.

We started a little booking agency that represented Shake, Uncle Walt's Band, Eliza Gilkyson, Bobby Bridger, and me. We built a booth and set up an exhibit at the annual Talent Buyers Convention in San Antonio: We didn't sell a single show. I picked up the tab. Gallagher and his silly smashing-watermelon act booked out for the whole year!

Benford talked me into making a trip to Missoula, Montana. He was "sort of" married to a woman who lived there, and he wanted to show me around. I had never been to Montana, and I was anxious to see that part of the country, so I caught a Frontier Airlines flight and flew into Missoula. While we were there, he cooked up the idea to produce a show for some charitable entity later that summer. He booked Eliza Gilkyson, Bobby Bridger, and me and somehow persuaded Hoyt Axton and Kris Kristofferson to appear as well! Michelle had graduated architecture school at Rice and was doing an internship at a firm in New York, so I flew her out, and we all went on an awesome rafting trip on the Clark Fork River.

The show sounded like a winning combination. There was only one hitch: There was hardly anyone in the audience. I remember so vividly when Kris came onstage for his show. He took one look at the audience and said, in his signature scratchy voice, "Oh well . . . there has to be a world for dreamers too!" It seemed that the projects Benford dreamed up were all moral victories of sorts. Our hearts were always in the right place, trying to do things to help people in need. It's just that financially most of them were disasters, and I was the one who always picked up the tab for the losses. Somehow, I managed to survive.

The original Sons of the Bunkhouse ran with me till toward the end of the summer of 1981. Billy Sink had developed a terrible drinking problem and was pouring down a fifth of vodka a day, so I contacted his folks in Arizona. They arranged for an intervention and took him to treatment.

Mike Hardwick settled in Austin and played with Jimmie Dale Gilmore and others, and ultimately went to work for the IRS. Paul Goad went to Ruidoso and Clovis, New Mexico, and I understand he was instrumental in the discovery of LeAnn Rimes. Billy Sink eventually went to Nashville and pursued a songwriting career. He succumbed to cancer at the age of forty-five.

I will always be grateful to those boys for their loyalty and support and the sacrifices they made to run with Gary P. Nunn and wear the A O brand. The origin of the brand that I branded my cattle with came from the company name I was using at the time: A O Communications, which stood for the "art of communications." Successful songwriting is the art of communicating. You gotta be tough . . . you gotta sleep in the back of a truck . . . you gotta be tough to wear the A O brand! David McKnight and I later wrote a song about it. I had to remain tough because the A O brand was mine. I spent the remainder of 1981 and the early part of '82 throwing together bands of local sub musicians, the most notable of whom was Junior Brown.

I invested in a funky beer and taco stand property on North Lamar called Taco Flats. A colorful local character, "Cosmic Carl"

Steele, and his wife Linda—who by that time had taken over the groove shack—ran it for me. I put money in but never took anything out other than all the bean burritos and tacos I could eat.

One night after a show in Dallas, Walker Carver approached me about booking me, and I entered into a loose agreement with him. I was flying back and forth to New York on a regular basis to see Michelle. J. J. Levy had departed, and one day I came home from a trip to find this beautiful and petite young woman sitting yoga–like on the floor of the living room, sorting papers.

"Well, hello, and who are you?"

She flashed a beautiful, disarming smile and said, "I'm Christy Ellinger, and I work for you now." Benford Standley had brought her in.

Christy was a member of a large artistic Austin family. She and her sisters were schooled in modern dance and theatrical endeavors, and several of her brothers and sisters had gigs as Disney characters who performed and made appearances locally. Christy played Minnie Mouse. She was a doll, with the most agreeable and pleasant personality, and her multiple skills were very suitable to my situation. She served me so very well, taking care of all my business and holding down the fort at Public Domain during my frequent trips out of town. Once again, I was covered by a loyal and faithful assistant, and I was so very thankful for it.

SAM LEWIS FROM SAN Angelo was an iconic figure in Texas. He was a fixture at the Terlingua Chili Cook-Offs and was responsible for my performing there for many years. He was called "Jalapeño Sam," after his line of hot sauces and his famous jalapeño lollipop! He was also known as "Armadillo Sam," as he maintained a string of "racing armadillos." He hauled them from coast to coast and staged "armadillo races" at fairs and festivals to the delight of children of all ages. He even went to England and raced them for the queen. Sam always treated me special, and like Hondo Crouch, offered me fatherly advice that I appreciated very much.

In the spring of 1982, James Michener was in Austin doing research at the University and writing a novel about Texas. I got a call from Sam Lewis asking me if I would like to join him and Mr. Michener for lunch at Terry Boothe's Headliners East at 406 E. 6th Street. Mr. Michener was writing Sam into his book because of his reputation as the "armadillo man," and they had become friends.

"I would be honored to have lunch with James Michener!"

Benford and I drove downtown and had a leisurely lunch with Sam and Mr. Michener.

ALONG TOWARD THE END of the lunch, my buddy Bobby Bridger dropped by. We were catching up on gossip and news when Bobby asked me if I would do a favor for him.

"Sure, what's up?"

He informed me that he had been entertaining a couple of theatre critics from New York. He wanted to know if he could hand them off to me, as he had some things he really needed to get done. I told him I'd be happy to entertain them. The two critics were a married couple and, as such, represented one half of the theatre critics in New York! Marilyn Stasio wrote for *The New York Times* and her husband, Dick Hummler, wrote for *Variety* magazine.

That afternoon, Bobby brought them out to Public Domain and introduced us. I asked them what they wanted to do, and Marilyn spoke up.

"We want to see the music scene in Austin we've heard so much about."

Okay . . .

I happened to be aware of the fledgling theatre activity going on at the TransAct Theatre on 6th Street through Daryl Perriman's girlfriend, Liz Montgomery, a wealthy heiress from Amarillo who was involved in the local theatre scene. We had attended a performance of an original, two-man show at the TransAct at her behest.

It was called *Greater Tuna* and featured Joe Sears and Jaston Williams, who played multiple characters—mostly women. It was very funny.

I asked Marilyn if they might be interested in seeing the play.

"Oh, no," she said. "We see off-Broadway shows four or five nights a week in New York. We want to hear some music!"

Okay, fine by me. I looked in the paper to see what was going on, and we headed out on the town in my old black checkered cab that I had picked up for $300 at an auction.

I took them to Clifford Antone's venue in the old Shakey's Pizza building on Guadalupe north of UT. Butch Hancock and Jimmie Dale Gilmore were performing. Marilyn and Dick were all smiles and having a ball. Then I took them to Steve Clark's original Waterloo Ice House on Congress downtown to see Uncle Walt's Band. They were blown away. At the end of the evening, I told them they could just stay at Public Domain so they crashed there.

The next night, I took them to Esther's Follies. Shannon Sedwick, the cocreator/owner, reserved seats for us and comped us tickets. Marilyn and Dick loved it. After the show, I called Walter Hyatt, and he and Champ Hood came out to Public Domain and played till the wee hours. Marilyn and Dick were beside themselves!

We got up and around the next morning, which was a Sunday. We drank coffee, and I cooked up some omelets for breakfast. They were going on and on about what a good time they were having and how much they had enjoyed the music the last couple of evenings.

Then Marilyn said to me in her heavy New York accent, "Gaaahree, I've been thinking I'd like to see the *Greater Tuna* play!"

"Marilyn," I said in my best Texas drawl, "They had their final performance last night. They just finished their second run, and nothing has happened, so they're closing down the show!"

"Do you think they would do a private showing for Dick and me?"

"I don't know. I can call down there and ask."

"Would you do that for us?"

I got on the phone and called the TransAct Theatre. C. J. McFarland, the manager, answered the phone.

In a hushed, conspiratorial tone, I said, "This is Gary P. Nunn. I have a couple of New York theatre critics here with me. They wanted me to ask if Joe and Jaston would consider doing a private performance for them. They really would like to see the show."

"They did their final performance last night. The boys have already left town. I can call Jaston and ask him," she said.

"Would you do that for me?" I asked.

She said she would try.

About a half hour later, the phone rang, and Jaston was on the line.

"What's going on?" he says.

I repeated the fact that there were two New York theatre critics in town who would like very much to see the show!

"I'll talk to Joe and see what he says. I'll get back with you."

He called back shortly and said, "We'll do it! When do you want to do it?"

"How about tomorrow night?"

"Okay, we'll do it tomorrow night!"

I turned to Marilyn and gave her the news. She was delighted.

Okay. We had a private showing scheduled on a Monday night. I contacted a few of my friends to see if they would like to attend so there would be some bodies in the audience besides us. I decided to go all out to try to make this a special event for them.

I called Tim O'Connor who owned a Cadillac limousine and asked him if I could borrow it for a night. Then I called Alan Lazarus, who had opened an Italian restaurant called Basil's at 10th and

Lamar, and filled him in on the situation. He offered to feed us dinner. That's about all I could think of. The next afternoon, I picked up the limo, and we loaded up and headed off to Basil's. Alan came out of the kitchen with his apron on carrying a couple of bottles of red wine and hors d'oeuvres. He sat down at the table and gave us the royal treatment.

We had a lovely Italian dinner, and then I drove the limo to 6th Street and parked in front of the TransAct Theatre. Much to our surprise, there was a line three deep wrapped around the corner waiting to get in the theatre! The word had gotten out. We were greeted and escorted into the theatre, which was already packed. Journalists from the *Austin American-Statesman* confronted us and asked for quotes regarding *Greater Tuna*.

Marilyn turned to me and said, "Gary P. Nunn, you must have a lot of pull in this town—you make one phone call and this place is packed!"

"Yeah, I do, don't I," I said, feigning exaggerated self-importance and braggadocio in my best Texas drawl.

Marilyn and Dick went back to New York and wrote rave reviews about the show, which immediately reopened for another run, sporting their reviews on the theatre front. They put Joe and Jaston in touch with their contacts in New York who helped them upgrade the quality of the production, including lighting, staging, and costumes.

It wasn't long before *Tuna* was booked for a run to rave reviews in Hartford, Connecticut. From there, they played the Theater in the Round in New York, and the rest is history.

In 1985, *Greater Tuna* was proclaimed to be the most produced play in the United States! Joe and Jaston went on to have fabulously successful careers over the span of thirty years. They created other *Tuna* shows like *Tuna Christmas* and *Tuna Does Vegas*. Norman Lear produced a *Greater Tuna* film, and they used my song "What I Like About Texas" on the soundtrack. I am very proud of the part I played in helping them get started.

ONE DAY, I WAS sitting at the piano at Public Domain. The phone rang, and Jerry Retzloff, the head PR guy for Lone Star Beer, was on the line.

"I need you to write another jingle for Lone Star."

Bob Livingston and I had written and recorded a spot back around 1973 called "The Nights Never Get Lonely" that had been a huge success for Lone Star. They even extended the ad's run as they enlisted the acts coming through the Armadillo to cut it as well. Freddie King cut it. So did the Pointer Sisters and the Chicano band Sonny and the Sunliners. The ad was quite successful, reaching across ethnic lines and helping to cement the association of Lone Star Beer, the Armadillo World Headquarters, and the Texas music scene.

I was thrilled to have an opportunity to write another spot for them.

"What does it pay?" I asked Jerry.

"Between $3,500 and $5,000."

Well, that was a no-brainer.

"Make it $5,000, and it's a done deal!" Jerry agreed.

I didn't want to write a traditional jingle for this project. I wanted to make it unique and different. So I waited for *it* to come to me.

I was coming back from a gig up in the Cuchara Valley in the mountains of southern Colorado, near the town of La Veta. I turned south on I-25 at Trinidad. As I passed through Raton Pass, great plains of golden grass stretched out before me as far as the eye could see. It was at that moment that I conceived the idea for the Lone Star song. I had been reading a good deal of Texas history at the time and was familiar with the geography and history of the state. I decided to transform myself and assume the viewpoint of a soaring eagle, with a vantage point that encompassed the entire state.

I drove on to Iowa Park, Texas, to visit my mom and spend the night. The next morning, I went into her living room, sat down at the piano, and wrote the song.

> You ask me what I like about Texas
> I tell you it's the wide-open spaces
> It's everything between the Sabine and the Rio Grande
> It's the Llano Estacado, it's the Brazos and the Colorado
> It's the spirit of the people who share this land
> Chorus:
> It's another burrito
> It's a cold Lone Star in my hand
> It's a quarter for the jukebox boys
> Play the Sons of the Mother-loving Bunkhouse Band
> You ask me what I like about Texas,
> It's the big timber around Nacogdoches
> Driving El Camino Real down to San Antone
> It's the Riverwalk and Mi Tierra's,
> Jamming out with Bongo Joe
> It's the stories of the Menger Hotel and the Alamo
> Repeat chorus:
> You ask me what I like about Texas
> It's bluebonnets and Indian Paint Brushes
> Swimming in the sacred waters of Barton Springs
> It's body-surfing the Frio, it's Saturday night in Del Rio
> It's crossing over the border for some cultural exchange
> Yeee Haaa!

———

"What I Like About Texas" from the CD *Border States*, 1986

It all came in a stream of consciousness. I just sang it out as it came to me, and I actually had to scramble to remember the words when the stream was over. I was so fortunate and grateful to have gotten it down before it got away. You have to be totally focused and undistracted when inspiration happens, or your best stuff will get away from you. It often happens to me when I'm driving, and I fail to get the idea recorded before it slips away, never to be retrieved—at least not in the same form.

We went back to Cerrillos for the recording. Jerry Retzloff joined us there and seemed to really enjoy the colorful adobe ambiance of the area. The Sons of the Bunkhouse played on the session.

For the radio spots, the ad was cut into three different ads, utilizing one verse and a chorus for each spot. When it began to air on San Antonio radio, I'm told that the radio stations were flooded with calls requesting "that Lone Star Beer commercial!" I knew right then that this was not just a popular radio commercial. I had a hit on my hands! I recorded it at the very next opportunity, and it has become one of the most popular tunes I've ever written—especially in Texas, of course.

AT THAT TIME, THE Lone Star Café was the happening place for country and Texas music in New York. I had been there on several occasions with Jerry Jeff, and it was the place to hang for Texaphiles and New Yorkers who wanted to sample a taste of the "Texas Thang" and were willing to pay $5 for a Lone Star Beer.

Kinky Friedman was the featured house artist, and he had the best country musicians in town backing him up. I surmised that while simultaneously writing murder mysteries, Kinky had a pretty cushy gig and got to play all the open dates he wanted, in addition to being first in line for the many good-paying private parties booked at the Lone Star Café.

One evening, I was hanging out there when the manger, Mort

Cooperman, cornered me with a proposition. He said Kinky was going to leave the gig come June 1. He asked if I would be interested in taking Kinky's place as the featured house artist.

I didn't have a band in Texas and was bouncing from one thing to the next. It occurred to me that a stint as a featured artist in a popular venue in New York City might suit me just fine. I could use the opportunity to get major visibility in the big city. If I could pull it off, I could enhance my career tremendously. I would have access to the same good musicians that backed up Kinky.

Kinky's show was based on his original songs. My approach would be totally different. I was thinking about getting together a repertoire of classic and popular country songs, as well as classic Texas tunes. Certainly, it would be an opportunity for me to test my skills, and I perceived it to be a once-in-a-lifetime opportunity to make a name for myself in a major market.

Mort Cooperman told me that if I could be in town by June 1, I could have the gig. I didn't bother to ask him what it paid or to request a written contract confirming our agreement. I was a my-word-is-my-bond kind of guy. I learned that lesson the hard way.

I hustled back to Texas and started preparing for the big move. I loaded up my little Chevy pickup with a minimum of baggage, a tumbling mat, a two-man dome tent, and took off for New York, with overnight stops in Little Rock and Nashville to visit Lukin. Michelle was living in a small apartment with a roommate, which eliminated it as a possible place to crash as the apartment belonged to her roommate's family. I figured I would crash wherever I could until I started making money and could get my own place.

I arrived on June 1 and called the Lone Star Café office to get things moving. I asked for Mort Cooperman and learned that he had left the city for a monthlong vacation. Uh-oh. Bad sign right off the bat. Not a good way to start a new gig. In Mort's absence, I found myself speaking to Cleve Hattersley, who had been left in charge.

Cleve, originally from New York, had migrated to Austin and played with a popular local band called Greasy Wheels. He and his wife, "Sweet Mary," the fiddle player I had called in to play on *¡Viva Terlingua!*, had followed Kinky to New York and were employed there.

"When can I go to work?" I asked Cleve.

He said, "Well, I'm working on some things . . . why don't you call me back on Friday?"

I was disappointed but not overly concerned, thinking I could hold out for a week till things got organized. I beat around town that week, staying with Marilyn Stasio and Dick Hummler and going out with them to see off-Broadway plays, slipping in with Michelle when her roommate was not at home, and as a last resort, checking in to the Midtown Holiday Inn where you could a get a room for between $50 and $60 a night.

Bright and early on Friday morning, I called Cleve. He said he didn't have anything for me yet. "Call me back on Monday."

I heard about another country music venue starting to happen in midtown. They had a cool scene going, and I began hanging out there. The boys in Kinky's band were playing a side gig there. The room had a dance floor and a youthful crowd of patrons swing-dancing and two-stepping. Actually, with the dancing, it was more to my liking than the strictly show-scene setup at the Lone Star Café.

Meanwhile, Cleve is telling me, "Call me on Monday . . . call me on Friday . . ."

He also told me that if I ever played in that club in midtown, I would never play in the Lone Star Café! *Whoa.* I started to get worried. This went on for about three weeks. I spent almost every evening in the clubs looking for a place to crash. When I couldn't find one, I would walk the streets and hang out till the early morning hours in underground subway stations listening to homeless derelicts proselytize.

My very last resort to avert sleeping on the streets with them was a $25-a-night flophouse room near Gramercy Park. The paint was peeling off the walls, but the sheets were clean. I didn't know it at the time, but this was a period when the streets of New York were at their worst with crime and homelessness. I'm lucky I didn't get my throat cut. I began to feel like a homeless derelict myself.

Still Cleve kept putting me off. At one point, I called him in desperation, and he said he had a date for me. "It's Monday night, July fifth!" I had been in town, practically living on the streets, for four weeks, but I was relieved. I got in touch with the musicians for rehearsals. I caught the subway to Queens to get with the bass player and to Brooklyn to rehearse with the guitar player.

Marilyn and Dick invited me out to their country cabin in Connecticut for the July Fourth holiday. We came back into town on the fifth for the gig. I did the show to a crowd of about seventy people. It wasn't very good. The band guys hadn't rehearsed the songs, and they all snorted cocaine before the show. I was stressed out from four weeks on the streets and their poor performance.

I called Cleve the next day to schedule the next date.

Cleve said, "Gary P., I can't book you any more dates. You don't have any draw in this town!"

I finally figured out that Monday, July 5, is absolutely the worst night of the entire year in New York! Those who aren't out of town to escape the heat are recovering from the holiday. I was so flustered that I didn't have the presence of mind to beg his pardon and respond, "I'm sorry, Cleve, but you're not the one who hired me. I need to talk to Mort Cooperman!"

I can only conclude that Cleve was determined that I wouldn't get the gig at the Lone Star Café. A great opportunity had slipped through my fingers, but I had learned valuable lessons.

As things turned out, it was probably for the best. If I had stayed in New York, no doubt my life would have taken me down another path, and everything would be totally different today.

Michelle was acquainted with Jim Lauderdale, who was doing a multiweek stint in Atlanta as a member of the cast of the musical *Pump Boys and Dinettes.* He offered to let me stay in his apartment while he was out of town. I stayed there a couple of weeks killing time while Michelle finished up her session at the architecture firm.

We loaded up my little truck and exited New York City. On the return trip, we took a leisurely tour through Pennsylvania Amish country. We continued on to Washington DC, where we camped in Greenbelt Park for $3 a night and spent three or four days visiting the museums and doing the DC thing. The tumbling mat and the two-man dome tent were our shelter and bed. From there, we went to Charlottesville, Virginia, to visit Monticello, Thomas Jefferson's estate, and then on to Nashville. We stopped off to see Lukin before completing the journey back to Texas.

THE MOST SIGNIFICANT EVENT of 1982 was Willie Nelson recording a song I had cowritten with Donna Farar in the early '70s. You may recall I mentioned that Karen Brooks was hanging out with the stars back in '76. At one of those late-night picking parties, she sang "The Last Thing I Needed, First Thing This Morning" for Willie. But nothing came of it for years.

In 1980, when Willie was making the movie *Honeysuckle Rose*, he showed up with members of the cast at one of my gigs at Steamboat Springs on 6th Street in Austin. He called me to his table on a break and introduced me to his costar, Amy Irving. He told me that he had always liked my tune, and he wanted to record it someday. Time passed until one day in the spring of '82, I received a call from my friend Jody Fischer, who was Willie's secretary/assistant. She told me that Willie was in the studio, and he wanted me to come out to the Pedernales Golf Course studio (aka "Cut 'n' Putt") and teach him the song.

I was just getting ready to head out to Bee Cave. Daryl Perryman

and Liz Montgomery were moving to New Mexico and abandoning a new refrigerator and a washer and dryer. They told me that
I could have them if I could pick them up within the hour. So I
detoured my trip to Willie's studio, went to Bee Cave, loaded the
appliances, and then went to the studio.

When I arrived, they were ready for me, and I went directly into
the studio and cut a demo version of the song. The musicians—
keyboardist Bobby Emmons, Mike Leach on bass, and Gene
Chrisman on drums—charted the song. I wrote down the lyrics for
Willie. He stepped into the studio, put on the earphones, and did a
single take.

Willie came back into the control room, fired up a doobie, and
listened to the playback. When it finished, he said simply, "I think
the vocal is pretty good." With that, he left the control room.

Naturally I was stoked about the whole thing. I said to producer
Chips Moman, "Hey, I have more songs where that came from."

Chips shot back to me, "Don't push it, kid!"

I didn't push. I just sat back and listened to the playback again—
to the four minutes and twelve seconds that changed my life!

The album *Always on My Mind* went multi-platinum. It was Billboard's Number One country album of the year for 1982. It stayed
253 weeks on Billboard's Top Country Albums charts, peaking at
Number One for a total of twenty-two weeks. It also spent ninety-
nine weeks on the Billboard 200 for all albums, peaking at Number
Two for three weeks. Willie released "Last Thing I Needed" as the
third single off the album. The other singles charted Number One.
Our tune went to Number Two on the Billboard Charts in January of 1983. Michael Murphey's "Wildfire" was Number One, and
Karen Brooks had a duo with T.G. Shepherd called "Faking Love"
that was at the Number Three spot.

Public Domain was turning out to be a productive domicile.
Maybe there was something to sleeping in a pyramid!

When Willie cut my song, he saved my financial life in more ways than one. Back in 1976, my Uncle Joe informed me that he was going to sell his four hundred acres of river-bottom land near Hanna. That property joined the land that my parents had purchased. I looked at the potential of increasing the size of our family's ranch if I bought it and decided that's what I would do. I was working with Jerry Jeff then and making good money. But following the break from Jerry Jeff, my income fell off dramatically. By 1982, I had fallen behind on my payments.

Joe informed me that if I didn't get caught up, he would have no alternative but to foreclose and reclaim the property. That would spell disaster for me. I would lose the $60,000 to $70,000 I had tied up in the property! Willie's cutting the tune saved me from ruin and allowed me to get caught up on my payments and eventually pay the note off. *Phew!*

God steps in and saves us from ourselves when we need it the most.

ALONG ABOUT SEPTEMBER 1982, I was still rocking along hiring sub players when I picked up occasional gigs. Walker Carver was booking me at Borrowed Money, a nice dance venue on Central Expressway in Dallas. It was a large, happening room in Dallas that played to a dance crowd that leaned toward Texas music.

My "Home with the Armadillo" song had put me up there somewhat, even though the song had Jerry Jeff Walker's name on it. That made it difficult for me to reap the full benefits of a hit record, as you might imagine, but it was his record after all!

One day, I got a call from Tommy Howard and Mark Webernick, who were playing in the house band at the Motherlode in Red River, New Mexico. They informed me that Mike Hearne, who was the primary front man for the Great American Honky Tonk Band, had been hired to go on the road with Michael Martin Murphey. They needed someone to fill his spot and would I be interested in coming to Red River for an extended six-nights-a-week gig?

You know, sometimes not having a regular band has its advantages. You can take opportunities from the outside that you normally wouldn't be able to accept. I jumped at the chance to spend time in the mountains of northern New Mexico and departed Austin, leaving Public Domain in the capable hands of Christy Ellinger. I relocated to Red River for the last week of September through the month of October.

I took the high-country back road through Ocate in Mora County to Eagle Nest. I liked that scenic route. Later, I learned it could be trouble as there were some outlaw locals who were known to highjack and rob people crossing that way. But I arrived in good order and settled in at the Bitter Creek Ranch, in one of the several log cabins nestled in the woods above Red River on the edge of the national forest.

They put me in Cabin 10, which slept twelve people. There was a pond filled with rainbow trout just off the front porch. Cabin 10 was after-hours party headquarters, and the band guys and I, along with other locals and beautiful blond ski bunnies who worked at Texas Red's Steakhouse, would go up there after the nightly shows at the Motherlode. Those were some of the most enjoyable evenings filled with laughter and music.

Everyone in New Mexico was a good dancer. They danced a unique blend of swing dancing and the two-step taught to them by Cisco Guevera, a local favorite in Red River who was on the ski patrol in winter and ran a river rafting business on the nearby Rio Grande in the summer. At the Motherlode, I became acquainted with a beautiful young singer-songwriter named Sara K. Wooldridge. I had met Sara that summer in Ruidoso. She had come up to Red

River and ended up staying the whole time I was there. She would sit in with the band and hang with us every night, and we became close friends.

Red River was an absolutely delightful place to spend the month of October. The days are sunny and warm, and the evenings are cool. The mountains are ablaze with the brilliant yellow of the aspen leaves turning. I had one of the happiest times of my life enjoying the Red River lifestyle and making music with drummer Tommy Howard, bass player Rick Fowler, and keyboardist Mark Webernick, whom I dubbed "Flaco" Webernick for his accordion playing. I beefed up my repertoire while I was there, learning the popular dance tunes that they used, and they became familiar with my songs, which proved to be critical in the not-too-distant future. All in all, it was a most enjoyable and beneficial experience.

Northern New Mexico became my very favorite place to vacation and ski, and I forged many friendships during that time that I enjoy to this day. But eventually the gig came to an end, and I came down off the mountain and back to Texas. One night at Borrowed Money in Dallas, Walker Carver sat down with me after the show, and we were visiting. He asked me if I had ever thought of playing in Europe.

"As a matter of fact," I told him, "I have been thinking about it for quite some time."

For a few years, I had been a member of a book club that featured books that were a little off the beaten path and focused on self-improvement, do-it-yourself subjects, and the like. I came across a book that really intrigued me.

The book was titled *The Secret of the Ages*. Hey, I wanted to know about the secret of the ages, so I ordered the book and read it straightaway. The gist of the book was that God gave us the power to create whatever we want in this world. All we have to do is create an image of what we want in our minds and focus and concentrate on that image. The more you focus and concentrate on the image, the more it sets up a magnetic-like force of thought that attracts the various component parts necessary to bring the image to fruition in the real world. It suggested that you write about what you want or draw pictures—analyze and list the components necessary to get where you want to go. Put a picture on your bathroom mirror. Focus on it every morning when you get up, and make it the last thing you think about before you go to bed. Pick a place you want to be and figure out a way to get there.

When you think about it, it makes perfect sense. For example, let's say you want to build a house. Well, first of all, you have to ask yourself, *What does the house look like?* You visualize it in your mind. The next step would be to draw a sketch of it. Then you go to the architect, and he draws the floor plans. The image has moved from your thoughts and has become a floor plan—something real that you can hold in your hands and focus on. The floor plan will reveal to you the various materials required to construct the house. The necessary components will begin to accumulate. The workers needed to construct the house arrive and start putting the parts together. The next thing you know, you're moving into your house.

So how was this house created? It was created in your mind, and you focused on the thought until the house was completed. From nothing, something very substantial has been created in the real world.

Contrarily, the absence of focused thought can lead to nothing—or worse yet, disorder, chaos, and confusion. The examples of the positive and negative effects of this way of thinking are infinite, but perhaps you get the idea.

But back to the subject I was discussing. I had read *The Secret of the Ages,* and I had deliberately employed the ideas espoused in the book, practicing by focusing on the idea of going to Europe just to test the theory. Now, here was Walker Carver, asking me if I was interested in doing just that.

He informed me that he knew a guy from Dallas, John Williams, who had immigrated to the Netherlands and started a country music club in Amsterdam. The guy had a band that toured regularly around Europe and England. Walker said he thought he could arrange a tour for me—with this fellow doing the organizing and supplying my band. In just a few weeks, he had arranged for me to fly to Amsterdam for a six-week tour of Europe! I was to depart January 1, 1983. I went back to Austin and started preparing for the trip. I sent over tapes of my repertoire so the band could start learning my material.

I had a New Year's Eve gig booked at Butterfield Junction in Abilene, and I got Junior Brown to play guitar and steel; Jimmy Marriott, my old compadre from the Shucks and the Sparkles to play drums; and Dale Dennis to play bass. We did an uneventful New Year's Eve show on a stage twelve feet above the dance floor with Michael Jackson blasting on the house system on the breaks.

Afterward, I drove overnight to Dallas, slept on Walker Carver's floor for a few hours, and caught a plane to Amsterdam on New Year's Day, 1983. The year had been an eventful one, even though I hadn't had a regular band. Those events had a direct and significant effect on the direction my life would take in the future.

Chapter 11

European Tours

I FLEW INTO SCHIPHOL Airport in Amsterdam on New Year's Day of 1983. It was the first time I had set foot on continental European soil. I was excited to be there.

I was also apprehensive about whether I would be received well and about what kind of band I would be working with. I still carried feelings of self-doubt about whether I had made the correct decision to continue on my musical journey. I had never really planned to make a career of it: But I always had some booking on my calendar, and I couldn't quit as long as someone was expecting me to show up.

My salvation was my audience. As small as their numbers were in the early days, my fans appeared to really like what I was doing. They would come up and tell me how they could relate to my music or how this song or that song reminded them of someone they knew or something that happened to them in their lives. I had always felt that I was a lot like other people; that there were common experiences and universal truths that we all shared and could relate to. If I expressed myself honestly, and if people took the time to listen, my conviction was that more and more people would identify with me and the experiences I was describing.

I had no radio airplay or promotion, but I thought if my small audiences liked what I was doing, then maybe there was a larger audience out there that would like it as well. If I could just hang on, maybe someday something would break for me. Communication with my audience was the bottom line.

John Williams, owner of the Last Waterhole, and my tour organizer, met me at the airport. He took me to his apartment in Amsterdam and got me settled in a room. Then we left for the venue, which was in the entertainment district, right in the middle of what is known in Mexico as "La Zona Rosa." It was culture shock for sure. The Dutch are very liberal in their social mores. In Amsterdam, a major seaport going back centuries, there have always been plenty of vices readily available to sailors on shore leave after long trips at sea. "Window-shopping" was a favorite pastime in the "District."

I was surprised, however, when I entered the place through its swinging doors painted like a Confederate flag. There on the walls were pictures of Willie Nelson and Jack Daniels and the like, and Doug Sahm and the Sir Douglas Quintet were playing on the system. The Last Waterhole was decorated like a typical honky-tonk in Texas. There was a hostel upstairs for young backpacking tourists to bunk in. Mostly they were kids from Texas who had gravitated to the familiar atmosphere of the Last Waterhole.

Like every bar in the area, there was a house dealer, who had a couple of British girls hawking his wares of hashish that came from various regions of the Middle East.

Patrick was a dreadlocked Rasta man from St. Lucia and a very likeable and sociable fellow. He would sit at the bar and roll one giant "blunt" after another, mixing the Lebanese Blonde or Afghan Gold with cigarette tobacco. This was common at all the tables, as patrons would be rolling and smoking and enjoying the excellent Amstel beer served on tap.

Taking all this in stride, I was introduced to the guys in the band.

The Pride of Texas was the house band at the Last Waterhole, and they played there on all the nights they weren't touring. There were two Americans, Larry Black, a piano player from Stillwater, Oklahoma, and a bass player, Charlie Bullington, who was out of Boston and had studied jazz guitar at Berklee College of Music. He had been assigned to play bass for my tour. There were also two Dutchmen: Rene de Falk, who went by the name of Lenny Falcon, on drums, and the derby-hat-wearing Cos Biel, a devotee of Buddy Emmons, who was recognized as one of the top steel players in Europe. All in all, it was a pretty good band.

We got busy and began rehearsing that first afternoon. After a couple of days, John Williams put me to work playing the evening shows at the Waterhole to prepare for the tour. The audience was a mixture of young American backpackers, Dutch country music fans, Middle Eastern–looking young men with the omnipresent traditional scarves wrapped around their necks, and a variety of European and British tourists who just happened in. Audience response was soft as they were totally unfamiliar with my music, and most of them were in a blissful state of inebriation.

One of our first gigs was a live radio show in a theatre in Utrecht in the south of Holland. The place was packed, and we got through the show without having any train wrecks. The closer for that show was none other than Lee Greenwood. His career was just getting kicked off in early 1983, and it was clear to me that, with that voice, he was going to be very successful! After the show, I went back to the lobby and sold a whole box of my *Nobody But Me* album at twenty guilders apiece.

We drove back to Amsterdam and played a few more nights at the Last Waterhole and a show at Camp Amsterdam, a NATO army base nearby. We went to Brussels, Belgium, and played in a Montana Mike's venue that was frequented by American soldiers assigned to NATO Headquarters. One fellow was a marine from

Oklahoma who guarded the American Embassy in Brussels. He was still upset about President Jimmy Carter's failure to rescue the American hostages in Iran. The next day, we played the NCO Club at the NATO Headquarters base nearby.

From Brussels we went to Paris. There was a Frenchman at the venue from Dallas—sounds funny, but it's true. I had met him at the Whiskey River in Dallas back in 1980, and he had told me about his owning a Mexican restaurant in Paris. I can't recall his name (Frank something), but do recall it was on Rue du Temple, not far from the Seine River and the Palais-Royal. It was a gathering place for American expats and tourists. We sat up in the corner of the restaurant and did our show. That's where I met John Phillips—the sports editor for the *International Herald Tribune*.

After the show, I stayed late and got into a heated discussion with an American guy who was a musician as well. He was going on and on about how it was impossible to gain any inroads in France because of the closed culture. I had had just enough wine and enough of people telling me what was and wasn't possible that I ended up shoving him off his barstool! The next morning, I did an interview with the music editor of the *Herald Tribune*. The headline of the article the following day in the *Herald Tribune* read, "I Knocked a Guy off His Barstool Last Night!" I guess I rednecked out! I was embarrassed and ashamed of my behavior and especially of having it published in the largest English-language newspaper in Europe.

The upside of the Paris experience was that I formed a lasting friendship with John Phillips. We corresponded for years, and I stayed with him on all my subsequent trips to Paris. He was a wonderful guy, a great writer, and I learned a lot from him.

Our tour of one-nighters took us to Bitburg and Spangdahlem, American air bases in Germany where we played the NCO Clubs. These gigs did not go over so well, as a majority of NCOs (noncommissioned officers) were black airmen, and they just could not relate to anything resembling country music and ignored us completely. We went to Emsland and played in a boomie shopping mall-type of venue arranged by Hermann Lammers Meyer, a German musician who was a regular visitor to Austin. Again, the stage was elevated way above the audience level, and that never works.

Traveling in a diesel cargo van, we got on the Autobahn and headed for Zürich, Switzerland. We stopped to sightsee a bit around Heidelberg University and then proceeded south past Baden-Baden. At the German–Swiss border, we were taken aside and funneled through a rigorous immigration examination, where we all had to present medical documents certifying that we had had the required vaccinations for communicable diseases, plus all information regarding what we were doing there, where we would be staying, and how long we intended to stay. After several hours, we were released and made our way to Zürich and checked in at the Hotel Hirschen, located right in the heart of the eight-hundred-year-old Hirschenplatz.

On the street level was a horseshoe bar with a few gambling machines on the walls, and in the back was the music venue that held 150 or so. The hotel rooms above were rather funky, but clean and comfortable. The bar served as a local watering hole for wealthy people who worked and did business in the nearby Börsenstrasse, where the Swiss stock market and major Swiss banks are located, and where a great deal of the world's wealth and gold is held in safekeeping away from prying eyes. It's funny how people like to be close to their gold. We were booked there for four weeks, twenty-eight nights in a row.

After getting settled in our rooms, we reported for sound check. Martin Schweitzer, the owner of the venue, was a most unlikely sort for a club owner. He was a professional pilot and flew private jets for Arab sheiks and people like Christina Onassis. He was a meek-looking fellow with a pale complexion, a skinny frame, and a slightly stooped posture—rather Casper Milquetoast in appearance.

His appearance was deceiving however. He was very intelligent, wise, and totally self-confident—and direct and outspoken in his demeanor. "Hallelujah, you redneck mother," was one of his favorite expressions along with, "Cheers, my dear, I'm only here for the beer," which sounded funny in his heavy Swiss accent.

During the sound check, he was very critical and kept telling us not to play so loud. After an hour or so of this, John Williams, a big, barrel-chested, intimidating sort of guy, got in Schweitzer's face and said, "Hey, MF, why don't you go sweep the floor or do whatever it is you do around here, and leave the sound check to us?" *Whoops.* Well . . . Martin was no shrinking violet, and he went ballistic! He told John Williams, "GET OUT! GET OUT NOW! YOU ARE FORBIDDEN TO SET FOOT IN THIS PLACE EVER AGAIN!" He blurted out a few expletives in German as well, some of which I recognized, like *"@#$%SCHWEIN . . . @#$%SCH-WEIN . . . @#$%SCHWEIN!"* Not a good start.

The Swiss had their ways about them, and they didn't tolerate brutish behavior. John Williams, the boss of our whole operation, and sometimes front man for the band, got fired and eighty-sixed for life before we even got the sound check done. Eventually we did, with Martin hovering over us. The four shows each night started at 8:00 p.m. sharp and lasted for fifty minutes precisely. The Swiss run by the clock, and no one should be surprised since they make the best watches in the world.

It was so strange those first few nights . . . the audience was stone-faced and totally unresponsive. It seemed like there was nothing I could do to elicit a smile or a reaction of any sort, and it was rather disheartening. I expressed my frustration to Martin Schweitzer after the show. He told me not to worry, as most of the audience didn't speak much English. "They're just trying to listen to understand the meaning of the words and decipher the nuances of your American expressions. Many of them take English lessons before they come to the show in an effort to better understand what the songs are about." I took a different attitude about it all after he explained the situation.

The first night we were there, I came down with a flu bug that laid me low with a violent case of nausea and dysentery. Then Christy called me from Texas to relay bad news. A steel player named Jerry Moore I had met in Santa Fe had been crashing at Public Domain. She informed me that he had stolen checks from my checkbook and had written several to himself totaling several thousands of dollars. He had forged my signature and cashed the checks at the drive-in window at my bank! Christy had been alerted to the scam when American Airlines called with the news that they had found one of the blank checks while cleaning a plane at Newark Airport.

I was devastated! It was difficult to deal with that knowledge and the violent illness I was experiencing at the same time. Still, I had to get myself together to do my shows every night. How I was able, I do not know. It took all I could muster to get it done, running to the toilet and throwing up during the breaks. Later, I would discover I was missing a vintage Martin 0018 guitar in pristine condition that would be worth a fortune today. It took me a week to recover from the severe gastrointestinal bug and get halfway back to normal. Turned out Moore was a cokehead, and I didn't have a clue. He'd be "counted sorry" by my Grandma Nunn.

Soon after we arrived in Zürich, John Williams sneaked up to my sick room without being detected. He asked me if I knew a female vocalist who might like to come over and be a part of the show. I replied that I did. Sara K. Wooldridge was just the sort of free spirit to do such things on the spur of the moment. John arranged for her flight, and she walked in the door of the Hirschen about noon the next day.

Sara K. was a gorgeous blonde with a disarmingly demure persona. She joined our show and did a few songs as a featured artist every night. She dressed in the coolest shiny rhinestone cowgirl outfits and cowboy boots and could lay down a soulful version of "Chain, Chain, Chain" that Aretha Franklin would have been proud of. She delighted the Swiss audiences and all the band guys as well, who were panting and waiting in line to pull her chain. But she was wise to the ways of the road and refrained from getting involved with any of them. Eventually, the Zürich audience warmed up to us as they became more familiar with our music.

At the end of each evening, the audience would be ushered out of the music hall, and the staff would serve us a typical Swiss family dinner and all the drinks we desired. The beer and the wine were of such excellent quality that only Americans would think of ordering whisky or other hard liquor. Some in our group did order Jack Daniels, which was looked upon derisively by the Swiss.

The staff, along with Martin Schweitzer and his wife, Maggie, hung out with us till the cows came home. We had some great times during those after-hour sessions, and we became familiar with the members of the staff—Chicho, Irma, and Silvia—as we spent so much time together. Sometimes, the guys would get back onstage and jam till the wee hours, with Charlie Bullington and Cos Biel blowing all the classic jazz lounge tunes, or Sara K. doing a dreamy version of "When Sonny Gets Blue" that would make you cry.

We would venture out on the streets after hours and walk to the Irish pub up the street or go around the corner to a club that featured New Orleans jazz musicians. Sadly, it was common to see a junkie crouched in a shadowy corner shooting up heroin. We would occasionally encounter a group of young German men marching down the street. They weren't goose-stepping, but it sounded like it with their heavy boots hitting in unison on the cobblestone streets as they sang loud martial-sounding songs that echoed off the walls of the Hirschenplatz. It felt quite intimidating, and we never knew if they were going to assault us—especially me in my cowboy hat, which I wore constantly. In Europe, the hat represented "J. R." and J. R. was the man they loved to hate and who represented everything bad about Americans. It was the epithet most commonly hurled in my direction.

By the time we finished up the four weeks in Zürich, we had built up quite a following and had formed many friendly relationships. There was a Swiss country band called The Rusty Nugget who came and sat in the front row with their wives and girlfriends almost every night. (Apparently, open marriage arrangements were not uncommon, and some of the wives were not shy about propositioning the guys in the band.)

One young woman on staff remained aloof and always looked askance at me during the month we were there. I would ask her for a coffee and she would reply, "*Humph*, make it for yourself." I recall her calling me *schlitzohr* one evening as I was leaving. I didn't know what it meant, but it didn't sound good.

WHEN WE FINISHED IN Zürich, we said our goodbyes and loaded into the van. I rode with John Williams in his Volvo that ran on LPG (liquid propane gas). We drove all day and most of the night to Calais, on the west coast of France, taking Sara K. with us. The appearance of the French countryside was so beautiful with every square inch perfectly manicured. In the predawn hours of the next morning, we drove the vehicles onto the ferry that would take us across the English Channel. In my mind, I tried to imagine what it must have been like for young American soldiers making the reverse trip on D-Day. As we approached the English coast, we had a beautiful close-up view of the White Cliffs of Dover. Then we entered the mouth of the Thames, sailed up the river, and disembarked in London.

When we went through immigration, John and I were detained.

All vehicles registered in the Netherlands were suspect due to the country's lax policies regarding drugs. An extensive interrogation and search was conducted on our luggage and the vehicle. John's big mouth prompted them to take him to a back room where he was given an anal exam. Scare *me!*

Finally, we cleared immigration and were met and escorted to Dingwalls, the venue where we were playing. John Williams planned to make a record and release it to promote The Pride of Texas and me in Europe. He had made arrangements to record the performance live that evening, so there was a lengthy sound check. I was exhausted from twenty-eight nights in Zürich; the sleepless, overnight trip to Calais; and the ferry trip across the Channel. I had to just sit and try to relax, regain my energy, and work on my voice during that long afternoon. With no sleep, we did the show and recorded it. The quality of the recording was about what one would expect from a project that was done with such little preparation. It wasn't bad, but in my opinion, it wasn't going to do anything to further either one of our careers. At best, it would serve as a document of where we were and what we were doing at the time.

We were on a circuit, as Dingwalls venues were scattered over Britain. From London, we went to Liverpool, a seaport city on the west coast, and, as everybody knows, the hometown of the Beatles. It was cool to drive by Penny Lane and other landmarks mentioned in their songs. I was reminded of the day I spent in Abbey Road Studio back in 1973.

From Liverpool, we made the short trip to Manchester. We played to good crowds. The music fans in England were interested to check out what this Texas music thing was all about. "London Homesick Blues" was greeted with mixed reactions. Some took minor offense, while others seemed to see the embedded humor and were able to appreciate it. We wrapped up the English leg of the tour and returned to Amsterdam.

We were there for a couple of days and then loaded into a tour bus for the last show of the tour, in Groningen, located in the very north of Holland on the North Sea. Groningen was the hometown of steel player Cos Biel, and there was a country music fan club there. On the bus ride, I got sandwiched between John Williams and John Phillips, who had come over from Paris. John W. wanted me to invest the $5,000 I had coming for the seven-week tour and become a full partner in the album project we recorded in London. They were putting the full-court press on me and were relentless.

I was not inclined to do it. Something was rotten, and I could smell it all the way from Amsterdam. First, I needed the money. Second, I didn't think the album had the potential to sell, and I probably would never recoup anything from it. I resisted, but they persisted. I had John Williams like a drill sergeant in one ear and John Phillips, whom I liked and respected, in the other. They hammered and hammered. They didn't relent, and I was stuck in the seat between them. By the time we reached Groningen, I was worn down, and I finally submitted. I felt like the innocent suspect who signs a confession just to get the investigators off his tail! I knew it was a bad deal. Consequently, I went home empty-handed after all the work I had done on the tour. The albums may still be in storage in Amsterdam somewhere. I do have a single copy worth $5,000 in my collection! It's for sale . . .

We did our show to a packed house in Groningen. Texas artist Clay Blaker and his band had driven over from Hamburg after their own show and turned up about the time we finished. It was good to see some familiar faces from home. We traded road tales for a while, and then our bunch loaded in the tour bus and drove back to Amsterdam. I flew back to Texas the next day exhausted and empty-handed. I was relieved to have the tour behind me, but I was still boiling inside over the Jerry Moore affair, and I was feeling weak and foolish for not standing up to John Williams and demanding the money I had coming.

WHEN I ARRIVED IN Austin, Christy picked me up and filled me in about the stolen check situation. I immediately began haggling with the bank about recovering the money paid out to Jerry Moore. They denied any liability, but for once in my life, I persisted, and eventually I was able to recover the funds.

David Wagnon, my artist friend from Santa Fe, had taken up residence at Public Domain. David was a painter but made his living primarily by dealing in antique Mexican architectural objects like Tarahumara pots, Mexican doors, tables, and chairs—all in great demand by people wanting to decorate their southwestern-style homes with genuine Mexican objects. He had a good business in Santa Fe but was looking to expand his market to Austin. Always willing to help a deserving artist, I provided him a place to hang and loaned him my extra pickup to make runs back and forth to Santa Fe and El Paso.

He immediately started remodeling Public Domain, ripping off the wall covering and exposing the natural rock walls behind. He cut a hole over the sink between the kitchen and the living room. He basically transformed the interior of a rented house. Being the decorator that he was, I suppose he couldn't help himself. His work did create more of a natural atmosphere, but it didn't do much for keeping the house warm in cold weather.

Years later, I visited the place for old time's sake, and it had remained the same. Even the old upright piano I had written many songs on was still there. That place should get a historical preservation seal for all the history that's happened there.

David's girlfriend in Santa Fe, Cecily Hughes, was in the art business, primarily selling expensive southwestern art to banks and fancy office buildings. She and her partner, Sara Jo Fischer, came to town to see a wealthy client who was building a high-rise office building in Austin. Ironically, it was the building constructed on the site where the Armadillo World Headquarters had been.

Their goal was to secure a deal to supply the artwork to decorate the building. David invited them to stay at Public Domain. Sara Jo and I became acquainted and struck up a friendship. She was a very attractive Jewish girl from Ohio but could have passed for an American Indian princess. She dressed to the nines for her wealthy clients and was very confident and outgoing. She had been a top sales associate at the prestigious Fenn Art Gallery in Santa Fe. We hit it off right off the bat.

I still had a lingering long-distance relationship with Michelle in New York, but the burden to maintain it fell entirely on me. I had supported her financially during her Rice years, paying her tuition and rent, and just putting money in her pocket. I was getting no attention or encouragement from Michelle, but a lot of both from Sara Jo. I made trips to Santa Fe at every chance. During one visit, she was house-sitting a beautiful home on Upper Canyon Road owned by her wealthy Austin client. We skied at Santa Fe and Taos and Red River, and our relationship blossomed. I was smitten and lapping up the attention she showered on me.

IN MAY OF '83, I was invited to Nashville to do a TV show. I contacted my friend Freddie Fletcher, Willie's nephew, for assistance. He agreed to put together a band to back me up. A young Gary Nicholson played guitar and Freddie played drums on the show. He was living on the Nelson family property in the Tennessee hills outside of Nashville, and he put me up in Willie's beautiful log cabin there on the property. I slept in Willie's bed! Then, I went out to Franklin to spend some time with Lukin, who was then seven years old.

Back in Texas, Pat Molac had walked in the front door of Public

Domain one day and asked me to do a benefit to preserve the old water tower in Gruene. He had purchased Gruene Hall and the old gristmill and was in the process of restoring the dance hall and converting the gristmill into a restaurant. I played my first show at the venerable "Texas's Oldest Dance Hall," which is situated on a bluff above the cypress-lined, green waters of the Guadalupe River just northwest of New Braunfels. It began a relationship that lasts to this day, and I still perform there several times a year. That was also when I started using Junior Brown regularly in my band, which I did for the next year and a half or so.

The river is famous for its excellent tubing, and Gruene Hall, the Gristmill, and the Guadalupe River have become some of the most visited tourist destination sites in all of Texas!

I am recalling those days by referring to my photo file of 35 mm black-and-white negatives and contact sheets, which is a virtual visual history of Texas musicians and the people who were in and out of my life during my travels. We were all so young and good-looking back then.[1]

In May of '83, I also produced a record for Melissa Javors with the guidance and assistance of Christy Ellinger. I had discovered Melissa at the Kerrville Folk Festival. She played piano and dulcimer, wrote the most excellent songs, and sang with an angelic voice. I was especially taken with her clean, intelligent, and expressive songwriting that dealt with love from an enlightened, feminine prospective. It also had a particularly Texas slant, which naturally I would be partial to. The album was titled *Just Beginning*. Melissa was a schoolteacher, and she had her students paint individual album jackets, each one totally unique.

---

1   When I complete this writing, I intend to focus on exploiting the thousands of photos I took with my little Canon Sure Shot. It's amazing how many really great exposures I got just pointing and shooting.

Christy arranged for an album release reception in the upstairs room of the Headliners East. Notables attending the reception were Sara K. Wooldridge, who had drifted to Austin following our European tour, and John T. Davis, whom I had helped get started in music journalism by giving him a job as a roadie for the Lost Gonzo Band. John T. went on to be the music writer for the *Austin American-Statesman* and is currently cranking out novels one after another. Also in attendance were Crow Johnson, a singer-songwriter out of Arkansas and perennial headline performer at the Kerrville Folk Festival; Nancy Griffith, who later landed a major record deal in Nashville and had Number One hit records like "Love at the Five and Dime"; Turk Pipkin, the six-foot-eight mime and master juggler who became a successful actor in the TV series *The Sopranos*; and author of books about Willie and master golf coach, Harvey Penick. And last, but certainly not least, the lovely and talented Christy Ellinger, my invaluable assistant and right-hand girl, who had taken the lead in working with Melissa to bring her project to fruition. Christy and Turk married the following summer. They cofounded the Nobility Project, which has raised millions of dollars to establish schools and infrastructure in Kenya, Africa, with which they are personally and intimately involved.

The caliber of the attendees at the reception speaks volumes as to the high regard in which Melissa Javors is held by her peers. I still pull out the record and listen to it on a regular basis. From the standpoint of the quality of songwriting, performance, and artistic expression, it ranks at the very top of my list of favorite records that I have ever been involved with.

MEMORIAL DAY AND THE Kerrville Folk Fest rolled around once again. I had been appointed by Rod Kennedy to the board of directors. It was the privilege of each board member to invite the artist of his or her choice to perform.

I selected Eliza Gilkyson. She came down from Santa Fe and made her first appearance in Texas. She was received with an overwhelming response and subsequently moved to Austin, where she enjoys widespread popularity. I'll take credit for her being in Texas and contributing to Austin's reputation as being the "Live Music Capital of the World." Christine Albert is another artist I persuaded to relocate.

During this period, I became acquainted with Murray Mead and Michelle Termohlen, a couple who had migrated from California to Austin. Murray was a successful entrepreneur who specialized in buying, refurbishing, managing, and selling motels for a profit. Many of you will remember the Villa Capri, located on I-35 near Memorial Stadium, which was one of his later projects. Murray and Michelle were active in supporting singer-songwriters and had taken on the talented Michael Ballew to sponsor. They took an interest in me as well, and we formed a close personal relationship that would have significant consequences in the not too distant future.

One day, John Williams called and offered to bring me back over to do another tour of Europe in June and July. The record was about finished, and he wanted me to come over to promote it. I had made some inroads and gathered a lot of fans on the first tour, so I reasoned that another trip might help me build on that and increase my visibility overseas. Plus, the idea of being a well-known Texas artist in Europe really appealed to me. I agreed to do a seven-week tour.

Sara K. joined us again for what was a repeat of the first tour, except there was much less activity in Europe in the summertime. We didn't return to England, but we made the rounds in Holland, Belgium, and Germany. We had significant downtime, as midweek dates were not available in the summer. I recall in particular a four-day layover in Koblenz on the Rhine River just west of Frankfurt.

We spent several days visiting the many castles sitting up high above the Rhine. There were wine festivals going on nearby, and we attended one that was celebrating the white wine harvest.

It was the first time I had the opportunity to soak up German culture, and it was on full display there. Newly made white wine was sold for one Deutsche Mark in soda bottles. Oompah bands were playing everywhere, and in the wine gardens, the German *volk* were singing traditional songs. Stocky blonde young women sang at the top of their lungs with their faces turning red from the exertion. At one point, Cos Biel, my Dutch steel player, leaned over and said in a low voice, "Gary P. (pronounced *Hah-ree P.*), now you can see for yourself the German mentality!" It appeared to me they were all having a good time! But memories of the war were still fresh in the minds of the Dutch. I made up the "Reggae Armadillo" just for fun in the hotel in Koblenz.

From there, we headed to Switzerland for another twenty-eight-day stand in Zürich. This time, however, we didn't return to the Hirschen but instead played another club that featured country music called the Nashville Sun. I was having a difficult time: The guitar they supplied for me was an Ovation gut-string. It was impossible to get the electrical ground adjusted properly, and every time I touched the microphone I would get shocked! It was totally distracting—as you can imagine—and very difficult to perform with the threat of being zapped in the lip every time you approached the microphone.

Unfortunately, my relationship with John Williams soured while we were there. His bullying nature began to be directed at me, and I was made to feel more like chattel rather than the name on the marquee. The record we had made was doing nothing, and the tour was long and tedious. I was not a happy camper. We returned to Amsterdam for the final week and played the Last Waterhole. John and I were totally at odds. He booted me out of the bedroom in his apartment, and I ended up sleeping on a mattress on the floor of an isolated, dingy, vacant room in his building.

One night, I was standing inside the entrance of the Last Water-hole on a break, when through the swinging doors walks Michelle! She was spending the summer at a villa in France. I was so lone-some and happy to see her that I threw my arms around her and hugged her for the longest time as tears ran down my face. She did not respond in kind and maintained a cool distance. That only added to my misery. She stayed a day or so, and even though I was in a total funk emotionally, I received no comfort from her.

Mercifully, the day finally came for my return to Texas. I did, however, this time, make sure I got paid. But my business with John Williams was finished!

BACK IN TEXAS, I vacated Public Domain, leaving it entirely avail-able for runaway fathers. I took up residence in the "Space," as we dubbed it. It was the entire upstairs part of a building at 501 E. 6th Street above the Balboa Restaurant that had been made available to David Wagnon by Terry Boothe. David painted the whole room white—including the floor—and moved in his artwork and stock of Mexican antiques. He constructed bunk beds for us to sleep on. There was only a toilet and washbasin up there, so we took our showers at Texas Hot Tubs that was located in the building just down the street on Waller Creek. For $3 you could rent a shower and a towel. Texas Hot Tubs was eventually closed down because of the AIDS scare that was beginning to sweep the country.

I spent the rest of the summer at the Space, and I lived an urban lifestyle in downtown Austin, which I had become used to after all the time I had spent in New York and Europe. We would put on private shows there and invite our friends. Artists like Sara K., Peter

Rowan, David Amram, and Junior Brown would drop by and perform. It was rather exotic living in an artist studio-loft with all the evening activity on 6th Street, which was just starting to develop as an entertainment district.

Sara Jo would come down from Santa Fe and visit while pursuing her art business, and we would stay at the Space. Invariably when she was there, Michelle would call in the middle of the night. Michelle's untimely reentries into my life spoiled my relationship with Sara Jo, who eventually had enough and gave me my walking papers. Soon afterward, Michelle finished her internship in New York and promptly called to tell me she was getting married! To make it worse, she flew to Houston the next day and showed up at a gig I had at Rockefeller's—and sat on the front row. Ouch! That was one of the toughest shows ever and extremely painful with her sitting right in front of me after she had so unceremoniously dumped me the night before. It took all the courage I could muster to cope with the emotions I was experiencing to get through it.

I was still involved with Taco Flats, the funky beer joint-taco stand on North Lamar. It was becoming well known as a popular hippie hangout and the site of the first Spamorama—a Spam cook-off spoof of the chili cook-offs that were proliferating around the country. It was promoted by Cosmic Carl and his wife, Linda, and it created quite a stir in town for the press.

Charlie Bullington, the jazz guitar whiz from The Pride of Texas, showed up and crashed at Public Domain. He played with me in the band that consisted of Junior Brown; Steve Mendell; Jimmy Marriott; and the fiddle-piano master Danny Levin. I even hired fifteen-year-old Monte Montgomery to fill in on guitar on a band trip to New Mexico.

Monte is the son of Maggie Montgomery, a perennial fixture and lovable character around Luckenbach. On the trip to Santa Fe, I showed him how to play the major scale with all four fingers.

Monte has become known worldwide for his mastery of the acoustic guitar. I ran into him recently at the Saxon Pub. He confided in me that my showing him that major scale fingering changed his life. It had opened up a new world of playing and led to the development of the unique style that he is known for today. As I've said before, sometimes the smallest things can have monumental consequences.

I was taking every opportunity to go up to the ranch in Oklahoma. By this time, I had accumulated quite a few cattle and was raising quarter horses. My brother Steve was living on the ranch in Hanna and looking after the livestock. We always had a couple of two-year-olds that needed breaking, and we would pair up and break them the old-fashioned way. Round pen training and horse whispering techniques were unknown to us. We would saddle up Old Joe, our dependable "bomb-proof" gelding. We'd put a halter and a bridle on and then carefully saddle the colt already "halter-broke" to lead. We would "snub" the colt's head to the saddle horn of the big horse. Steve would get on Old Joe, and I would carefully mount the colt. Having the colt's head snubbed high to the saddle horn by the lead rope prevented him from bucking, as he couldn't get his head down. Steve would put Old Joe in motion and off we'd go—from the house and down toward the river! After a good workout in the sand of the riverbed, the colt would tire and follow without resistance. At some point, Steve would reach down and unlatch the lead rope. The colt would follow, not realizing it had been freed.

From that point on, it was just a matter of putting miles on him. Rubbing and petting him to accustom him to being touched. Mounting and remounting. Picking up his feet and such. And feeding—that's important! We broke numerous colts that way, and they all became gentle and usable horses. I was always happiest when I was riding or working with horses.

ONE NIGHT BACK IN Austin, I was at Eddie Wilson's Threadgill's restaurant, just a block or so north of Public Domain on North Lamar. I was there to see Kenneth Threadgill perform his Jimmy Rogers yodeling act he was noted for. Eddie had named the restaurant for Kenneth. It was the site where Kenneth had run his beer joint in the old gas station building back in the '60s. Kenneth gave Janis Joplin her first gig in Austin there before she went to San Francisco and became a superstar.

I met VelAnne Rowland that night. VelAnne (aka Velta) was a rip-snortin' Texas gal from Hamlin, Texas, who would have given Annie Oakley a run for her money. I've always been attracted to characters, and she definitely was one . . . forever going on about the rebellious escapades she'd had . . . chuckling at her own stories . . . and at the same time, so sincere.

Her favorite story was about how she had dated the black quarterback in Hamlin just to ruffle feathers and poke a finger in the eye of conventional mores. She'd say, "Goddamn Jeep, why don't you marry me?" [She always called me "Jeep"!] I got some oil wells in Hamlin . . . we could live on the ranch . . . Yee-haw!"

I'd tell her, "Hell's bells, Velta, where do I get in line? You have a cowboy boyfriend, a tattooed punk rocker kid with spiked hair boyfriend, a yogi boyfriend, a hippie boyfriend . . . just where you gonna work me in?" It was all in good fun. VelAnne was a lifeguard at Barton Springs pool. She gave me a key to the back gate, and I would sneak in and go skinny-dipping after the pool had closed. That was where I began my lifelong love affair with Barton Springs and lifelong friendship with Velta.

I went back to New York to do a benefit show in a Broadway theatre that featured all Texas artists. The show's lineup was the dancer and choreographer Tommy Tune, an Austin product who had made it big in New York; the band and cast members of *The Best Little Whorehouse in Texas*; Joe Sears and Jaston Williams with *Greater Tuna;* and me. During the show, I sat backstage with another Texas expat, New York society columnist Liz Smith, and Debbie Reynolds.

The next day in the *New York Daily News,* Liz Smith wrote a piece about the show. This is what she wrote about me:

> "Gary P. Nunn could be the next Willie Nelson or Christopher Cross if anyone would take the time to notice his enormous talent!"

I would never presume to make such a claim, but it sure was gratifying to have someone of Liz Smith's stature do so. I couldn't help but compare the review of me by the society columnist for a major New York City newspaper with the treatment I had gotten at the Lone Star Café: In the end, my destiny was to be in Texas.

Chapter 12

Enter Ruth

IT WAS GETTING ON toward the end of 1983 when I got an invitation to perform on *Austin City Limits*. "London Homesick Blues" had been its theme song since 1974.

I had played on *ACL* with Jerry Jeff and in other configurations and was featured in an all-star lineup (available on YouTube) that included Ray Benson, Steven Fromholz, Marcia Ball, Tracy Nelson, and Jerry Jeff and the Lost Gonzo Band. But I had never performed there with my own show. I didn't have a regular band, but I knew the one group most familiar with my material was the Great American Honky Tonk Band in Red River. I gave them a call. They accepted enthusiastically and volunteered to bring fiddler David Coe with them. Junior Brown joined us on guitar and Herb Steiner on steel. Peter Rowan sat in with his acoustic guitar and mandolin, and Sara K. Wooldridge for harmony vocals. I invited Eliza Gilkyson to make a special guest appearance and sing a duet with me of her great song "Tennessee Road," which I had cut for the *Nobody But Me* album.

The day before the taping, the guys flew down from New Mexico. I rented a studio, and we rehearsed for the show. The next day, we reported early to the *ACL* sound stage on the University of Texas campus. It was exciting, but I was a nervous wreck. We did the taping to a packed audience, many of whom were my close personal friends. The band played flawlessly, and I managed to deal with my stage fright. We got through the show without having to do a single retake and got a standing O! The show was touted by Terry Lickona, the show's producer, as one of the best *ACL* shows to date. I know because I heard him say it on Paul Pryor's morning radio talk show a few days later. My friends Murray Mead and Michelle Termohlen were so excited about it that they approached Bill Arhos, the executive producer and creator of *Austin City Limits*, about the possibility of producing an album from the show, and he readily agreed.

We mixed the record down, and it went into production. We used a Lisa Law photo for the front cover and a Scott Newton photo for the back. Murray and Michelle proceeded to follow through with all the production details. Before the end of the year, we had the record—titled *Home with the Armadillo–Live at Austin City Limits*—in our hands. Murray and Michelle brainstormed another unprecedented idea: They arranged with *ACL* to create a video ad that was aired on successive shows. It offered my album for sale to a national audience through a telemarketing company in California. Slim Whitman and Boxcar Willie had enjoyed phenomenal success in England by selling records via television.

I thought that ship I had been waiting for was finally about to come in.

But the folks at *Austin City Limits* and the telemarketing company, who both had a piece of the action, had set the telemarketing price at twenty-eight dollars! *What?* You could purchase an album in the record shops at the time for eight or nine dollars! It was priced way out of the market and didn't sell at all! A giant opportunity for me had been squandered. On the positive side, I did have a new product in my catalogue, a recording of "London

Homesick Blues" with my name on it, and the active support of Murray and Michelle.

I was notified by BMI that "Last Thing I Needed, First Thing This Morning," was one of the "most played songs of the year," and I was invited to attend the awards ceremony. Ray Benson was also receiving an award for Asleep at the Wheel, so he flew with me to New York, and we attended the awards ceremony together. Willie Nelson's *Always on My Mind* received BMI's Album of the Year Award. Even though I hadn't had a regular band to work with, 1983 turned out to be a very eventful and productive year!

EARLY IN 1984, I got a call from Martin Schweitzer in Zürich, asking me to come back for another twenty-eight days at the Hirschen. Using The Pride of Texas was out of the question, so I was faced with deciding who to take. I asked Junior Brown, then fiddler-pianist Danny Levin, and on bass, Dale Dennis. At the time, I didn't know a drummer available that I could depend on, so I opted to not take one. I bought a nice Ovation acoustic guitar and figured I would keep time myself. The absence of loud banging drums would please Martin Schweitzer anyway. Sara K. couldn't make the trip, so I invited local female vocalist Megan Coleman to fill that spot.

The second time at the Hirschen was much easier. The staff and the audience were familiar with me, and the outstanding musicianship of Junior, Danny, and Dale made it easy to connect with the audience. I featured Danny on fiddle with the "Orange Blossom Special" and other standards that he could rip! I featured Junior Brown, who played steel guitar in the classic form, and of course on vocals in the Ernest Tubb–style for which he is so well known today. The total package made for a much better show.

One night toward the end of the stretch, we were spending a typical after-hours, after-dinner evening in the venue, enjoying the pleasant company of the staff. I was feeling no pain myself, and I clinked a glass and begged for everyone's attention. "Since y'all have been so good to us, I want to invite you all to come and visit me in Texas. We'll ride cowboy horses and sleep in Indian teepees!"

At that point, Ruth, which was the name of the lady on staff who had called me a *schlitzohr*, sauntered up, got close to my face, and said, "I need an American passport. Why don't you marry me and take me to Texas?"

"Well," I replied, responding in the playful spirit in which I assumed she had spoken, "That's the best offer I've had all day . . . I need a wife . . . let's get going!"

Her friends were zeroed in on it, and they came forth with the likes of "Yay!" and "Hooray!" and "You guys go for it!"

"You be serious?" she asked.

"Dang right I'm serious. [I'm still playing.] I've chased every single girl in Texas and couldn't catch one. You want to get married? We'll just get married!" Again, I'd spoken words that, having left my lips, could never be retrieved.

She continued, "Can I have my cats?"

Not knowing the extent of what that meant I said, "Sure, you can have your cats."

"Do you work hard?"

The Swiss work ethic was admired worldwide at that time. "Yes, I work hard," I said. That wasn't completely untrue.

"Do you make a lot of money?" she continued.

"I hope to make a lot of money, and what I do make, I'll bring home to you!" That elicited a few handclaps and cheers.

After a brief pause, she said, "Well, okay then. Get up on that table, turn around, and let me have a look at you!"

I did, and apparently, she liked what she saw. That was the first time we had had a conversation to speak of, but what a conversation! The expression, "Let's cut to the chase" comes to mind, and a very short chase it was. In less than a minute's time, we were transformed from virtual strangers into fiancés—more or less.

"Don't flinch," Jerry Jeff used to say. I didn't, and it would turn out to be the best thing that ever happened to me! The next few days we hung out together. She took me skiing at the nearest ski resort, and I got my first taste of the Swiss Alps. In a few days, we finished our twenty-eight days. The guys in the band flew home, and Megan Coleman and I boarded a train for Paris. Turned out Megan had fallen in love with Sean O'Brien, the owner of the Irish pub up the street from the Hirschen, and she ended up marrying him and staying in Zürich.

Ruth and I parted with plans to pursue the idea of our getting together. I asked her to come over so I could show her my life, and she could see my goals and plans and decide if she still wanted to get married.

BY THIS TIME, I had vacated the Space downtown, and David Wagnon had returned to Santa Fe to work as a set designer on *Silverado*. I retained Public Domain just to accommodate anybody who needed a place to stay and rented an efficiency duplex at 1201-1/2 Baylor Street. It cost $150 a month and had just enough room to put my office in the front and a bed in the middle room. As always, I rarely ventured into the kitchen.

Ruth would call me from time to time with the question, "You still be serious?"

"Yes, I be serious." I was in too deep to pull out now anyway.

I made a trip to Brussels and played with a band of Germans at the Ancienne Belgique. It normally takes about a year to get a band in shape, so you can imagine how we sounded after a one-hour rehearsal with guys who speak little English.

After that, I went straightaway to Amsterdam to hang out for a few days. It had become familiar territory, and I stayed at a small hotel in the "District." The girl living in the room next door was an artist. She would leave her door open, and I could see her room was filled with excellent paintings. One day, she knocked on my door. She came in, and we struck up a conversation. She was Dutch but spoke good English. After a bit, she asked me to give her twenty guilders. If I would, she said, she would go get some cocaine and then we could "make it in the bed!" Then it struck me that she was a "working gal," and giving her money would not be a wise thing to do.[1] She was somewhat charming and very persistent. Finally, just to get rid of her, I gave her the twenty guilders and told her to take it and go.

She was back in ten minutes. She had not bought cocaine, but heroin, and she proceeded to get out the spoon and the lighter and the syringe right there in my room! I thought I was going to throw up, and I ordered her to leave. That was the one and only time I have ever been exposed directly to anything like that.

I came home and headed straight to Red River for another short run at the Motherlode and spring skiing. My show on *Austin City Limits* was due to air, and Sara K. and all the band guys who played on the show were there. We were hyped up about it and in a celebratory mood. The Red River regulars showed up to join in. We set up a TV in the bar. *ACL* was using the occasion as a fundraiser for PBS and had a bank of phones and operators in the studio taking calls for contributions during the show.

I was stoked by the whole situation. For one night, Gary P. Nunn was the undisputed star of the show! Then, I got a brilliant idea. I would call the show personally and make a donation pledge, hoping

---

1   Cousin Milton used to say, "One working gal is worth three rent houses!"

to help out the fundraising effort and get a little bump PR-wise. Maybe they would put me on the air live, and I could encourage folks to pledge! I could just hear the person emceeing the fundraiser announcing live on the show, "Ladies and gentlemen, we have a special treat for you. Gary P. Nunn is with us live on the phone and wants to make a pledge to support PBS!"

I went out to a phone booth outside. Giant fluffy snowflakes were falling. I dialed the 800-number and reached the phone bank in the studio.

"Austin City Limits, may I have your name please?"

"Hi, this is Gary P. Nunn, and I'd like to make a pledge."

"Who is this? I didn't catch your name," the operator said.

"This is Gary P. Nunn. I'm watching my show, and I want to make a pledge."

"I'm sorry, I didn't catch your name. Would you mind repeating that for me?"

"THIS IS GARY P. NUNN!" I said, practically screaming into the phone.

"Could you spell that for me?"

"Just forget it!" I yelled, banging the phone receiver two or three times before I hung it up.

I walked back into the Motherlode covered with snow and feeling a bit deflated. It was my big night. I was on nationwide TV. I was the star of the show they were using to raise money for PBS, but my name didn't ring a bell with the lady on the phone! It's kind of funny in retrospect. There I was, all puffed up and full of myself but at the same time totally vulnerable to the opinion of an unknown woman at the other end of a phone line. It was a good lesson in humility, and my feelings of deflation were totally unjustified (I know that now) because I was, after all, THE STAR OF THE SHOW!

In April, I got on a bus with the lineup from the Kerrville Folk

Festival to attend the Crawfish Festival in Beaumont. Beto and the Fairlanes, Robert Shaw, Townes Van Zandt, and David Amram, the avant-garde composer of movie themes from New York, were all on the bill. Junior, Danny, Dale, and Jimmy Marriott backed me up.

And Texas Governor Mark White proclaimed Gary P. Nunn as the Official Texas Ambassador to the World!

RUTH ARRIVED IN AUSTIN having disposed of all her belongings in Zürich. I picked her up at the airport and took her straight to the old El Rancho on 1st Street (now named Cesar Chavez) for Mexican food and showed her the sights around town. The next day, I took her to Barton Springs pool and told her she might see some topless bathers there. "*So . . . ?*" she replied. I took her to Texas Hatters to meet Manny Gammage, and he made her a hat. Then, we went out to Luckenbach, and from there, to San Antonio to see the Alamo. We went to Ruidoso, Santa Fe, Taos, and to the ranch in Oklahoma. When we approached the Red River on the Oklahoma line north of Sherman, I told her to get out her passport as we were about to cross the border into Indian Territory. She thought I was serious and got out her Swiss passport! The purpose of all this traveling was to give her an idea of what life with me would be like and to give her a chance to escape. We attended Christy and Turk's wedding at Steiner Ranch, and then it was Kerrville Folk Festival time.

Benford Standley, forever the promoter, had talked the people at a newly constructed high-rise bank building on Congress Avenue into giving us floor space in a storefront to retail a line of "Gary P. Nunn Guacamole Apparel." Inspired by our trip to Guatemala, I had the idea that hip clothes could be designed using the colorful textiles I saw there. We teamed up with Oakleaf Annie, a seamstress friend, and she created all sorts of fashion items utilizing the hand-woven Guatemalan fabrics. On paper, it appeared as if I were becoming quite the entrepreneur, with a Mexican food restaurant and cantina (Taco Flats) on North Lamar and a line of designer clothes sold exclusively in a high-rise bank building on Congress!

Ruth and I settled into a Central Austin lifestyle, living in the three-room efficiency duplex on Baylor. The hike and bike trail had an entry spot on nearby Shoal Creek. I settled into my routine of running round Town Lake and swimming a lap in Barton Springs. Our love affair blossomed—despite its unusual budding. A few months later, she visited a doctor for a check-up. She came out and said, "I be pregnant!" Well, that settles that. Looks like she was going to get her American passport for sure. I was thrilled! I'm not sure that she was at that moment.

Soon after that news, I got an offer from Mike Barrow. Mike was a halibut fisherman in Seward, Alaska, and the son of my good friend Mary Lou Barrow, whom we dubbed our "redneck mother"! He said I should come up and do a single gig at the Yukon Bar in Seward and salmon fish for a couple of weeks. The idea of an Alaskan adventure appealed to me. After all, how many chances do you get to go fishing in Alaska and make money at the same time?

I invited my buddy Herb Steiner, who was an avid fisherman. We flew to Anchorage and drove down to Seward. We would perform during the short three hours of darkness, and then get on the *Espidon*, a seventy-five-foot sailing vessel, and sail out for an evening of daylight. We'd wake up about 10:00 a.m. at the dock and head out on Cook's Inlet to salmon fish for a few hours. The "silver salmon" (Coho) were running, and we'd catch a mess of seven- to ten-pounders in no time.

We visited the local glaciers and went out on day sails in the Gulf of Alaska. We hired a bush plane, landed on a lake in the Alaskan wilderness, and camped in a forest service cabin. The pilot lent us an outboard motor he carried on the plane, and we mounted it on a small boat there. For three days, we went out on the lake and fished for grayling. The water was so clear you could put your lure right in front of them, and they would bite every time. It was a great adventure.

Townsend Miller, the music writer for the *Austin American-Statesman*, was also on that trip, and this gives me an opportunity to say a few words about him.

Townsend was a stockbroker in Austin and a passionate fan of country music who would make the rounds visiting all the venues with live music several nights a week. He persuaded the *Statesman* to let him write a weekly column covering the local music scene. This was a significant event and had a profound impact on the growth of Austin's music reputation. Up until that time, all kinds of music was happening in the clubs, the fraternity houses, and the Armadillo World Headquarters, but there was little or no media coverage except for the local rags, which were ignored by the public at large. Radio stations took no note of local talent.

That all changed when Townsend started covering the local scene. He wrote for no salary and did it just because he loved it. "If I can't say anything good, I won't say anything at all," was his motto. When he started writing about the local singer-songwriters and musicians and the places they were playing, it was the spark that started the fire. When one type of media takes notice, others follow suit, and the fire spreads. Townsend Miller's contribution to the Texas music industry cannot be overstated!

We returned to Austin from Alaska just in time to be invited to play for a political rally on the steps of the Texas Capitol for Walter Mondale, the Democratic candidate for president. Ann Richards, Jim Hightower, Bob Armstrong, and all the Democratic movers and shakers were onstage.

JUNIOR BROWN CONCEIVED OF designing a special guitar that merged a guitar and a steel guitar into one instrument. He discussed the idea with me, and I agreed that it sounded like a great idea. I encouraged him to pursue it. I had bought a couple of inexpensive Fender guitars from Ray Hennig at Heart of Texas Music. They were similar to the old Fender Mustang that was popular when I was a kid. I gave Junior one of them, and he took the neck from that guitar and incorporated it into the first prototype built by Michael Stevens. It turned out great, suited Junior's classic country style perfectly, and freed him up from having to switch from guitar to steel.

I also had a hand in securing Junior a position at Rogers State College in Claremore, Oklahoma, to teach in the music school there and study under the great Leon McAuliffe, who played steel with Bob Wills. Later, I put him in touch with Michael Taylor, an Oklahoma friend of mine who had moved to Hawaii, who arranged for Junior to go there and immerse himself in traditional Hawaiian steel. I've read interviews with Junior where he mentions how these two events were instrumental in the development of his career and playing style.

Around this time, a new club opened up in town on 6th Street called Texas Money. I started playing there on a fairly regular basis, as did Rusty Wier, T. Gozney Thornton, and others who leaned toward country. One night, Larry Hagman, who played the part of J. R. on *Dallas*, was in the audience, a guest of Murray Mead's. As he was leaving, he dropped a one-hundred-dollar bill in the tip jar on the stage and said, "If you ever take those glasses off, you're going to be a star!" That made me feel good, and my thoughts went back to all the grief I had experienced in Europe being called "J. R."

Danny Levin had been with me since before we went to Zürich, but one night he informed me that he was going to drop out. He introduced me to a talented fiddle and guitar player named Erik Hokkanen, a young man in his early twenties who had just moved from Florida. Erik's previous gig was being the "Fiddling Bear" at Disney World. He came up to the dressing room at Texas Money and pulled out his fiddle and auditioned for me. His extraordinary talent was so obvious. I hired him on the spot! Erik played with me regularly for the next couple of years. He is one of the most gifted and creative players I've ever worked with.

Benford Standley and I put together a benefit for the Texas Runaway Hotline at the Texas Opera House. It featured Rusty Wier, Steven Fromholz, B. W. Stevenson, Ray Wylie Hubbard, Rattlesnake Annie, Michael Martin Murphey, and me. That was probably the most concentrated lineup of Texas talent to share the same stage since Willie's picnic at College Station in '74!

Things continued to rock along without major incident till near Christmas. I came home one day, and Ruth asked me a very unambiguous question in her direct Swiss manner. "When we be married?"

"Well, any time you like . . . how about tomorrow? What day is this?" I looked at the calendar, and it was Wednesday, December 18. The next day was the nineteenth and, for some reason, that number didn't suit me. "How about the day after tomorrow, the twentieth?"

I called my friend Laura Mendenhall, who was the pastor of the Central Presbyterian Church in downtown Austin. She and her husband, Chuck, and a group from their congregation frequently came out to the Broken Spoke to dance. We got acquainted and became good friends, so she was the first to come to mind to marry us. I called the office at the church, and she answered the phone.

"Laura, this is Gary P. Nunn."

"Uh-huh, *who* is this?" she said, in an incredulous tone.

"This is Gary P. Nunn, and I was wondering if you would marry me."

"I'm already married!" she exclaimed. "This is a joke, right? Who is this?"

"Laura, this is really Gary P., and I was wondering if you could marry Ruth and me on Friday the twentieth." She had a cello recital in the sanctuary that day, but if we could be at the church, she would perform the ceremony afterward. So on Friday morning, I bought Ruth a corsage, and we dressed up and went to the church.

We listened to the recital, and then Laura signaled us to join her down front. She had arranged for her organ player to play some music and serve as the witness. We exchanged our vows there, with just the four of us in attendance—a first-class church wedding. Afterward, we walked to the Austin Hotel and had lunch and returned to the place on Baylor to begin our marriage together. There was no honeymoon—only a lifetime of happiness in our future.

We enrolled in Lamaze classes and waited for the baby to come. Julian Phillip Nunn was born on July 7, 1985 at the birth-ing center at Brackenridge Hospital. They put Ruth on the bed during her labor, but she found it intolerably uncomfortable to lie down, so she went through her entire labor standing up using the bed for support. She ended up delivering while sitting on the floor! It was quite a humorous scene watching the doctor down on his knees checking her progress at floor level. When the baby arrived, the nurse put him in my arms, and I welled up with fatherly pride, said a silent prayer of gratitude to God for Ruth's safe delivery of a healthy child, and made the comment, "He smells like barbeque!"

Ruth has never let me forget that.

Obviously we needed more room. Ruth discovered a nice, big house right down the street for rent at 1208 Baylor. It was just across the street from Michael Brovsky's office. The rent was $850 a month.

My expenses were starting to get out of hand as I was still paying rent at Public Domain and making payments on a rent house I had in Wichita Falls that went unrented. We lived at the big house on Baylor till after Julian's first birthday. I was being eaten out of house and home with payments on three different places. That was not my modus operandi.

MY COUSIN TOLLIE BOY Nunn was quite a character. He was 100 percent Okie and damned proud of it. He had an Ag degree like his dad, and he was a cowboy/horse trader/character if there ever was one. He would "ride the blacktops" around Oklahoma and knew all the cowboys. He used to throw Tollie Nunn parties and 500 people would show up. He bragged back in 1976 that more people in Oklahoma knew him than knew Jimmy Carter. He had horse-trading deals and partnerships and breeding fees all over the state the likes of which no one could ever unravel.

The point is, he was well known and well liked all over the state and had a hell of a following. I figured with his connections, we could team up, and I could add Oklahoma to my territory and live my fantasy of being a cowboy too. I had always dreamed of living on the ranch, so I suggested to Ruth that we move there and cut down on all our expenses.

We arranged to buy a double-wide and have it set up on the ranch. After thirteen years, I finally let go of Public Domain. We vacated the house on Baylor and set up housekeeping on the ranch in Oklahoma. My brother Steve was married with a son the same age as Julian, and he took up residence in my rent house in Wichita Falls. I took over possession of the ranch and adjacent family property that totaled eight hundred acres. I had accumulated fifty mother cows or so by selling the bull calves and keeping the heifers and slowly building up a herd.

We had four pretty, well-bred quarter mares, and I would send them to a good Oklahoma Star, Leo-bred stallion owned by our neighbor Charlie Schropshire. Charlie always kept good stallions down there, and he would breed our mares for $50 with no mare-care fees. We always had foals coming that I would break and sell to locals who came around looking for well-bred gentle horses at a cheap price. I'd sell them broken to ride for $500.

I had my hay round-baled, and I made enough to get my animals through the winter. I bought an old International Harvester 956 diesel tractor to move the round bales as I was doing the feeding in the winter—no tractor cab, no heater, and no turtle and rabbit decals on the dash. I can tell you, it could be miserable feeding in the winter, but I enjoyed it and took pride in doing a job that had to be done.

I added the titles Cattleman and Quarter Horse Breeder/Trainer to my resume. I somehow forgot to add farm laborer, chainsaw operator, and fence builder to the list.

I was commuting back and forth to Texas every weekend—an 800-mile round-trip to Austin. I did that from 1986 till 2003. I'd leave out on Thursdays and make the trip to Austin, where I'd stay with my bachelor friend, Bob Honts, who was a county commissioner in Travis County.

Bob had a nice house on Comanche Trail, just above Hippie Hollow. He was, as county commissioner, primarily responsible for having Hippie Hollow and Windy Point converted to county parks, and for having FM 2222 expanded from a dangerous, winding, two-lane road, to a four-lane highway from Balcones Drive in northwest Austin all the way to Highway 71. People called him the "Road Warrior." I bunked at Bob's house on my weekend trips to Austin or wherever the gig was for many years.

My bands would last a year or so maybe, and then they would leave to take other gigs or perhaps just got weary of all the traveling.

We were doing regular trips to the Little Bear in Evergreen, Colorado, and making runs from Port Aransas to the XIT in Dalhart and all points in between. By then, I had two little Chevy pickups, one for me and one for the band. In the midst of all this, my old friend Bill Walker from Arkansas offered to produce another record for me at Grady Trimble's studio in Little Rock. We used the top Little Rock musicians, with Andrew Frye on piano. Andrew and I are still in touch today, and he sits in with me on occasion.

I would make my weekend trips to Texas and drive back to the ranch on Sundays. Monday morning, I would drive the four hours to Little Rock, go into the studio, and start recording. We'd work long hours on Tuesdays and Wednesdays. I'd return to Hanna on Wednesday evening. Then, on Thursday afternoon, I would get on the road back to Texas. It took me six weeks to complete the album, and as you can tell, I didn't see much of Ruth or my young son.

The record turned out to be really good. I cut songs by a variety of artists: Junior Brown, Red River writers Michael Hearne and Rick Fowler, Rick Cardwell, Brian Burns, George Ensle, and Arkansas writer Frank Wood. I also cut my own "Think I'll Go to Mexico" and the first studio version of "What I Like About Texas." I titled the album *Border States* and released it in 1986. I was using a band based in Oklahoma City: Cleve Warren, Rick Reynolds, and Billy Shephard. I would drive from the ranch to Oklahoma City, pick the guys up, go to Texas for the weekend, deliver them back to OKC, and drive back to the ranch. Eventually this became too much for all of us, and we gave it up.

That year Ruth decided she wanted to put on a chili cook-off/music festival at the ranch. We called it the "Terlingua North Summer Social and Chili Cook-off." She got busy and more or less single-handedly made it happen. I had become acquainted with an Oklahoma band called The Great Divide. They wanted to make a record, and I suggested they get Lloyd Maines to produce it, which they did. They volunteered to come to the ranch and build the stage, as three of them were ranch hand cowboys and had welding skills. Mike McClure was the front man and principal songwriter—but not a welder, so he looked on and kept us entertained while the stage was constructed.

We had a great turnout of between 500 and 600 people who came from all over to camp out in a pasture and enjoy the music and the chili. The Great Divide broke out from our festival and soon were touring in a bus and headlining others' festivals.

The next year, Cross Canadian Ragweed called Ruth and asked to play Terlingua North. They did and went over big. I ran into them again soon thereafter in Stillwater, Oklahoma. I had a show at Gruene Hall the next night, and I told Cody Canada that if they wanted to, they were welcome to come sit in on my break. Dang if they didn't show up in Gruene the next night! I put them on. It wasn't long before they became one of the biggest names in the so-called Red Dirt Movement!

The next year at Terlingua North, it was Pat Green. He had opened for me as a single at a show in Lubbock, and I saw him at a private Labor Day party at the Welsh Ranch in Riesel, Texas, and again at the Sons of Hermann Hall in Dallas. He was bursting with energy, and I sensed his potential to go places. Ruth invited him to appear at Terlingua North, and the next thing you know, the hottest thing was Pat Green! It seemed that all three of these acts soared after playing Terlingua North. James Hand was another unknown at the time that we had come up to play.

In 1989, I went into Fire Station Studios in San Marcos and released a record called *For Old Times' Sake*. One by one, as the band guys peeled off, I went back to subbing musicians, and I did manage to make a record every two or three years.

FOR YEARS, DAVID CARD'S Poor David's Pub on lower Greenville Avenue in Dallas had been the main venue where Texas songwriters performed. It was primarily an acoustic listening room that catered to a folk music audience. Steve Layne, Ricky Davis, and Gary Delz came on board around 1990, and we had a pretty good run. We recorded a live CD at Poor David's and released it in 1991. Then a new club started up that had a profound effect on expanding that market.

John Bailey opened up a room on Industrial Boulevard in Dallas called the Three Teardrops Tavern. He featured acts based primarily in the Dallas–Fort Worth area, giving exposure to songwriters who were just starting out and who wouldn't have any exposure otherwise. He got the club off the ground rapidly with a brilliant idea: He sold Schlitz Beer for $1 a can! It quickly became a favorite watering hole for the young professionals working in downtown Dallas, police officers, and music fans. As I already had a name, I became a regular featured artist, and I drew some big crowds.

The Three Teardrops began booking local songwriters like Tommy Alverson, Eddie Burleson, Brian Burns, and Ronnie Spears, as well as classic country acts like Johnny Bush and Leon Rauch, formerly the singer for Bob Wills.

Tommy Morrell, one of the greatest steel guitarists on the planet, would sit in regularly.

Roy Ashley, the program director for Dallas's community-sponsored radio station, KNON, got involved and started doing promotions and broadcasting shows. It raised the visibility of all of us and the Three Teardrops became the focal point for the Texas music scene in Dallas. And it had room enough to dance!

The Three Teardrops ended up influencing the Fort Worth scene as well. Phillip Murrin opened the Longhorn Saloon in the Stockyards using the same format. Two major Texas markets were opened for our kind of music, and they contributed greatly to the expansion of our audience and territory.

My publishing and recordings catalogue was growing slowly.

One night in San Antonio, Paul Jones, a local record-store owner, asked me about doing another record. A year or so prior, a songwriter by the name of Larry Joe Taylor had approached me and asked if I would publish his material. He had written a few pretty good songs that showed a lot of promise, so I agreed to work with him. It seemed that gave him a creative boost, and he started writing really good songs in quick succession. We cowrote a few together. Many of them had a Tex-Mex Texas coast theme as if inspired by Jimmy Buffett. Songs by Geronimo Trevino, Brian Burns, Joe Pat Hennen, Tommy Alverson and others that fit the theme were building up in my publishing company as well, so I decided to do a concept record for Paul Jones using those songs.

Steve Layne, "Little" Ricky Davis, and Gary Delz made a good little four-piece band that could cover a lot of ground. We went back into the Fire Station Studio and cut the record I titled *Totally Guacamole*. Paul Jones released it in 1992 on Campfire Records, a new record label that he formed with his attorney partner, Jim Hoffman. *Totally Guacamole* was my very first CD (as opposed to vinyl!), and it was received very well. But with no promotion, its reputation never reached beyond the boundaries of Texas.

Larry Joe Taylor went on to be a stable force in the Texas music scene, and he created the largest music festival in Texas. Tommy Alverson, Brian Burns, Davin James, Geronimo Trevino and others went on from that point to have successful and productive careers. I hope that my recording their songs and shining the spotlight on them contributed to that in a positive manner.

THE NEXT TEN YEARS are somewhat of blur. Time flew by. I was commuting a thousand miles a week from Oklahoma to Texas and back. Musicians, as usual, came in and out of the band with frustrating regularity. It was one step forward and two steps back every time I had to find and train new ones.

I was visiting my friend Don Holland at his ranch in Brownwood, Texas, one evening after a show. We were sitting around a fireplace when one of his sons asked, "Why don't you release a greatest hits record?"

I replied, "Well, if I did, what songs would go on it?"

The boys proceeded to reel off a list of tunes they thought had to be included. I wrote down the list and gave it to Paul Jones. Paul contracted Jim Franklin, the famed "armadillo artist" to create the cover, and in 1997, we released a Gary P. Nunn *Greatest Hits—What I Like About Texas* CD on Campfire Records. To this day, it's still the best seller of all the recordings I've made.

I LOOKED AROUND ONE day, and Julian was starting school at Hanna, and then he was graduating from junior high. There were only four kids in his class. Naturally, he was the valedictorian! He wanted to play football, so we transferred him to Eufaula High School, and he played on the team that produced the Selmon brothers and J. C. Watts.

Then I looked again, and he was about to graduate from high school. He had spent his summers as a camper at Camp Stewart in Hunt, Texas, and later became a camp counselor. One summer, we sent him to Hawaii to do home construction for old friend Mike

Barrow. I had missed the greater part of his growing up, as well as Lukin's. Ruth had been home alone for all those years. Those are my greatest regrets.

One day I arrived in Houston on a flight from France. I called to let Ruth know I had arrived safely back in the country.

"Hello dear, I'm back." There was a brief pause, and I sensed something was not right.

"What's going on?" I said.

"Mister Nunn." Uh-oh. When she says Mister Nunn, I know it's serious.

"Mister Nunn, you are a callous person," I understood her to say.

Wow, this is a heck of a welcome-home greeting! I can't imagine why she would call me a callous person.

"What makes you say that? I'm curious to know."

"Because I sold all your *Gott*damn cows! Every time you leave, your cows get out on the river, and people come barking at me, and I have to go get them back, and I'm not going to do it anymore!"

There was nothing I could say back to that. I was officially a cowless cowboy.

I didn't blame her. She was alone and had to deal with all the problems that arose. She also wanted a gun. She had been in a shooting club in Zürich, and she knew how to handle and shoot a gun with proficiency. I'd bought her a little .22/410 "over and under," but I dragged my feet about buying her a pistol. I came home once and found a dead possum hanging on the gate and another one hanging from the doorknob by a piece of twine around his neck. That possum had a bullet hole right between his eyes! I think she was sending me a message.

Then there was the time I came home, and Ruth met me at the door. She had her hands on her hips, and she proclaimed, "When this boy graduates from high school and goes to college in Texas . . . you can live on this ranch if you want to, but I won't be here!" Well that was a plain enough message. She had been by herself too many years. She had done everything from covering the double-wide in cedar shingles to putting on a metal roof—everything to make ours a nice home. She ran the ranch almost single-handedly. She had had enough isolation.

The time had come for us to move back to Texas.

Epilogue

DETERMINED TO FOLLOW THROUGH on her idea to leave Oklahoma early in 2003, Ruth began making trips back and forth to Austin looking for a house to buy. She wanted to live in the country, so she looked in the Hill Country from Wimberley to Burnet. She also looked in the piney woods of Bastrop east of Austin. Our friend Angela Tharp's dad was a real estate agent, and Ruth engaged him to help her find something that would suit her. She found a fifteen-acre piece of property in Burnet County outside Marble Falls that had no house, but it did have a water well. Looking for a builder, we stopped into the David Weekly Homes showroom in northwest Austin: It didn't take her long to settle on a beautiful model, and we made the deal to have a house built.

By the time Julian graduated from high school, the house was completed. He went to Camp Stewart as a counselor for the summer, and we packed up and moved from the ranch. Julian enrolled in college at Texas State in San Marcos. It was tough for me to leave the ranch and abandon my dream of establishing a "Kids' Farm," but I had to face reality.

I have a saying about that. "You can deny reality, but you can't avoid the consequences of denying reality."

I never dared to dream it would be possible for us to have a home built, but Ruth had the vision, and her focus and determination made it happen.

It was a good example that the tenets set forth in the book *The Secret of the Ages* were valid. All we have to do is create an image of what we want in our minds and focus and concentrate on that image. Ruth created a beautiful home for us. From Day One, she made all kinds of improvements. She laid rock for flower beds and planted gardens, flowers, and trees; she added on porches and decks; she built outbuildings; she did landscaping, painting, and remodeling. She cooks like a European chef and sets beautiful cuisine on the table every evening. She has been my steadfast partner, taking care of all our business during my many absences and serving for years as manager and booking agent. If I had looked the whole world over, I couldn't have found a better partner and helpmate. The Lord steps in and blesses us when we need it the most if we just "don't flinch."

From 2003 till the present, I have stuck to my guns and not let setbacks stop me. It's been a steady process, and I have used any setbacks I've encountered as learning experiences. We've made progress by being true to our word, avoiding making promises we couldn't keep, and paying our own way—just trying to be productive citizens, as Uncle Samuel would say.

I have been blessed with good health, and I have driven over two million miles alone without an accident—knock on wood! "Success is survival," as Leonard Cohen told me many years ago.

As I wind down this narrative, I am reminded of a line by master recording engineer/musician/producer Tommy Detamore, who once said, "Recording projects are never finished . . . just abandoned!" That's the way I feel right now.

I said at the start that I was going to write off the top of my head and see what came out. I have consulted none of my journals or notes, only my file of photographs, to remind me of the places I have been and the people I have encountered along the way. There are so many stories—too many to include them all.

I have attempted to relate the stories of the events and characters that represented turning points in my personal life and music career that have guided me to this point here at the end of April 2017. With that, I say, "Adios amigos," and until we meet again, I will remain your

Friend for life,
Gary P. Nunn

The End

Acknowledgments

I AM HUMBLED TO have been recognized with many honors over the years. I want especially to express my appreciation to Governor Rick Perry for proclaiming me the Official Ambassador of Texas Music back in 2007.

I have witnessed the phenomenal growth of the Texas music industry, for which I have quietly worked since that fateful evening in 1972 when Michael Murphey offered me a job at a time when I had almost given up.

I am proud of the role I had and the opportunity to play. It came natural to me. It gives me a great deal of pleasure to see artists I have had the privilege to be associated with grow in their talent and be successful. I am very grateful to the writers of the songs I have recorded and published, as they are my real heroes. I'd be proud if they considered me to have played some positive role in their careers.

I want to thank all the musicians I've had the privilege to work with, without whom I couldn't have played a single show. I love and respect every single one of you.

There are countless personal friends who have contributed so much to this story. I assure you that you are very much loved and appreciated and certainly not forgotten.

I would be remiss if I failed to thank my main man, John (Hondo) Burris, who has been the "Trail Boss" of my outfit for the past ten years. He possesses all the admirable traits associated with the ideal cowboy. His limitless contributions, commitment, and loyalty—along with bassist Ric Ramirez, guitarist Derek Groves, and Russ Patterson—have been key to the tremendous growth in business we have experienced since we've been working together.

Also, I must thank D. Foster, who came on board to help me with social media and promotion. His efforts have increased our visibility exponentially in nine short months. This has given me new inspiration and motivation to persevere at a time when I was seriously considering retirement. He is responsible for prompting me to write this book, and, I must say, I have thoroughly enjoyed doing it.

GARY P. NUNN DISCOGRAPHY

Nobody But Me	Campfire Records 1980
Home With the Armadillo Live at ACL	Campfire Records 1983
Border States	Campfire Records 1986
For Old Times' Sake	Campfire Records 1989
Live at Poor David's Pub	Campfire Records 1991
Totally Guacamole	Campfire Records 1992
Roadtrip	Campfire Records 1994
Under My Hat	Campfire Records 1996
Greatest Hits—What I Like About Texas	Campfire Records 1997
It's a Texas Thing	Campfire Records 2000
Greatest Hits Volume II	Campfire Records 2001
Something for the Trail	Campfire Records 2004
Texas Music Legends	Live at the Majestic Theater Mack's Yasguir 2005
Taking Texas to the Country	Campfire Records 2010
Christmas Time in Texas	Campfire Records 2010
One Way or Another	Campfire Records 2010

SONGWRITERS

Jerry Abbott	Donna Sioux Farar
Janie Alverson	Lucky Floyd
Tommy Alverson	Rick Fowler
Ray Austin	Martin Fuller
Tommy Barnes	Eliza Gilkyson
Mike Blakely	David Gilstrap
Rick Boyette	Bret Graham
Karen Brooks	John Hadley
Junior Brown	Michael Halvorsen
Clyde Buchanan	Michael Hearne
Brian Burns	Joe Pat Hennen
Gary Callahan	Frank Hill
Rick Cardwell	Daniel Huff
Guy Clark	Walter Hyatt
Benny Craig	Jon Ims
Randy Crouch	Patricia Jackson
Don Crum	Davin James
Bill Cuswell	Jay Johnson
Johnny Divine	Jimmy Johnson
George Ensle	Kevin Johnson

Steven Kundert	Shake Russell
Eddy Lee	Curtis Ryle
Robert Livingston	Mike Silar
Jim Lunsford	Bobby Smith
Stan McElrath	Jimmy Stadler
David McKnight	J. Stafford
Maggie Montgomery	Daron Stegall
Levi Mullen	Hank Stegall
Michael Martin Murphey	Travis Stegall
Milton X. Nunn	David Stewart
Steve Nunn	Kenny Bill Stinson
Larry Nye	R.B. Stone
Rich O'Brien	Larry Joe Taylor
M. O'Dorne	Geronimo Trevino
Len Pollard	Scott Walker
Chuck Pyle	Steve Walters
Willis Alan Ramsey	Brad Williams
Red Willow Band	Rocky Wimberly
Luke Reed	Frank Wood
Thomas Michael Riley	Charlie Wright

About the Author

GARY P. NUNN is a renowned Texas country music singer-songwriter whose career began in the 1960s with the Fabulous Sparkles. Today he is a Texas institution and is considered one of the fathers of the progressive country scene that started in Austin in the early 1970s. One of his most famous songs, "London Homesick Blues," was used as the theme song for the popular television show *Austin City Limits* for two decades. Nunn's songs, such as "The Last Thing I Needed, First Thing This Morning" and "What I Like About Texas," have been recorded by artists from Jerry Jeff Walker and Michael Martin Murphey to Rosanne Cash and Willie Nelson. With a continuing array of successful solo albums and an army of fans, Nunn has made a permanent mark on the Texas/Southwestern/Country/Folk music scene and draws devoted fans wherever he plays.